Linux® Performance Tuning and Capacity Planning

Jason Fink

Matt Sherer

Kurt Wall

SAMS

201 West 103rd St., Indianapolis, Indiana, 46290 USA

Linux Performance Tuning and Capacity Planning

Copyright © 2002 by Sams

International Standard Book Number: 0-672-32081-9

Library of Congress Catalog Card Number: Not yet available

Printed in the United States of America

First Printing: August 2001

04   03   02   01   4   3   2   1

Trademarks

Warning and Disclaimer

ASSOCIATE PUBLISHER
Jeff Koch

ACQUISITIONS EDITOR
William Brown

DEVELOPMENT EDITOR
Mark Renfrow

TECHNICAL EDITOR
Kurt Wall

MANAGING EDITOR
Matt Purcell

PROJECT EDITOR
Natalie Harris

COPY EDITORS
Krista Hansing
Rhonda Tinch-Mize

INDEXER
Erika Millen

PROOFREADER
Plan-It Publishing

TEAM COORDINATOR
Vicki Harding

INTERIOR DESIGNER
Dan Armstrong

COVER DESIGNER
Aren Howell

PAGE LAYOUT
Ayanna Lacey

Contents at a Glance

Introduction   **1**

PART I   **Introduction and Overview**   **3**
1   Overview of Performance Tuning   **5**
2   Aspects of Performance Tuning   **15**

PART II   **Performance Tuning Tools**   **43**
3   Popular Unix Performance-Monitoring Tools for Linux   **45**
4   Linux-Specific Tools   **69**

PART III   **Performance Monitoring Techniques**   **83**
5   Apparent and Nonapparent Bottlenecks   **85**
6   X Window Performance   **99**
7   Network Performance   **119**

PART IV   **Tuning and Performance Mechanics**   **153**
8   Job Control   **155**
9   The Linux Kernel   **163**
10   Disk Configurations for Performance   **195**
11   Linux and Memory Management   **211**
12   Linux System Services   **223**

PART V   **Capacity Planning**   **233**
13   Thinking About Capacity Planning   **235**
14   Methods for Capacity Planning   **261**

PART VI   **Case Studies**   **279**
15   Case Studies: Web Server Performance   **281**
16   Where to Go From Here   **291**
Index   **295**

Table of Contents

Introduction   1

PART I   Introduction and Overview   3

1   Overview of Performance Tuning   5

What Is Performance Tuning? 6
Why Consider Tuning?..7
What Can I Tune?..7
Defining Performance-Tuning Objectives 8
Identifying Critical Resources 9
Minimizing Critical Resource Requirements 9
Reflecting Priorities in Resource Allocations...10
Methodology...11
    The Beater Box Theory 11
    Local Documentation 11
    Under the Gun Versus Proactive Mode 11
Roles of the Performance Analyst 12
The Relationship Between Users and Performance 13
Summary...13

2   Aspects of Performance Tuning   15

Operating System Structure 16
Kernel Architecture..18
    CPU Scheduling 18
    Program Loading...20
    Process and Thread Management 22
Virtual Memory Overview 23
Filesystem Caching..25
I/O Overview 25
    I/O Performance Management 26
    Layers for File I/O..26
NFS Performance 27
Methodology...28
    Assessment 28
    System Configuration 28
    Application Configuration...29
    Performance Expectations 29
    Known Peak Periods 29
    Sudden Changes 30
    Duration of the Problem 30
    Understanding the Options 31

Measurements 31
    Queue Versus Load Average 31
    Per-process CPU Metrics 32
    Metric Documentation...32
    Metric Accuracy 33
    Qualitative Versus Quantitative Measurements....33
Interpretation and Analysis 33
    Compute Versus I/O-Intensive............................33
    Application Architecture 33
    Speed of CPU 34
    Type of Disks..34
    Managing Disk Space 35
    Identifying Bottlenecks 36
Tuning or Upgrade? 38
    Determine Particular Bottlenecks 38
    Determine a Simple Test for Measuring 38
    Do Not Tune Randomly 38
    Look for Common Causes...................................39
    Prioritize Goals 40
    Understand the Limits of the Architecture 40
Risk Evaluation and Tuning 40
    Different Levels of Risks.....................................40
    Kernel Changes 40
    Service Changes 41
    System Reconfiguration 41
    Time Versus Benefits...41
Conclusion 41

PART II   Performance Tuning Tools   43

3   Popular Unix Performance-Monitoring Tools for Linux   45
The Scope of These Tools and the Chapter 46
Interpreting Results and Other Notes 47
All-Purpose Tools 47
    The top Utility 47
    vmstat...50
    xload and xosview 51
    uptime 53
Benchmarking Your Disks with Bonnie 53
Other Tools 55
    ps 55
    free 60
    time 61

Some Network-Monitoring Tools 61

    ping 62

    traceroute 63

    Using the Sniffer tcpdump 64

  ntop 65

  Summary 67

4 Linux-Specific Tools 69

The sysstat for Linux Distribution 70

    iostat for Linux 71

    Additional iostat Options 73

  ktop and gtop 74

Using the /proc Filesystem to Monitor System Activities 79

Other Free Utilities 82

Summary 82

PART III Performance Monitoring Techniques 83

5 Apparent and Nonapparent Bottlenecks 85

There Is Always a Bottleneck 86

User Expectations 86

Performance Agreements 86

Tuning CPU Bottlenecks 87

    Hardware Solutions 87

    Software Solutions...88

    General Application Tuning 89

Specific Clustering Solutions 89

    Beowulf 89

    MOSIX 90

Tuning CPU-Related Parameters in the Kernel 90

Tuning CPU-Related Parameters in Software 91

Memory Bottlenecks...92

    Hardware Factors..92

    Factors to Keep in Mind 95

Conclusion 97

6 X Window Performance 99

Analyzing the X Server's Performance 100

    Understanding x11perf 100

    Using x11perf 102

Measuring the Results..104

Tuning the X Server for Local Use 104

    Increase the Server's Priority 105

    Verify the Server Configuration File..107

Decrease Color Depth or Display Resolution 107

Disable Unused Modules and Server Extensions 108

Use Chipset-Specific Configuration Options 110

Rebuild the Server 110

Load Fewer Fonts 111

Use a Font Server 113

Upgrade the Server 113

Upgrade the Hardware..114

Tuning X Desktop Performance 115

About Those "Desktop Environments..."......................................115

Improving X Client Performance 116

Summary..118

7 Network Performance   119

Overview of Network-Performance Issues..120

Hardware Methods 120

Application Network Tuning 122

Examples: Database Work..122

HTTP Speed-ups 123

The Value of Knowing Your Domain 123

Tuning Samba 124

Filesystem Buffers..125

Fake Oplocks 126

Caching getwd Calls 126

Hiding/Vetoing Files 127

Considering Packet Transmit Size..127

Raw Reads and Writes...128

Socket Options..129

Write Cache Size 129

Tuning NFS..130

Tuning NIS 132

Making Kernel Changes to Improve Performance..............................132

Device Backlogs 133

Disabling ICMP..133

Local Port Range 133

Path Discovery..134

Fragmentation Thresholds 134

ECN 134

Keepalive Times 135

tcp_sack 135

Urgent Pointers 136

Window Scaling..136

Large Windows 136
TCP Timestamps 136
Bonding..137
Enforced Bandwidth Limitations 141
New and Interesting Capabilities 143
TUX 143
Zero-Copy Networking 144
High Availability/Load Balancing 145
Tools 147
Ethereal 148
tcpdump 149
Netwatch 149
SNMP 150
Testing Tools 150
Conclusion 152

PART IV   Tuning and Performance Mechanics   153

8   Job Control   155
Background Mode..156
The at Facilities..157
Using at..157
Using batch 158
Using cron 158
The cron Format 159
nice and renice 160
The nice Command..160
The renice Command..161
How nice Comes into Play 161
Summary..161

9   The Linux Kernel   163
Why Alter the Kernel?..165
Modular and Monolithic Kernels 165
Tuning via the /proc Interface 169
Data-Presentation Areas 172
Modifiable Parameters..172
Filesystem Limits 172
Kernel Parameters 173
Network Manipulation 174
Virtual Memory..175

Recompiling the Kernel 178
  Getting the Sources 178
  Configuring the Kernel 180
  make dep, make bzImage, and Similar Commands 183
  Installing the New Kernel 184
  Choosing the Right Drivers 187
  Changing Driver Configuration 188
  Patching Your Kernel...188
  Trapping Kernel Oopses 193
  Summary 194

10 Disk Configurations for Performance   195
Managing Disk Space..196
  GFS/SAN...196
  LVM...198
Disk I/O Utilization 202
Swap Strategies...204
Using RAID 204
Software RAID 205
  Understanding the Limitations of the Bus 207
Alternative Solutions 208
Summary 209

11 Linux and Memory Management   211
Determining Physical RAM Requirements 212
  Single-User Systems 212
  Multiuser Systems 213
  RAM Requirements...214
  Getting Additional RAM 214
Swap Space 214
  Calculating Swap Space 215
  Assigning Swap Space 215
  Managing Swap Space 216
  Configuring Swap Space 216
  Swap Priorities..218
Swap Partitions Versus Swap Files..218
  Swap Files 219
  Swap Partitions 219
Advanced Topics...220
  Industry Guidelines 220
  Application Effects and Memory Operations 221
  The Crash Test Dummy...221
Summary 222

12   Linux System Services   223

A "Typical" `inetd.conf` File 224

The Internet Server `inetd`..224

TCP Wrappers...227

The `rc.d` Scripts 228

The Role of Other Files in `/etc/rc.d`..230

Starting, Stopping, and Restarting...231

Summary 231

PART V   Capacity Planning   233

13   Thinking About Capacity Planning   235

What Is Capacity Planning? 236

Never a Quick Fix 237

Having a Global View of Requirements 238

A Twofold Approach 239

Grounding Planning Reliability in the Real World.......................240

Classic System Requirements...241

Application-Specific Requirements 241

Actual Versus Potential Needs..242

Pay Attention to Requirements and Administrators 244

Structured Approaches 245

Thinking Outside the Box...246

The Interrelationship of Performance Tuning and
Capacity Planning 247

Planning May Preempt the Need for Tuning 247

Predictive Analysis Versus Actual Results 248

The Never-Ending Need for Data 249

Quality Versus Quantity..249

Ways of Gathering Relevant Data...250

Data Storage: When Enough Is Enough 251

Tuning the Data Collection Process 252

How to Evaluate Your Need for Capacity Planning 253

Large Enterprise 253

Medium Business 255

Small Technical Outfits 257

Summary 260

14   Methods for Capacity Planning   261

A Blueprint for Capacity Planning...262

General Principles..262

Gathering Requirements 262

Gathering Statistics 262

Achieving a Global View...263

Using Upcoming Technologies 263

Identifying the Way Forward.......................................265

Software and Hardware Requirements 265

Determining Planned Component Update Points 266

Handling Configuration Management Migration 267

How to Develop a Structure 268

Determining Who Is Involved 268

Creating the Group 268

Outsourcing 269

Ensuring Flexibility in the Future.....................................270

Building a Contract 270

Handling Project Management 270

Navigating Political Aspects 271

Knowing Your Application Needs................................272

Commercial Products 273

Network Analysis Tools...273

Pollers 274

Example 275

Summary..277

PART VI   Case Studies   279

15   Case Studies: Web Server Performance   281

Web Server Performance 282

The Symptoms..282

The Quick Checks 282

Some Quick Guesses 282

The Web Server Culprit...283

Possible Solutions 283

A Classic Memory Problem 283

The System Configuration...283

The Beginnings of a Problem 283

Detailed Analysis Says… 284

Quick Solutions 284

Changing the Disk Configuration(s) 284

Increasing Network Latency..284

A Day in the Life of an FTP Server 285

The First Look 285

And the Answer Is…...285

Another Memory Problem 285

The Symptoms..285

Tracing the Problem 285

Finding a Solution 286

Conclusion 287

Linux Virtual Server (LVS) Walkthrough...287

Concept 287

Assumptions 287

Configuration...288

Summary 289

16   Where to Go From Here   291

World Wide Web Resources 292

Magazines, Journals, and Newsletters 293

Newsgroups and Mailing Lists 293

Summary 294

Index   295

About the Author

Jason Fink has been involved with computers and electronics since 1984 when he blew up a power supply he tried to "improve" in high school. Since then he has worked on mainframe systems, Unix clustered LANs and a variety of other interesting networks and systems. He contributes to the Open Source community in various manners.

Matthew (Matt) Sherer has been fixated with computers for years, starting with a Laser128 back when Apple-compatible machines were all the rage. This fixation resulted in a degree in Computer Science from Juniata College in Huntingdon, PA, and a discovery of UNIX and Linux along the way. Upon graduation, he spent some time in the government contracting world for a while before succumbing to the lure of commercial work. He spends a large portion of his time following all things pertaining to Open Source and Free Software, attempting to project their impact and assist in making sure that they are chosen over more limiting solutions whenever possible. Matt can usually be found behind his monitors either hacking or catching up on news about the latest code. If he's suspiciously not at his machine, chances are good that he's off travelling to some distant corner of the world.

About the Tech Editor

Kurt Wall has extensive technical experience, including programming and administering Unix and Linux systems. He is the author of Linux Programming Unleashed, Linux Programming Unleashed, 2nd Ed., and Linux Programming by Example. He is also a contributing author for numerous other books, user guides and papers. In addition, he has been technical editor for too many books to list here. Kurt is the Vice President of the Salt Lake Linux Users Group, former President of the Informix on Linux SIG of the International Informix Users Group, and former maintainer of the Informix on Linux FAQ.

Dedication

Acknowledgments

There are far too many people to thank to list here. However, here is the short list: Many thanks to Linus Torvalds and the Open Source Community at large.
—Jason R. Fink

I would like to thank those at Sams Publishing for considering an unknown by bringing me onto the project, specifically William Brown and Mark Renfrow for getting me up to speed on how the whole process works. And thanks to Jason Fink for doing the legwork involved in bringing the book up to the point where I came on board, providing me with a framework to just dive into.
—Jason R. Fink

Special thanks go out to my parents, friends, and other family members, who calmly watched me spend so much of my time growing up playing around with computers, always with the glimmer of hope that someday I would do something constructive with it. Also, I would like to show appreciation to the faculty and networking staff at Juniata College for giving me so much and for so bravely letting me administer their systems. Without all of the lessons learned there (most of them learned the hard way), I don't know where I'd be.
—Matt Sherer

Tell Us What You Think!

As the reader of this book, *you* are our most important critic and commentator. We value your opinion and want to know what we're doing right, what we could do better, what areas you'd like to see us publish in, and any other words of wisdom you're willing to pass our way.

As an Associate Publisher for Sams, I welcome your comments. You can fax, e-mail, or write me directly to let me know what you did or didn't like about this book—as well as what we can do to make our books stronger.

Please note that I cannot help you with technical problems related to the topic of this book, and that due to the high volume of mail I receive, I might not be able to reply to every message.

When you write, please be sure to include this book's title and author as well as your name and phone or fax number. I will carefully review your comments and share them with the author and editors who worked on the book.

Fax:	317-581-4770
E-mail:	`feedback@samspublishing.com`
Mail:	Jeff Koch
	Sams Publishing
	201 West 103rd Street
	Indianapolis, IN 46290 USA

Introduction

The art of performance tuning has been around a very long time. Most people are aware of performance tuning with regard to activities such as race car driving. The race car driver, engineers, and team in general work together to make the car work as efficiently and fast as it can with the singular goal of winning the race in mind.

Notice that I said the art of performance tuning and not the method or perhaps procedure of performance tuning. There are several reasons why performance tuning is much more of an art than a hard-coded method. First, it is old. Performance is relative to how any task is done, which means that humans (and many other species as well) keep improving the way they do things. Second, performance tuning requires skills that are not always associated with computers. For example, as I write this, I am using a word processor on a Linux system. That alone is a very mechanical process and does not really require a great deal of skill. The practice of performance tuning requires additional skills outside of the scope of just knowing how to invoke a particular utility or command. It requires a degree of intuition and a great deal of subjectivity. The performance analyst must understand what is really happening and why.

Linux-based systems of course are no exception to the rule of want for high performance. The primary reason many organizations use Linux is to squeak out all those performance gains on hardware that will be in place for a very long time or that is older hardware already in place.

In this book, the performance analyst will be introduced to the concepts behind performance monitoring and tuning, considerations of performance tuning, and methods of monitoring in order to understand monitoring results and actions to take.

Not only does this book walk through methods, practices, and applications, but it does so in a compact and human readable way so the performance analyst can have a readily accessible volume that is easy to use and understand.

In addition to these, the book also examines several practical case studies that explain real-world situations when performance problems arose and how the analyst addressed them.

Last and not least, although this book has strong recommendations for actions to take in almost every possible performance problem area, it is still more of a guide than a set of rules. In essence, it introduces the reader to concepts, methods, and solutions with solid examples. However, I can tell you for sure that you will encounter situations that are not in this book or perhaps not documented anywhere at all. Hopefully with insights gained from this book, you will be able to tackle the unknown with confidence or at least a really great reference.

Introduction and Overview

IN THIS PART

1 Overview of Performance Tuning 5

2 Aspects of Performance Tuning 15

Overview of Performance Tuning

What Is Performance Tuning?

In the simplest sense, performance tuning pretty much involves what it sounds like: making something (in the case of this book, a Linux-based Unix machine) run more efficiently. A phrase to remember here is "more efficient"—later in this chapter, we take a good, hard look at real efficiency.

Performance tuning certainly sounds simple enough, but there are nuances to performance tuning that many people are quite surprised to hear about. As an example, the definition of "fast" is almost completely dependent upon perspective. I briefly studied computer usability, and the first lesson I learned about speed where computers are concerned is this simple golden rule:

"It depends...."

This rule has a strong role in performance evaluation. A simple example might be the difference in performance that a user on a remote network might see, compared to a user on the local network (especially if there is a great deal of network traffic). A more complex example might arise when someone using a Web page on a system that you maintain is running a client system that is older than that of the given Web site—in this case, performance certainly will be different.

When you think of performance tuning, many times your mind is immediately drawn to altering kernel subsystems or parameters to make the system perform better. Although those are actions that you might have to take, in many other situations, things as simple as repairing a SCSI cable can make a world of difference. (This actually happened to me on a larger enterprise system. I once had a system that had been up for nearly 200 days when it suddenly began developing disk I/O problems. My first step is almost always a visual inspection. Because the system had been up for so long, I had not really "looked at" the hardware for a while. I discovered that a SCSI connector's cable was loose and that some of the shielding had become unraveled. This caused a resistance problem on the cable and thus affected the performance. Luckily, I had a spare cable.)

In reality, performance tuning is a process as a whole. It could also be said (arguably) that there are two types of performance tuning:

1. Proactive
2. Reactive

That is, the system administrator is in one of two modes: either carefully planning and monitoring the system continuously or trying to fix an immediate performance problem. Most administrators run in both modes. (These two rules pretty much apply to any job. Either you are dormant until called upon, or you are continually striving to make the process better. In performance tuning, this has a very special connotation because the general health of the system is very important.)

By virtue, performance tuning is also boundless. It is not necessarily constrained to a particular system on a network or to systems that have multiple-channel disk interfaces. Again, the problem might not be related to the core operating system at all.

Why Consider Tuning?

Well, aside from obvious reasons, such as a system that might be running incredibly slowly, the most important reason is to improve system performance and enhance efficiency. The rewards that can be gained from a well-tuned system are pretty clear. For example, an order-entry system can now process orders faster because some part of the system has been enhanced through performance tuning. This means that more entries can be pushed through, so production increases. In most organizations, this means savings of both time and money.

Performance tuning need not apply only to organizations, either. As a good example, a user might work on large programs that require a great deal of disk and processor I/O subsystems. Trimming the kernel and enhancing the disk I/O subsystem can help the programmer speed up compile time.

The list of examples can go on forever, and there are very few good reasons why you should *not* tune a system. The only imaginable case might be one in which the system administrator is too inexperienced to tune the system. Some other reasons might include uptime requirements, corporate policy, vendor support agreements, or other influences that are external to the sysadmin or the "shop" in general.

What Can I Tune?

In a nutshell, you can tune whatever you want. Most Linux performance tuning revolves around the kernel, with perhaps the biggest exception being aspects of the X Window System. As mentioned earlier, however, the kernel itself is not always the only the thing that requires tuning. A few examples of tuning outside the kernel itself are changing hardware parameters on the hardware, tuning the video driver within X Window, changing the way disks are organized, or simply changing the way a particular process is performed or engineered.

The kernel is divided into parts known as subsystems. For the most part, these subsystems are all based on input and output (I/O). The main subsystems you will find yourself tuning are these:

1. CPU
2. Disk
3. Memory

That is not to say that these are the only subsystems (there's also the sound subsystem, for example), but the three mentioned here are normally the subsystems that a system administrator will need to troubleshoot in relation to the system itself. The networking subsystem is also of great interest to the administrator.

How these subsystems affect the user's experience and each other is very important. For example, one problem might *mask*, or hide, another. Suppose that the system appears to have heavy disk usage. However, upon closer examination, you discover that it is also doing an unusual amount of paging to the same disk(s). Obviously, this will result in heavier disk usage than under normal circumstances. That does not mean that disk I/O is all right; it only means that some sort of memory problem could be the culprit instead of disk I/O. This is the essence of performance monitoring and tuning.

The kernel subsystems and their relations will be discussed in detail in Chapter 10, "Disk Configurations for Performance."

Defining Performance-Tuning Objectives

As stated earlier, the most obvious reason for performance tuning is to solve an immediate performance issue. However, it is generally a good idea to also have long-term performance objectives. The reason for this is simple: There is always room for improvement somewhere. You also might have uptime requirements—a system simply might have to work a little under par for a period of time until the system administrator can work on it.

This type of performance tuning falls under the proactive category of tuning. As a good case example, imagine that you want to upgrade BIND to a newer release in a networking architecture so that you can benefit from some enhancement. Obviously, you cannot just replace an organization's BIND services on a whim. Some degree of planning must take place before you take any actions.

Long-term objectives might be simple: Find a way to speed up tape drives so that backups will take less time. Other ones might be incredibly complex, such as improving an entire network infrastructure, which is discussed more in Chapter 7, "Network Performance."

As you can see, performance tuning even in proactive mode can be very time-consuming yet extraordinarily rewarding. The benefits of performance tuning obviously include a faster system, but often a well-tuned system also is a bit more stable. As an example, a kernel that has only the drivers that a system needs is much less prone to error than a generic installation kernel.

Identifying Critical Resources

When troubleshooting system problems, it is generally a good idea to know which parts of a given system are the most important. That does not necessarily mean just the hardware itself—or the kernel, for that matter. Knowing what the most important resources of a system are helps when you're setting priorities (which is discussed later in the section "Reflecting Priorities in Resource Allocations").

Determining what is most important can be difficult. The following is a small example of how important it is to understand critical resources.

One system that I maintained for a long time was my personal Internet gateway server. This was a demand dial-up system that I configured to act as a router, a firewall, and a nameserver for my home network. Obviously, my most important resources were networking services and security. I did not spend a great deal of time examining the disk subsystem because all the firewall really did with the disk was write log files. I also did not have any additional applications or X Window on the system.

Most operating systems are a bit more complex than a simple router/firewall, but not necessarily less important. A large database server has a great deal to contend with, especially if the database must do a lot of complex number crunching. In a case like this, almost all kernel subsystems are equally important.

Minimizing Critical Resource Requirements

Knowing what the system's critical resources are helps, but a system administrator can do even more before beginning to tune the system. One of the best ways to enhance the performance of a Linux system or any Unix system is to eliminate everything that you do not need in terms of unused services and software.

As stated earlier, some obvious things that might not be required on the system are simple things, such as X Window. A case in point is an FTP server: There is no need to load X Window on it because the sole purpose of the server is to store and transfer files.

Other items that can be removed include any services that the system does not need. For example, if a system's only task is to run a MySQL server, then services such as sendmail and a Web server simply do not need to be running because they are not used. This is discussed in greater detail in Chapter 13, "Thinking About Capacity Planning."

After unrequired services and software have been turned off, the next step is to look at simple items in the kernel that might not be needed. A good example in the kernel is drivers that you do not need. This might seem daunting to a new administrator because the kernel can be hard to understand, but after even some minor examination, you can sometimes find entire subsystems that are not needed. Once when I was customizing a Linux kernel for a workstation, I found several subsystems that I did not need, such as amateur radio and DSL subsystems. I removed all unrequired drivers that I could identify to strip down the kernel and enhance performance.

So what does all this achieve in terms of critical system resources? Obviously, not running services that are not required frees up resources. A trimmed kernel will load faster, and, in some cases, depending upon what drivers were removed, the kernel will work faster.

Another very important aspect of unrequired services running on a Linux system is that unrequired services are almost always unmonitored services. This is a rather serious security threat. Turning off unrequired services improves system security as well as performance.

Reflecting Priorities in Resource Allocations

The previous two sections discussed how to determine priority components of the system and how to remove or disable components that are not needed. By doing so, you free the system to focus more on handling the important processes. Unfortunately, sometimes you must go beyond those steps to ensure that a system is performing to the best possible standard. For instance, you must understand which resources require the highest priority and determine how these relate to system-wide resource allocation.

That might sound fancy, but it is not that difficult. Let's look at a really simple case. Imagine that a Linux system is configured to perform two tasks:

1. Run a php3-enabled Web server with a MySQL back end on the same server
2. Serve as an FTP server for Linux updates (meaning temporary files)

Php3 is a layer that can access the server or another server using its own language. In the case of this particular server, it will be communicating with another server running a MySQL-driven database.

Both services are needed, and this system is the one that can do them the best. It is quite obvious that the php3 to the MySQL Web server should have the highest priority. By allocation, I mean that it might be a good idea to limit the amount of disk space that the FTP processes have, to free them up for the MySQL processes. This is perhaps another oversimplification, but the idea remains the same: The allocation of resources should be proportionate to priorities. Essentially, they should directly reflect the planning or allocation of current resources.

Methodology

How you approach performance tuning is pretty much up to you. This book is a guide to performance tuning, but it is not a rule set. Some practices might be worth noting before we delve into all the different areas of performance tuning.

The Beater Box Theory

Many Linux system administrators keep a spare "crash test dummy" box lying around. I refer to this practice as the "beater box theory." The idea of the beater box is simple: Test as many changes on it as you possibly can before altering a Linux system that is in production.

For instance, imagine that you wanted to change some network parameters on the fly to make a php3 to MySQL (and back) server perform a little better. If you have a beater box, you can easily test several or all of the changes on that system to see the effects. The inherent problem with beater boxes is emulating the exact load that the system will be under. This is next to impossible unless you have an exact clone of a production system facing the same load. The beater box still retains its value, though, especially when low-level kernel changes such as filesystem parameters or networking parameters can be very volatile. In these cases, testing the effects of changes ahead of time can at least give you an estimation of the impact.

Local Documentation

Although many people simply abhor writing local site documentation, it is a necessity.

This is not to say that documentation must always be something that you simply cannot live with. If you have total control over a Unix system, then the system documentation is pretty much under your control, unless otherwise directed. This means that you can use something as complex as some sort of database or something as simple as a written or text file log.

This can actually be an interesting side project, if pursued properly. For instance, I once wrote a simple Perl program to enter and retrieve information about system changes that I made. It was an interesting learning experience because most Perl programs that I had written up to that point revolved around writing temporary reports about the system or automating certain tasks. I had never really dealt with creating permanent records and querying those records.

Under the Gun Versus Proactive Mode

Methodology plays an important role when a system administrator comes under serious fire—take my word for it. I was once maintaining a Unix system that used BIND for its resolution. Unfortunately, the named server had two different address classes in it without different zones. This meant long reverse lookups when remote users were connecting, resulting in a long time to connect. The immediate fix was to tell the particular server not to use DNS until the name-server could be fixed. That particular action showed grace under fire, as a quick short-term fix for a long-term problem. Of course, that's not always the best of circumstances.

In the most extreme cases, when troubleshooting spans hours, the most important thing that the system administrator can do is keep his cool and stay reasonably focused.

When I maintained mainframe systems, I also was completely responsible for the hardware. Many times I was troubleshooting (especially interfaces) when I was under serious pressure to resolve a problem. When a troubleshooter is under a great deal of stress, objectivity can be somewhat skewed. I found myself dreaming up strange theories to explain to my supervisor what I thought was happening. I have come to learn that simply saying "I am not exactly sure what is wrong, but I am working on it" is the best route to take. (I have not yet grasped at straws on any Unix-based system, including Linux.)

Documentation pertaining to system problems and corrections can come in quite handy in pressure-cooker situations. A problem likely has arisen before (especially on recently deployed Linux systems), so if it is documented, the solution is not very far away.

Roles of the Performance Analyst

Watching systems definitely requires wearing different hats for different situations. Anyone who has administered a Unix (or Linux or BSD) system knows this quite well. Your role as the one responsible for the well-being and performance of the system should make you quite familiar with the many-hats concept.

You might say that the roles match the problem scope: Sometimes you are faced more with a matter of diplomacy and education than with tuning a system. When a programmer writes an inefficient program, is the system to blame? When a user has so many aliases loaded in his .alias file or login scripts that it causes account problems, is the system to blame? If an Internet connection provider's server is too slow, is the fault in your Web server? Of course not. All these situations require a good ability to communicate and understand.

Aside from these roles, the performance analyst (typically the system administrator) also must be able to ascertain the difference between disk I/O problems and swap thrashing, network configuration (as illustrated by the named problem), and local network configuration.

You must understand precisely what you are troubleshooting and then know how to react to users. In the best of environments, you are isolated from the user barrage; in the worst, those users will be visiting you every 10 seconds. Finding the focal point of the error and acting appropriately (and nice) to the users is the key to success.

The Relationship Between Users and Performance

One particular practice of performance tuning that is not often discussed is user expectations and the capability of the systems administrator to relate those expectations to real values. Some might even suggest creating a written document that spells out what user expectations should be versus what they really are. This practice has largely gone by the wayside because of the much more dynamic nature of systems in this modern age. (Of course, the phrase "modern age" is quite relative.)

Piled on top of the modern mania of slapping systems together from commodity hardware (a purpose to which Linux and many other free Unix-like operating systems are quite well suited) are newer infrastructures that have multitiered applications. Explaining how a midtier Web server talks to a client and the top tier database server can be a daunting task.

A good example, of course, is when dealing with Web pages. Static Web pages that are designed in a minimalist manner have a tendency to download to the browser client much faster than dynamically generated or filled Web pages that are connected to a database engine. Although you might understand the inherent differences between these systems, most users do not. The key to success in managing user expectations was already mentioned in a previous section: diplomacy.

Along with diplomacy must come a willingness to teach users in a way that's not condescending—and that can be incredibly difficult. You must remember that, as a system administrator in any organization, if you are servicing someone other than yourself, you are in a customer relations–oriented position. This might be a severe hassle, but take the time to ask a user exactly what his job is and how it works. You likely will not understand a great deal of what that user tells you.

One approach that I have found most rewarding is to make users feel like I am empowering them somehow, even if I'm using just trivial knowledge about the systems. Sometimes this approach is as easy as explaining in simple terms why some things do what they do. Additionally, a little self-deprecation never hurts; users love the human touch.

Summary

This chapter touched lightly on what performance tuning is and offered some very broad examples of it. The next chapter looks at the different aspects of Linux performance tuning in greater depth and detail.

Aspects of Performance Tuning

Operating System Structure

Linux's overall structure, which is invisible to the user, is similar to that of other Unix systems in terms of its structure. Nearly everything on the system can be viewed as a file. This paradigm is apparent throughout the system, from interaction with real files to kernel tuning. Programmatically, most work is done through a file interface. Everything from network sockets, streams, interprocess communications, hardware driver interaction, and standard file operations is handled through a file interface. For nearly any operation, work is most likely to be done through some sort of file handle, allowing users and developers to adopt a common method for working with the system rather than maintaining different models for interaction with different aspects of the system.

Let's look at an example. Programmatically, if you need to get the kernel's revision number, it can be retrieved through open/read (and hopefully close) calls on the file /proc/sys/kernel/osrelease. (This is through the /proc filesystem, a pseudo-filesystem that hooks directly to the kernel and is discussed in depth later.) To get information on the contents of /etc/hosts, you would use these same calls. Likewise, if your code needed to communicate with another machine over a network socket, the same read (and write) calls would be used. Regardless of the activity in question, the Linux/Unix model will likely present the data through the common file interface. This yields simplicity and also provides clean mechanisms for interaction with everything from normal files to kernel performance metrics.

One of these areas that will be discussed in more depth later is the buffer cache. The buffer and page caches ride under the file system interface and provides a way for the system to transparently buffer as much data as possible within the available memory. This means that the system does not always have to use the underlying physical storage as directly as the user requests it, for both reads and writes, whether it is a network mount or a local disk.

In the case of file reads, the caches can maintain copies of the data requested in memory, preventing expensive disk reads. For writes, they can buffer data temporarily to prevent slowdown while the physical medium is being updated. This results in a more intelligent medium during writes and a more responsive system from the user's perspective. A highly visible example of this in action can be seen by copying a large file to a mounted floppy disk. The drive's mechanisms cannot physically keep up with the write request, but the data becomes temporarily cached, allowing the user to continue on and do something else. Eventually, the data is synchronized to the medium, whether it is through a normal superblock flush, a forced drive sync, or the action of unmounting the floppy disk in question.

Another concept that deserves an introduction here is the /proc interface. Linux follows the Unix filesystem concept of having a root filesystem, /, and various mount points and directories of varying depth below that. The /proc directory off the root of the filesystem is a pseudo-filesystem that doesn't reside on any disk; the kernel presents some of its internals and subsystem statuses to the user through a filesystem interface. Embedded within these directories is data on various kernel subsystems. Some of this data is read-only because it provides only a view of the kernel's current status with respect to different components. However, as will be covered later, many files under /proc also can be used to modify kernel behavior. Think of /proc as a filesystem that acts as an interface as needed and uses the common Unix file model, as explained earlier. For example, you can retrieve the currently supported filesystem types by looking at the contents of /proc/filesystems, as in this example:

```
# cat /proc/filesystems
nodev    sockfs
nodev    tmpfs
nodev    pipefs
nodev    binfmt_misc
nodev    proc
         ext2
         iso9660
nodev    smbfs
nodev    autofs
         reiserfs
nodev    nfs
nodev    devpts
```

This is a common list that you might find on a standard Linux machine. This was done on what might be considered a low-end server, a dual PIII-600 with 512MB of RAM and several 20GB SCSI drives. Regardless of the machine, this list (or the other basic concepts) won't vary too much, if at all. In this case, most of these filesystems don't need to be handled directly. For example, sockfs was originally written so that permissions on ports under 1024 could be granted to normal users. binfmt allows the specification of native handlers for various types of files present on the system. For example, you can configure your Java installation to handle applets natively so that the applets themselves can be run, rather than having to specify the binary to handle them.

In reality, most administrators need only make sure that the normal filesystems are present to handle the formats on the various drives and network mounts. In this case, the native filesystems needed are ext2, reiserfs, NFS, SMBFS, iso9660, autofs, and procfs. Traditionally, ext2 has been the native filesystem used on drives in Linux machines in most environments. These days, to minimize downtime, journaling filesystems are becoming a primary focus because their recovery time during a hard reboot is mercifully short. For this reason, reiserfs is coming into play on many production systems: It handles crashes more effectively and can offer better performance in many applications, including storage of many small files. NFS and SMBFS allow network mount points to NFS servers and Samba or Windows servers, respectively. iso9660 is needed for interaction with CD-ROM drives. autofs is used to automatically mount various filesystems on demand. As described earlier, procfs allows a view of the kernel internals; although it is not a traditional filesystem, it still exists as a mount point and, therefore, a filesystem in the kernel list.

It should be noted that this list is not all-inclusive and that it might vary greatly, depending on your environment. You might need other filesystems that Linux supports, such as NTFS, Coda, ext3 (the next version of ext2, mainly a journaling upgrade), or a host of others. This depends on what your kernel has compiled support for and what modules are present in memory.

Also embedded in the /proc interface are current statistics on what the memory subsystem is doing, current maximums for SYSV settings, environment settings for all currently active processes and other useful information on the current system load. For example, given a process ID, you can look into /proc and see exactly what started the process, what its environment is, what it is linking to, its process capabilities, and much more. The applicability of some of this data will become apparent later.

Kernel Architecture

This section briefly discusses some of the concepts behind technologies present in the Linux kernel and shows how they are used in the real world. In reality, nearly all of this happens behind the scenes and does not have to be handled directly. However, the concepts are important to keep in mind when you're thinking about tuning concepts.

CPU Scheduling

The internals of the Linux scheduler are too complex to be described here, but an overview is needed to give perspective on what is going on beneath the hood. Most programs don't need to be scheduled beyond what the scheduler picks for them, but occasionally this does need to be done. Interaction with process scheduling is done with the nice command-line utility or with the system calls nice and setpriority.

The scheduler breaks down real time into a unit called an epoch. Within that, the epoch is divided among processes that need to be run so that the processes present their time among the current time epoch, as long as each one has time left in its current quantum. A process's CPU time into a unit called a quantum. Units of time are divided into epochs. When all currently runnable processes are finished with their quantum, the scheduler determines a new time epoch and divides the time within that to get the quantum for each process. Depending on priority of each process, it could get the default amount of time or more, if it has a need for it. Real-time processes (which have very explicit timing and scheduling constraints) are assigned static priorities and are never changed by the scheduler. Normal processes are given dynamic priority, which can shift based on the amount of time that they have left in the current epoch, their weighted priority. Their values relative to other pending processes are also taken into account.

(If you're interested, looking at the kernel call goodness() can paint a clearer picture of what is considered when selecting different processes.)

Quantums also can be divided up. If a process is waiting for a disk to spin up, it is placed back in the task queue and retains the remaining part of its quantum for activity when the drive returns the requested data. At that point, the process is rescheduled and uses the remaining bits of its quantum for that epoch.

In general, there are three types of processes: real-time, interactive, and batch. As mentioned earlier, real-time processes are those with specific scheduling needs. Although Linux is not a true real-time operating system (RTOS), it can accommodate what is a softer version of real-time operating. Work is underway to raise Linux's support of real-time operations, but because this generally applies to embedded systems, it won't be covered in detail here.

The other two types, interactive and batch processes, are normal user-run processes that have varying scheduling needs. Interactive processes are what the user generally works with visibly, such as graphical applications and editors. Batch processes can be anything from databases to daemons. Although the kernel doesn't really have any idea about whether an application is interactive, it can tell whether it is I/O-bound or CPU-bound. Interactive applications, such as editors, are I/O-bound because they act on various I/O operations such as keyboard interrupts and mouse movements. Because these I/O events happen rarely in kernel terms, priority is deferred to I/O bound processes in general, to provide better visible performance to the user. The rest of the time is given to the CPU-bound processes.

On SMP systems, each processor runs its own instance of the schedule function. The schedule function looks for a balance between getting full utilization of all processors and using each hardware cache to the fullest. To do this, processes that are running on a given CPU most likely will remain on that CPU because hardware caches on that CPU present quick access to data that the process will most likely need. So, if CPU 0 is running process A and CPU 1 becomes free, process A might not be immediately moved over to CPU 1 because CPU 0 will probably provide better results for the process's data when it does get scheduled. The larger the hardware cache is, the more convenient it is to keep a process on a given CPU—the scheduler will take this into account.

It also should be noted that interactive processes get a higher priority than batch processes, to make interaction with the user more palatable. Because batch jobs, by default, are penalized slightly, it could be beneficial to run them at a higher priority to make up for this. For example, if you want to speed up the work being done by process ID 4322, the following would set its priority to 5 (nice and renice work with a value set from –20, the highest, to 19, the lowest):

```
# renice 5 -p 4322
```

Or, if you wanted to kick off a process at a higher priority (higher numerically, but lower in terms of how important the job is), you would do so like this:

```
# nice -n -10 tar czf file.tar /usr/local
```

By default, nice works by running a process at a lower priority (adjusted upward by 10, which is the default—running the same command without the 10 still would have changed it to 10 instead of the default 0 priority). This reverses the priority by −15 for starting the tar command, meaning that it would start work at a higher priority than normal.

As mentioned before, most users don't need to specify scheduling for processes, especially if the box doesn't operate at full load. Also, normal users can't raise their priority too high—that responsibility is given to root or, under the capabilities model, users capable of using CAP_SYS_NICE. In general, users can reschedule jobs only between 0 (base) and 20 (max), while root can shift jobs into the −20 to 0 range. This should be done only to help specific process performance constraints, though, because the scheduler will make sure that everything gets all the time that it needs eventually. Exceptions to this occur when real-time processing enters the picture or when a user wants to get a job done at a faster rate and when the act of modifying a job's priority doesn't negatively affect the throughput of the system's jobs.

Program Loading

This is handled transparently to the user and should never have to be dealt with, unless libraries are not found. (When executing a program, either from the shell or from within another program, this process is handled through the name generally passed as a call to execl, execve, or a similar system call. Refer to the man pages for more information on how this works.) Shells handle all of this transparently; check with a general Unix programming book for examples on how to make the calls yourself with your own code. Although this might seem slightly esoteric for general use, it is important to understand that binaries, libraries, and other elements are glued together. That way, you can better understand what work is going on under the hood when the kernel does process management, and you also can understand how memory is used when dealing with shared libraries.

This can be a call directly to a binary or to a script of some kind. This call is started with #! and the path to the interpreter needed to run the script, such as Perl or sh, as in #!/bin/sh. The kernel handles the internals of this system call, loads any shared libraries, and ends up with an executable image of the binary in memory, either the binary called or the interpreter, in the case of a script. The internals of what goes on here are beyond the scope of this chapter, but the result is a process running the command for which you asked.

Let's step back a moment and look at linking. Essentially, the process is exactly what is says, which is rare in the computer industry. If your binary depends on external libraries, the system needs to bring those dependencies into view of the binary, to create a complete running image in memory. This dependency is generally served through shared libraries, which are noted in the executable as being external and are brought together at runtime. Errors can pop up if the linking stage fails. For example, if the program that you want to run depends on the presence of some libraries and the kernel doesn't know where to look for these libraries, the linking will fail because the binary called won't have any way of making the needed library calls.

For the most part, libraries are installed in places such as /lib, /usr/lib, /usr/local/lib, and /usr/X11R6/lib, but you could be working with a product that doesn't want to keep its libraries with the rest of the system, for version reasons. Check with your vendor's documentation on what to do in this case, but you generally can take two routes. First, you can add the directory where the libraries exist to the linker's list of library locations: This is in /etc/ld.so.conf. Add the directory to the file, and run either of these commands:

```
# /sbin/ldconfig
```

or

```
# /sbin/ldconfig -v | less
```

You will be able to see what libraries the system sees by default (the -v switch indicates verbose output).

The other route is to define the environment variable LD_LIBRARY_PATH in the environment of the calling process. This is used to specify extra directories to check for libraries when you don't want to expose the whole system to the library. If you want to test the new version of a product but not introduce the new library to the whole system and break the existing version, this is a convenient way of doing so. Here's an example with the bash shell:

```
# export LD_LIBRARY_PATH=/home/user/newlib
```

Now, when you run the program in question, the linker knows to look for the library in /home/user/newlib, but the system as a whole has no idea that the new libraries are even an option. In reality, this is not optimal because it relies on specific environments on a per-user basis, but this is perfectly fine for testing before deployment.

Another way of giving hints to the linking process is to use the environment variable LD_PRELOAD. This can be used the same way as LD_LIBRARY_PATH, but it enables you to specify libraries to be loaded first. This is an easy way to specify which libraries are loaded first. If you have a library that traps file-interaction calls and then passes them to the real C library, you can specify your library with the LD_PRELOAD variable. When programs run and perform file operations, the linker makes sure to use your specified library for calls to open(), close(), read(), write(), and so on, rather than using the normal ones specified in the C library. This can be invaluable in adding libraries that enable you to hook into a program to see what it is doing, watch file statistics, or do a myriad of other things.

There are other ways to alter the linking process, but this covers most of the common operations. Refer to a guide on C programming under Unix for more operations you can use with the linking process.

This might seem like a fairly complicated section that you, as a user or administrator, shouldn't have to deal with directly. This is true, although it does help to have an understanding of how it all fits together. Simply put, you've got binaries that are executed via a set of system calls, which, in most cases, depend on external libraries. Through a couple of optional linking mechanisms, the linking process links these libraries (from the disk or the shared image in memory) with the binary into a usable executable image. The resulting process is executed by the kernel based on various priority levels and scheduling rules determined by the process itself and other work happening on the system. This is enough for most users to understand, although the minor details can come in handy occasionally. Next, you'll look at threading models and how they affect the process mechanisms just examined.

Process and Thread Management

Two general methodologies are used when using Linux and threading: user-level threads and system-level, or POSIX, threads. Before going more in depth on this threading, you need a standard description of it.

Processes are heavy, particularly in terms of memory usage, and the work involved in switching between them in the kernel is significant. In addition, in any system that requires a decent amount of work, there needs to be some interaction among components of the system. This can be done with processes, but it takes some effort. Processes also tend to block single operations (such as disk access or network waits) for a large portion of their time. It would be useful to allow other work to be done while some part of the system is waiting on a resource.

Enter threads. Threads share the same space for resources, but each one has a different path of execution. Among the benefits of threads, sharing data becomes much simpler (although definitely not foolproof). Memory requirements also are lighter because, rather than having a few hundred processes running along, you can get away with one single process that is executing multiple paths of execution internally. Coordinating different operations becomes easier to handle because each thread can easily access mutex variables controlling what gets to do which operation and when. If multiple processes were doing the work, both processes would have to either maintain separate instances of the data or work through a shared memory system to coordinate modifications.

Linux allows a couple methods of handling threads. Using POSIX threads is one way, and this method generally is preferred because POSIX threads are considered portable to almost any modern Unix system. Under this scheme, threads created by your process are handled by the kernel, through the linux-threads component of glibc, which should be part of your distribution. This way, the user doesn't have to worry about scheduling at all. The kernel treats the running threads as lightweight processes and just schedules them as if they were normal running processes. (From a shell, you'll be able to see the individual threads as normal processes.) Internally, the kernel knows that these are threads, not processes, so it doesn't replicate all the data that normally would be duplicated if the thread really was a full-fledged process. The user ends up with large savings in memory overhead, compared to the full process model.

The other method is to use user-space threads, as implemented by GNU pth. This API looks virtually the same as POSIX threads for most operations, but the threading is done entirely within the scope of the single parent process. Within the program, a scheduling system arbitrates all the threads on behalf of the process. The kernel never has any idea that multiple threads are running within the program, and it schedules the whole process as a normal job.

User-space threads are generally not the first method people go with—POSIX is simply more portable and scalable. However, if you know, for example, that your data is likely to reside on one CPU's hardware cache, using user-space threads provides a nice way of ensuring that your process will stay on that CPU because the scheduler will lean toward that CPU. You save the overhead of having the scheduler try to run threads on another CPU that might need data on the local hardware cache. User-space thread swapping also is lighter than kernel-level scheduling, so speed gains can be achieved. It's a matter of choosing the right tool for the job at hand.

Another important difference between the two systems is that only POSIX threads can scale to SMP systems. Because user-space threads reside within the space of a single program, they cannot use multiple CPUs at the same time. On single-processor systems, they can give better results, but on a four-way system, the most that they can use is all of one processor. POSIX threads, on the other hand, are scheduled by the kernel and, because the kernel knows how to schedule across CPUs, can utilize all CPUs at the same time, with more scheduling overhead. Taking these factors into account when designing a system can have a large impact on how the system behaves in the field. In general, POSIX threads are the better choice for most operations.

Virtual Memory Overview

With today's memory prices, the importance of having large amounts of swap is lessened. But when you're deploying a machine that could be severely overloaded, it's always good to have a large amount of swap space just in case. The traditional rule is to have double the amount of physical memory, although, if you consistently use it, that's generally a sign that you need more memory.

The virtual memory system is largely handled by the kernel. The most you should have to do with it in terms of administration is to add and delete swap files, as needed. Command-line utilities are the easiest way to do this: swapon and swapoff should cover your needs. There are two general ways of handling swap: One is by explicitly partitioning your drive to contain a swap partition. This is preferred because you can format that partition as a swap device and because it provides the cleanest interface to the disk.

But you might have already allocated your drives, and now the system is overloaded. There is no free space to create new partitions for swap space. What do you do? Simple: You can use a regular file as swap space, although it will be layered on top of your regular filesystem. This is not preferred but it needs to be done in some situations. Here's an example of how to do this on a running system:

```
# dd if=/dev/zero of=/tmp/swapfile bs=1M count=100
# mkswap /tmp/swapfile
# swapon /tmp/swapfile
```

The first line creates a zeroed file of 100MB. Next, mkswap turns that file into a valid swap-file. Finally, swapon turns it on, and instantly you have another 100MB of swap space on your system. Just make sure that you add the file on a disk that still has enough space left for it. (Also make sure that you place the swap in a proper place—make sure that it's on a drive that has room to grow and that isn't already heavily loaded by other I/O requests.)

Keep in mind that you should put the new entry in your /etc/fstab file so that it is used from now on. Otherwise, the swap will be active only for the current boot. When you reboot, the file still exists and is already a swap file, but you will need to rerun swapon to enable it. Here's an example entry for /etc/fstab:

```
/tmp/swapfile  swap swap defaults 0 0
```

I recommend placing it in a more meaningful location than /tmp, though. Also remember that swapon -a and swapoff -a are convenient ways of enabling and disabling all swap specified in /etc/fstab. Disabling swap space is rarely needed in most situations, unless you are looking to reclaim some disk space and know that the system load is low.

One final note on swap space: When programs or data are swapped out, they remain so until the system or user needs them again. So, if your box starts swapping under heavy load but then still seems to have swap usage afterward, don't be alarmed. This is just the kernel leaving existing memory free for more useful operations. If the data can live in swap for an extended period of time, it's probably safe to assume that you really weren't using it in the first place.

Filesystem Caching

Linux aggressively caches filesystem data, sometimes to the alarm of users. Typing **free** from a shell gives you something like this:

```
              total        used        free      shared     buffers      cached
Mem:         387404      282208      105196       71652      166284       40364
-/+ buffers/cache:        75560      311844
Swap:        801552        5576      795976
```

Looking at these numbers, you would guess that the system has roughly 387MB of RAM and is using 282MB of that. You would think that the box is running low on memory and that it's time for an upgrade. But that's just the caching within the kernel, utilizing the free memory for disk caches. Note the second line, which is the system memory usage without the buffer and page caches—roughly 75MB, which is more in line with expectations. For a quick idea of the different caches, think of the buffer cache as being a cache of the raw blocks on the disk, and think of the page cache as being a cache of various files that are in use on the system. Requests for sequential sectors on a physical device might be cached by the buffer cache. The page cache would handle a series of requests made for the same section of a file that has been assembled in memory from what might have been discontinuous locations on disk.

As the kernel is handling various data, it buffers as much as it can within the available RAM to save time on consecutive accesses of that data. As the system load grows and applications request that memory, the buffer caches shrink so that more memory is available to user-space programs. In general, using these caches can greatly improve system responsiveness, without any special code needed to take advantage of it. Later in this chapter, you will see an example of how to tune the buffer cache if you need to boost system performance.

Incidentally, these caches tend to find bad memory rather quickly (as will memory-intensive operations such as using GCC to compile the kernel). If you load an operating system that doesn't cache as aggressively as Linux onto the machine, and if the box never uses all the available RAM, no fault is ever seen. But with Linux installed, faults occur frequently, and they can be wrongfully attributed to the kernel misbehaving. A good test of this is to build the kernel. Between the memory-intensive compiler and the caches, the system ends up using all memory in one form or another fairly quickly.

I/O Overview

Your I/O subsystems should get a lot of attention, in the planning stage and during the tuning process. The right hardware needs to be in place to effectively handle the system's needs. At the same time, it needs to be managed so that configuration changes down the road can be handled with little or no disruption. This section looks at some management factors to keep in mind.

I/O Performance Management

Most of the details of I/O performance management are covered in later chapters that discuss the various utilities for monitoring and interacting with different I/O subsystems. A general overview is needed at this point, though. The most important thing to keep in mind when managing your I/O is the underlying architecture. Know exactly what you want to get out of the system, and determine whether the system is going to be up for the load.

For example, if you're looking to do video streaming, don't use a slow disk. If you want to do operations that could be done in parallel, get an SMP box. This might sound simple, but it is very important to know whether you're fighting a bad application configuration or whether you are running up against a wall because of the physical capabilities of the hardware. If you have too many devices on the PCI bus pushing too much data across it, delays and missing data are likely possibilities, and no reconfiguring of the kernel, tools, or applications will fix the problem. Make sure that the hardware can handle what you think a peak load will be.

Sometimes the easiest way out of an I/O bottleneck is to change the way you're doing the work. Rather than do all that file work on a real disk, configure the system to use ramdisks and keep all temporary storage there. This can speed interaction with that data and, at the same time, reduce the strain on the disk set underneath.

Layers for File I/O

The Logical Volume Manager (LVM) was introduced to the kernel in the 2.3 development cycle, and it provides a clean way of handling layered file operations. You can picture the LVM as sitting on top of the filesystem layer. It can join multiple disks to create single growable virtual disks. This can be done at runtime without interrupting normal work on the filesystem that users or applications are using. If your /home drive is filling up, you can use the LVM to add another disk partition to the set; as it is joined, the /home partition usage will drop proportionally. Put simply, this removes the need for painful repartitioning in the future as certain disks fill up and need to be reconfigured.

There are other means of layering file operations as well. Within the kernel is a filesystem interface called the VFS layer. This provides a clean interface for user applications to interact with mount points, regardless of whether the filesystem in use is ext2, ntfs, nfs, cramfs, or something else. The software RAID implementation also fits within this layer and can be used to provide RAID across drives without having physical hardware present to do the work. Interestingly, there are also filesystems such as PerlFS that sit behind this interface and allow normal file operations to be done on remote HTTP sites. For example, you could use the command `cat /mnt/perlfs/http/www.cnn.com/index.html`, and the file would be retrieved and cataloged for you as if it was were a local file residing on a local disk. Allowing filtered I/O like this can open all kinds of interesting possibilities without forcing you to reinvent the wheel when interacting with the data; it behaves as a file, just like everything else.

NFS Performance

Historically, Linux's NFS support has been lacking. However, many improvements were made late in the 2.2 series and also in the 2.3 to 2.4 development cycle. The NFS support currently provided should be enough to satisfy most users, as long as security is taken into consideration. In general, NFS over public links should be done through some sort of encrypted tunnel. If they're using NFS over a slow link, some users might want to mount with the `timeo=n` option. The n value is .7 of a second, which is the length of time that the subsystem waits before retransmitting a request. If you are on a slow line or have many gateways between you and the server, raising this could help prevent rebroadcasts and duplication of effort. The maximum value is 60 seconds.

Now let's consider the normal case in which you are fairly close to the server and there is a normal LAN between you and it. Mounting with the `rsize` and `wsize` parameters can help because this will buffer your data more efficiently before pushing it over the network. Here is an example:

```
#mount -o rsize=1024,wsize=1024 server:/mnt/nfs /mnt/nfs
```

This mounts the server's /mnt/nfs export to the /mnt/nfs mount point, using an `rsize` and `wsize` of 1024. This will make sure that transfers are handled in groups of 1024 bytes. In reality, most users jump these values up to something more like 8192, although your needs might vary. If the network card doesn't support buffer sizes as specified, the mount might not behave correctly. If this is the case, reduce the block size until things start to look normal again. A good test of the speed is to do time tests—time the creation of a given file size over the network. Something like this will do the trick:

```
# time dd if=/dev/zero of=/mnt/nfs/test bs=1M count=50
```

Do this several times to get a decent average of the elapsed time for each copy. Also note that NFS does use the buffer cache as explained earlier, so raise the count parameter until you are pushing so much data that it cannot fit comfortably within the buffer cache. Depending on the NIC and the underlying network, playing with the `rsize` and `wsize` parameters might be needed.

After tweaking the parameters, if you're still not getting the results you need, consider alternatives. Although NFS is stable and common, it has been around for a long time and might not be the best solution. Samba and Global File System (GFS, a mechanism for multiple machines to share access to the same physical drive space without forcing the user to deal with the synchronization problems) could be worth looking into as possibilities. HTTP access to the files through a Web server on the remote box might be an option as well, depending on your needs.

So far, you've seen a lot of subsystems and learned how they relate to the overall performance of the system. You've learned about different layers of I/O, network performance issues, memory management, buffering, swap utilization, and how the system pieces together components at runtime into processes. On their own, these factors can appear complex, especially because they interact with each other. (Processes can force the buffer cache to shrink or cause swap files to be used, which will utilize your I/O subsystems.) As you will see in the next section, these factors must be taken into account and must be handled systematically to effectively plan and manage your system.

Methodology

Systematic decision making is key to designing a capable system. If you build the system with the wrong ideas in mind, there is no way you can recover from the decisions made up front. These ideas apply to any system that you might be building, whether or not it is constructed with Linux in mind. Approaching design without clear and precise goals is like running into a battle without a battle plan. You might come out alive, but don't count on it.

Assessment

Assessing tuning needs is a complex issue, with possible wild goose chases if you're not careful. Determining that the system is not working at the speed it should is generally a fairly obvious conclusion. Determining why requires a stringent approach to the problem. If it looks like the system is slow when it comes to file accesses, you might guess that the disks or drive mounts are at fault. But the database providing the file location lookup could be swamped. Determining the root cause of the problem requires considering all aspects of the system. If that weren't enough, it also helps to be able to keep all the different load factors in mind at the same time. (If this was really that easy, why would you need a book on the subject?)

System Configuration

Know the system's configuration. If you're tracking performance issues and don't realize that the machine in question has a slow drive subsystem, you'll be chasing a red herring indefinitely. Keep in mind kernel capabilities, the hardware present, and the state of the installation. Linux boxes can run for years, but the installations tend to go out-of-date very quickly, considering the rate at which development occurs in the field. Unless the box is regularly updated, it could be outdated for what you are trying to get it to do. For example, if you are trying to deal with files larger than 2GB, you will need a recent (at the time of publishing) version of the C libraries and preferably the 2.4 kernel. If the box has been just working away for the past two years in the server room without updates, it's probably going to need some work.

Application Configuration

Like system configuration, this largely depends on the situation, particularly the application in question. It is unwise to assume that just plugging an application into a system will give you optimal performance. Sure, it'll work, but when it comes to tuning it and the system for performance, it helps to know the application well enough to know what you can do to help performance. A perfect example of this is Oracle. Anyone can install Oracle without a problem and get it running, but to really get it optimized for speed, you need to know how to tune both the application and the underlying operating system. You need to know how to split data files across drives, poke at the /proc interface to make sure that SHMMAX is appropriate, and so on.

The point is that configuration for speed is a larger issue than just clicking a "go fast" wizard. You need to take as many factors into consideration as possible and then test your tuning ideas under as many types of loads as possible.

Performance Expectations

Make sure that you build expectations into the specification of the system at the hardware level first. When that is in place, getting the software up to speed is a matter of expertise, if it doesn't perform as needed out of the box. The most limiting thing you can do is to build a hardware solution that isn't up to the job. No matter how much software work you do, you'll never recover from the inherent design flaws of the system. If possible, calculate the raw amounts of data you'll need at any stage. If you're trying to make sure that the disk array provided will be fast enough, determine what the maximum number of megs-per-second throughput needs to be, and compare that to the specification of the array. It should be obvious whether the hardware will be up for the task. Also figure in some legroom for feature growth down the road.

Known Peak Periods

Will the system be capable of handling the peak system load? Always build up the system to be capable of handling the heaviest load, preferably with minimal performance loss. If enough leeway can be built in to assume a constant operation at peak loads, so much the better. As the system grows, being capable of handling the upswing without an absolute immediate replacement of core components (hardware or software) can be a lifesaver in a production environment. Consider a stock-trading system that is operating at 50% load across the cluster and 85% at peak usage. After a massive media campaign, what used to be peak operating rates are now the norm, and there is still room to keep things going until all the new hardware comes in.

Sudden Changes

As mentioned previously, there can be sudden upswings of requirements. The system needs to be capable of handling this. Make sure that there is adequate spare CPU power to handle peaks, and also enough redundancy to handle losses of nodes. There are many ways to handle this: through GFS clusters, with the Linux Virtual Server project, and so on. The optimal system can have spare nodes offline that can be swapped in automatically at a moment's notice. For something like a Web cluster using GFS with a Fiber Channel switch, failure of a given node is not severely detrimental to the system overall. In a database environment, database clustering is a good option to have.

Another type of sudden change to hit a system is a new rollout of software, whether it is your in-house system or new versions of software involved. It is impossible to overstress the importance of serious testing of every bit of every piece of software before it gets dropped into production. Nothing is as wasteful as trying to recover from a failed installation of some software because it wasn't tested enough. With a large enough system, an hour of downtime due to this kind of glitch can be devastating. If possible, do the work incrementally and maintain the old software configurations in case you need to revert back. If you're upgrading kernels across the cluster, keep the old images around so that you can boot back to them if you need to. Perform the upgrade slowly, and watch for disturbances along the way.

Of course, the environment doesn't always allow such a nice, easy change. Depending on your needs, you might be forced to drop in many modifications at the same time, any of which could cause a dozen different types of problems. In any case, back up anything and everything that you can. Nothing is foolproof, and having a handy tape backup can save you if the change goes awry.

If changes start happening to the system that weren't planned, things can get very messy unless the problem is approached with a clear head. Determine when this began. Is it only during a peak load that the symptoms are evident, or is it consistent over time? Was there some "trivial" update somewhere that was thought to have no impact outside its scope? This is most often the cause. Some small part of the system gets a small tweak, and you think that it doesn't affect anything but itself—sometimes, though, this can cause serious problems.

Duration of the Problem

If problems start occurring in what seems like a random sequence, don't lose your cool. Look at when and where it is happening. Again, is it only under heavy load? Does it happen only in the morning? Resolving these kinds of problems involves relying heavily on specific knowledge of the system in question. If the data that is processed first thing in the morning is a different type than what is handled throughout the rest of the day and the problem occurs only at 9:00 A.M., it's probably a fair assumption that the problem lies in the data.

Understanding the Options

Know what options are in front of you. If possible, have multiple options built into the design of the system. Say that the Web servers are getting swamped, but the disk array that is serving that group is still okay. If the Web servers were designed to be dropped in as serving nodes in a cluster, that option is an easy one to take.

If you don't have any quick recourse for the problem, look carefully at the problems present. Has everything grown too far beyond the original scale? It might be time for a redesign of some of the core systems to handle the new load. Maybe the problem has scaled up so far that you need to switch architectures at this point to handle the amount of data involved. Maybe a couple slight tweaks here and there, such as tuning the Web servers or updating the drive array with better throughput, will solve the problem.

In the end, finding the right solution will depend greatly on understanding the system at hand. If you don't have a tight grip on how your system works, no amount of tweaking will help you. The best that you can hope for is to tweak random components of the architecture until you hit the one that was causing the problem in the first place. Insight into how the system works, combined with a clear understanding of where you want it to go, should be enough of a catalyst to get pretty much any problem solved. The section "Identifying Bottlenecks," later in this chapter, includes a rough path of checks to follow when trying to identify bottlenecks.

Measurements

No performance data is worth anything if you don't know how to interpret it. Given a few data points and how they relate to the system, along with baseline metrics of at what values the system should be operating, it becomes easy to build a view of the system's current and projected usage rates.

Queue Versus Load Average

The queue is the current runtime queue for processes. Load averages are measurements of this metric over 5-, 10-, and 15-minute intervals. The runtime queue is a count of the number of processes ready to run at any given point in time. A value less than 1 is optimal. This means that there is never a process sitting in the queue waiting to be run. When the load averages start to creep over 1, it means that there is always a process ready and waiting to be scheduled, which implies that something in the system is being delayed. In some cases, another CPU will solve the problem and make sure that there is a better chance of schedulable time. There are several ways to watch this data—through vmstat, top, and uptime, and so on. Using uptime is the cleanest way to just get the load average data:

```
# uptime
1:34pm  up 61 days,  3:12,  1 user,  load average: 0.00, 0.16, 0.19
```

As you can see, this is a lightly loaded system. If the first number had been something like 5 rather than 0.00, it would have meant that a current load of five processes was waiting for work. If the second and third numbers were similar values, there would always be a work backlog and a very obvious bottleneck. In this case, you should look into how to distribute your load over different machines or upgrade your processor, or look into SMP machines.

Per-process CPU Metrics

Standard utilities can get this data for you. Graphical utilities such as xosview will display it with X, or top will show you through a shell login. For example, top will give user, system, nice, and idle statistics for each processor, updated based on how often you tell top to update. (Hit S and enter a number to change the display update rate. Any number, including a decimal fraction, is valid.) Information about each processor can be retrieved from the /proc interface, as in the following example:

```
# cat /proc/cpuinfo
processor    : 1
vendor_id    : GenuineIntel
cpu family   : 6
model        : 8
model name   : Pentium III (Coppermine)
stepping     : 6
cpu MHz        : 863.975
cache size   : 256 KB
fdiv_bug     : no
hlt_bug        : no
f00f_bug     : no
coma_bug     : no
fpu     : yes
fpu_exception    : yes
cpuid level    : 2
wp          : yes
flags        : fpu vme de pse tsc msr pae mce cx8 apic sep mtrr pge mca
cmov pat pse36 mmx fxsr sse
bogomips     : 1723.59
```

This can be useful when determining what capabilities are present in the hardware. If you're running CPU-intensive work and the application can take advantage of extra instruction sets such as MMX and SSE, the /proc interface ensures that the CPU can use it.

Metric Documentation

All the utilities to pull metric data are documented in more depth in Chapter 3, "Popular Unix Performance-Monitoring Tools for Linux." More in-depth data also is available in the man pages for the individual utilities themselves, with data on every possible configuration switch.

Metric Accuracy

To get these statistics, you need to interact with a running system. By interacting, such as running top, you are also altering the system. You might be just adding another process to the run queue, but it does shift the numbers slightly. In terms of overall trends, though, the data retrieved in analysis can be counted on to give you a good overall view of the system resource usage.

Qualitative Versus Quantitative Measurements

Make sure that you are recording statistics of relevant data. Don't keep 1000 records of vmstat data over the span of an hour when you're really just interested in overall CPU usage through the course of the day. You'll reduce your interaction with the system and get only the data you need. Make sure to look everywhere for helpful data: You might not get anything particularly interesting from top, but by watching the /var/log/messages file as the system hits peak load, you might see some kernel messages come through. That one-line warning message (maybe a kernel driver module dropping a warning) can be more informative than watching a CPU usage meter for an hour.

Interpretation and Analysis

If you are chasing a problem, try to approach it objectively. If you go into the research process with a clear view of what you think the culprit is, most likely you will look at the numbers so that you see what you want instead of what is really there. Objectivity is key in resolving tuning issues quickly and easily.

Compute Versus I/O-Intensive

Applications tend to fall into one of two categories: Either they are bound by the speed of the CPU or they are bound by the speed of I/O, whether it is a disk, a multimedia device, a printer, or something else. Accommodations can be made on either side to help matters, and expectations must be kept in mind when dealing with either type.

Application Architecture

The architecture of an application can have large repercussions in how it interacts with the system and, in the larger scope, how it scales. Given a number-crunching scientific application, it is most likely CPU-bound. Scaling it requires either multiple CPUs or a clustering capability within the software. Linux projects such as MOSIX can work around the lack of this kind of capability, but they are not foolproof; depending on how the application is written, they might not help matters at all. Likewise, if the application is entirely disk-bound, such as a movie viewer, spreading it across machines won't help, but getting a faster disk subsystem (or multiple controllers and spreading the load) can send performance through the roof. Keep this in mind when selecting applications for your project, and fit them with your hardware needs.

Speed of CPU

This might sound simple, but it can get out of control in many ways. As usual, it depends on your needs. If you're running a static Web site on a decent network connection, something like a T1, you're safe with a 486. If you're doing large amounts of processing, a two- or four-way machine could suit your needs and might be cheaper than purchasing a single-processor machine with today's fastest chip. Building a cluster, either a Beowulf-style set with custom code or a load-balancing Web farm, might be appropriate. This depends entirely on your needs.

If you're looking at something that could end up being embedded somewhere, the ARM architecture might be the way to go. Looking at the higher end? As of this writing, both Intel and AMD are moving toward a 64-bit architecture, while HP and Sun have been there for years. The Linux kernel is currently ported to about 20 different architectures. Finding the right one depends on your budget and target need.

Type of Disks

Once upon a time, there was a clear distinction in drive types. If you were building a desktop or a low-end system, it was assumed that you would deploy IDE. For a decent server, SCSI was the default. But now, with the advances in the IDE specifications, the current crop of disks can compete with SCSI in some applications. Ultra 160 is the current high end in the SCSI world and is still the weapon of choice when building a decent server. SCSI benefits from a more intelligent bus scheme, and this can show whether you have multiple applications attempting massive writes at the same time. An example of this is command reordering. If you have several applications bursting data at once, the requests would normally send the drive head all over the disk, wasting time. With command reordering, the requests are organized so that the writes that are close to each other physically end up being executed in sequence, reducing the strain on the drive.

The next step beyond SCSI is Fiber Channel. Fiber Channel technology offers several bandwidth improvements over traditional SCSI and allows physically separate drives to be connected easily. (Ultra 160 SCSI allows up to 25 meters, while Fiber Channel allows separations in the kilometer range.) Many vendors use Fiber Channel as a connection mechanism to drive arrays that are backed by SCSI disks, which allows many machines to connect easily to the same physical drives. Combined with GFS, a Linux clustering filesystem, allowing many machines direct write access to the same physical hardware becomes feasible.

On the other end of the drive spectrum are solid-state drives, which historically have had smaller capacities but a much higher cost. The advantage is that there are no moving parts, which yields large increases in drive speed. Typically, they are used for embedded systems because of their smaller form factor, but the price differential is falling. As a result, these drives might find their way into other uses soon. If you need to build a cluster of machines for intensive CPU work but minimal disk interaction, using a small solid-state drive on each box would greatly increase the CPU per square foot ratio.

Linux offers solid support for all these types of disks and will even support a compressed filesystem on a smaller drive, as in the case of a solid-state drive. If you're looking to build something with very high availability, Fiber Channel access to a RAID array is the way to go: It gives you shared access to a common disk pool, fast interconnects, and consolidated drive management. For most servers, IDE and SCSI can be used interchangeably, although if you know that the box is going to be disk-intensive but you don't want to drop money on Fiber Channel, SCSI will give you the biggest performance gain.

Note that although Linux supports a wide variety of drive types, in many instances software tuning will do the trick. Refer to the later chapter on drive performance for specifics on how to tune your existing hardware to get the most out of it.

Managing Disk Space

As mentioned before, the LVM integrated into the kernel as of version 2.4 is a great addition to Linux's drive- management suite. It allows easy integration of existing unused drive space into an already mounted filesystem. Planning your system around the LVM is a good way to ensure expandability as the system grows.

In terms of managing the drives themselves, there is a large industry push toward storage area networks (SANs). These offer high-availability drive space, with high-bandwidth connections, all collected in a central location. Rather than having 10 servers in your server room, all with separate RAID cards and individual storage and backup mechanisms, a SAN puts all these drives together in a common pool. This can seemingly introduce single points of failure, but the hardware in the SAN should be fault tolerant in all cases, usually to a degree greater than what would be seen on an individual machine because the failover hardware is more effectively used. Depending on your needs, a SAN can be configured to replicate between physical locations. Generally, each machine that needs access to the drives gets a Fiber Channel card, connecting to a Fiber Channel switch that allows crossover to the drive array. This keeps drives co-located, simplifying storage management immensely. Also, by having all the drives in the same physical location, you can connect a single tape loader to the SAN and back up the data directly, without transporting large amounts of data over the network during backups. This speeds the backup process and reduces the impact on your operational network.

For a lower cost, it is also feasible to get a normal storage array, perhaps with a SCSI interface, and place a server in front of it that exports the drive set to the rest of the network over something like NFS or Samba. This keeps the drive management centralized but introduces a single point of failure. Using a shared SCSI system, two machines can be plugged directly into the system so that one can take over in the event of a failure. However, this is still a secondary solution to a Fiber Channel switch. If all interested machines have direct physical access to the drives, the load of all that data being transported over your network is reduced. Although Samba is feature-rich, it is known to be a fairly chatty protocol, and it can impact the performance of your network if all data is being transported over it.

The gist of all of this is that storage is again heading for the centralized model. As the system grows, the savings begin to show in management overhead. The days when every machine had all the hardware within it and managed itself are slowly disappearing as the concept of a SAN really takes hold. Many of the larger vendors support SANs with Linux nodes.

Identifying Bottlenecks

Identification of bottlenecks is a difficult task, to say the least. Depending on software interaction, simply looking at the memory usage and finding the culprit generally doesn't work. As usual, this involves knowing the system and what might be causing the slowdown, depending on the current load across different aspects of the system. If you're looking for a rough order of what to check, a good sequence might be the one shown here. (This isn't to be taken as gospel, but it's a decent enough gauge. If the path to the problem is fairly obvious, it might not make sense to follow all the checkpoints every time.)

- **CPU**—Look into what is using the CPU and when. Look for obvious abuses.
- **Memory**—Look for abuses of memory on the system, according to various usage loads.
- **Swap**—This interacts with memory, of course, but make sure to note various levels of swap usage over time.
- **I/O subsystems**—Note usage levels of all involved I/O subsystems, such as IDE and SCSI busses, proprietary interfaces that applications depend on, and so on.
- **Application settings**—As noted previously, it is of paramount importance that you know your environment and how your applications should be configured. In the end, this will likely be the source of many bottlenecks.

Resource Saturation

Saturation can occur in many forms. One is that the disk could be full, or approaching full. Generally, most filesystems start to experience degraded performance after usage goes over the 75% mark. Memory could be overextended, and the box could be swapping severely to recover. In extreme instances, when the kernel has absolutely no other recourse, a process killer could be activated that will look for the most likely culprit of the memory loss and then kill it off in an attempt to get the box back into a usable state. There have been many arguments about whether this is a valid approach, and it can be enabled or disabled within the kernel, depending on whether you feel that this is a safe last-ditch effort. Personally, I have had it kick in several times in the process of testing code, and it has done a great job of getting the machine back in a usable state without a crash. Otherwise, because my box was remotely installed, I would have had to wait until someone at the location facility could reset the machine for me.

Resource Starvation

Saturation and starvation are related concepts, with a slight difference. Think of resource saturation as having a subsystem that is overworked, or saturated. Starvation is the problem of having processes that are waiting long periods of time for resources to which they need access. In most cases, starvation is a byproduct of saturation, although that doesn't necessarily have to be the case. Resource starvation can be as much an example of broken code as it is of an ill-equipped system. If a process is constantly blocked, waiting for a resource, and the scheduler never sees that it can be scheduled in, this is generally because another piece of code has locked that resource and hasn't given it back. Avoiding deadlock of this type is not the kernel's job; if a single process wants to hold on to a device indefinitely while another process waits for it, the code is either broken or misconfigured.

If the machine in question is misconfigured, it doesn't have the hardware that it needs. In this case, the fact that one process is locking a device and a second process is waiting for one might be because the machine should have two instances of the device in question. This depends on the task at hand and is generally a solvable problem. Likewise, if the Web server tries to create another child but fails with an out-of-memory error because the system can't physically allocate anymore RAM, this is a simple issue of a machine not having enough hardware to do the job.

Unsatisfactory Response Time

This is a fairly obvious problem, usually detected when users start asking why the system isn't behaving correctly. Most of the time, this becomes an instance of a system that has grown and is resource-starved; the problem is solvable with more hardware of some form, depending on the symptoms. If users are connecting to the database but are blocking until the machine has a chance to answer the request, it could be a simple problem of increasing the maximum number of connections in the database or adding memory to the machine so that it can serve the new influx of users causing the increased system load.

Tuning or Upgrade?

Users are screaming and the system is fully loaded. What do you do? Spend another fruitless day tweaking configurations, or just break down and buy more hardware?

Determine Particular Bottlenecks

Understand your system. This is your mantra. If database access is slow but the machine's memory, CPU, and disk look fine and the database relies on information halfway across the network, that remote repository might be the culprit. If you know how the system components interconnect, tracking problems should be a matter of deduction, not trial and error. You also should see if there is a single bottleneck involved or the possibility of multiple snags in the flow. Keep in mind that in fixing each snag, each problem should be handled independently, and system tests should be run after each fix to determine what actually was the culprit. Never apply multiple fixes to the same problem at the same time. If you're lucky, it'll just fix the problem, and you'll never know which was the real bottleneck. If you're unlucky, the "fixes" could break things in a way you never expected, resulting in a system that is more broken after the fix than beforehand.

Determine a Simple Test for Measuring

When trying to trace a problem, always look for a simple test metric that tests a certain component but is unlikely to stress other ones. By interacting with the system, you're bound to the Heisenberg principle, but minimizing the effects is always in your best interests. Consider the case in which drive speed is in question: The database is slow, and the consensus seems to be that data throughput to the drive isn't quite up to par. Let's bring out your good friend:

```
# time dd if=/dev/zero of=/mnt/file bs=1M count=200
```

This creates a 200MB file on the disk in question. Make sure that you use a file size larger than your system's memory so that you can be sure that you really are using the disk, not memory. Do this several times, and average the results. Figure out the throughput rate based on your elapsed time and file size, and compare this to the advertised speed of the drive in question. Does it match? If so, the drive is up to speed and the problem is elsewhere. Apply this same kind of test for a single component against the next most likely culprit, and eventually you'll track it down.

Do Not Tune Randomly

A few rules should always be applied when tuning. The first and most important is that you should never tune more than one subsystem at a time. This should be adhered to without fail, as tempting as it is to try to save time by applying several fixes at once. You might just cause another problem, obscuring the problem that you might or might not have just fixed.

Here's an example: You need to make sure that the buffer cache is being used correctly. The kernel allows you to play with the buffer cache via the /proc interface. For nearly all uses, the default kernel configuration should be sufficient, as reflected by this:

```
# cat /proc/sys/vm/bdflush
30    64    64    256    500    3000    60    0    0
#
```

These values correspond to the buffer cache data within the kernel. The first number, 30, represents the percentage of the cache that needs to be dirty before the cache is flushed. You can update this file by echoing new values to it. Assume that you want to try raising the percentage to 100 before a flush would happen:

```
# echo 100 64 64 256 500 3000 20 0 0 > /proc/sys/vm/bdflush
#
```

As you can see, you have done two stupid things. First, we have set the percentage to 100, which effectively disables the buffer cache. This might help performance because it will use more of the cache before incurring disk overhead. But you have done something else at the same time—you set the third-from-last number to 20 rather than 60. This corresponds to the number of seconds between flushes of the superblock. So, on one hand you probably increased performance by raising the usage percentage, but you've probably hurt performance by forcing more flushes due to timeouts. Have you solved the original problem? No one knows.

Note that these values are documented in /usr/src/linux/Documentation/sysctl/vm.txt. Also, here is a set of values that some people have found to be beneficial for increasing performance in relation to the buffer cache:

```
# echo 100 5000 640 2560 150 30000 5000 1884 2 >/proc/sys/vm/bdflush
```

Compare these values to what you might need, and check with the documentation for each field to see if it might be the right combination for you.

Look for Common Causes

This might sound like common sense, but when you are tracing a bottleneck, look for common causes. Take the time to step back and ask yourself what all the problems are. If they all seem to be related to drive I/O, check the storage array. If you have all the drives housed in a SAN and one of the raids has corrupted itself and is trying to rebuild, there will be a noticeable performance degradation until the recovery is complete. This could result in multiple degradations throughout the system. Try to disassociate yourself from the problem directly and focus on the possible causes. Many hours have been lost being so frustrated with the problem that the simple solution was completely overlooked.

2

ASPECTS OF
PERFORMANCE
TUNING

Prioritize Goals

At any given time, multiple problems will need to be solved. Make sure that you systematically weigh these troublemakers against what has the most impact for the largest number of users, and act accordingly. At the same time, make sure that you do not allow problems themselves to become resource-starved. Finding a balance between high-priority new problems and low-priority old problems is difficult, but this needs to be done to make sure that, over time, every pending problem is solved.

Understand the Limits of the Architecture

Linux has come a long way in scaling to both large and small systems, but sometimes the architecture and the system just aren't the right match. At some point, it might still make sense to drop the money on a high-end Sun machine and make the jump to the stronger UltraSPARC architecture. If you're a Web-hosting facility, it might be worthwhile to jump on the IBM S/390 bandwagon and centralize all your offerings. Intel's instruction set is aging, but it has had several facelifts to keep it around until 64-bit systems are ubiquitous. As of this writing, this is still at least a year out, and even then there will be advantages to scaling up past the current Intel architecture.

Risk Evaluation and Tuning

Tuning, even when done with care, involves making changes to a production system. There will always be risks with this, no matter how careful you are in preparing yourself. Balancing the risks with the payoffs is difficult, but, if approached with care, it can be done with minimal impact.

Different Levels of Risks

Depending on what needs to be tuned, different levels of risk are involved. These can range anywhere from a full outage to a split-second glitch for a couple of users, to nothing at all.

Kernel Changes

Kernel changes can be done seamlessly, if handled correctly. If the running kernel was built with support for loadable modules and has the core subsystem enabled for most devices, most driver upgrades can be done to the kernel without a reboot. Underlying SCSI support needs to be enabled as a module, though, to dynamically load a driver module for a controller. Nearly all distributions ship kernels with these switches on, and it is easy enough to do yourself if you are building your own kernel, as explained in Chapter 9, "The Linux Kernel."

If you do need to completely replace the kernel, as in a full version change, a reboot might be in order. Coordination around downtime for the box can keep unexpected problems from surfacing. Also, it is always a good idea to leave your current kernel as a runnable option at boot so that if something goes wrong, a simple reboot will get you back to the old configuration without a problem. That said, if possible, the kernel upgrade and testing should be done on a similar nonproduction system beforehand, just to make sure that there is no problem with any of the hardware drivers or general configuration differences. If you are running a production kernel (as you should), any problems that arise most likely will result from a misconfiguration of the kernel because it is very rare for a bug to enter a kernel in the stable series.

Service Changes

This is a riskier undertaking. Changing services generally implies some downtime, and a lot of things can go wrong, most of which are usually out of your control. If possible, deploy some machines in the new facility to make sure that the network and environment are prepared correctly for you. DNS propagation can take some time, so it is good to have machines answering at both sets of addresses to minimize confusion during the swap.

System Reconfiguration

Reconfiguring various parts of the system can have different effects, depending on what is changed. Changing the IP address of a machine can break the listener configuration for an Oracle database because it won't be capable of binding on the next restart. Although automatic upgrades are nice in theory because they reduce management overhead, they can cause problems if software present on the box relies on specific versions of underlying utilities. Always keep all aspects of the system in mind when performing an upgrade of any part of the machine.

Time Versus Benefits

You might have found a way to get an extra 1% out of the disk array, but it would require downtime to implement, and the array is already working at only half utilization. This is an extreme example, but it's something to keep in mind when considering modifications. Does your solution impose unnecessary risks for minimal gains? Does it really justify a week of research and testing to get that extra couple of bytes per second through the network? Keep all of these factors in mind when weighing your current set of goals and needs.

Conclusion

This chapter has thrown a lot of information at you by covering many different aspects of the system. You learned about everything from threading methodologies to drive hardware configurations—it might seem like a bit too much to handle at once, but it's important to keep everything in mind when looking at performance-tuning issues. The broadest scope needs to be taken. Then diving into the act of actually taking measurements becomes an important step in finding and eliminating bottlenecks. In the next chapter, you'll take a closer look at the tools you need to get an accurate view of your system.

Performance Tuning Tools

PART

II

IN THIS PART

3 Popular Unix Performance-Monitoring Tools
  for Linux   45

4 Linux-Specific Tools   69

Popular Unix Performance-Monitoring Tools for Linux

Before the Linux kernel, there was Unix. Well, okay, there were a lot of different flavors of Unix, but most Unix systems came from Hewlett Packard's Unix HP-UX to Sun Microsystem's SunOS and Solaris. In addition to the commercial variety, there were also other free Unix operating systems. The Berkeley Software Distribution (BSD) was the main free Unix; it later spawned three flavors of free Unix systems: OpenBSD, FreeBSD, and NetBSD.

Without going into too much historical detail, it is safe to assume that the art of performance tuning has been around a long time. To better enable the system administrator in the task of performance tuning, many tools were created on these systems well before the Linux kernel became as popular as it is today. Almost all of those tools have been ported to or rewritten for use on Linux-based operating systems. The reverse also is true: Many of the newer tools initially developed on Linux-based systems have been ported on to other flavors of Unix. This chapter looks at some of the more popular Unix tools that have been ported or rewritten for use on Linux systems.

> **NOTE**
>
> For more information on the history of Unix, go online and search `http:www.yahoo.com/` or `http://www.google.com/`. Many Web sites chronicle Unix and Unix-like operating systems history.

The Scope of These Tools and the Chapter

Take my word for it: A plethora of other performance-monitoring tools are available for Linux and other Unix operating systems. This chapter takes a look at the most common of these tools. Indeed, an entire book could be written on every single performance tool ported to or written on Linux systems. The unfortunate truth, however, is that the book would never be up-to-date because so many are added almost daily.

This chapter is divided into four generic sections of tools:

1. All-purpose tools
2. Disk benchmark tools
3. Network monitoring tools
4. Other tools

It is important to note that we do not break down the tools by subsystem alone because there are very few subsystem-specific tools. Many performance-monitoring tools can monitor all the subsystems or, as was noted in Chapter 1, "Overview of Performance Tuning," the big three: CPU, disk, and memory.

Interpreting Results and Other Notes

Before delving into how each tool works and what the returned information means, I have to throw out a disclaimer. Most performance-monitoring tools used in a somewhat random pattern can sometimes yield random results. It is quite common for documentation that comes with a tool to state that scripting with it might yield better long-term results.

To better understand this, think about real performance and perceived performance. Even the system administrator can be tricked into "freaking out" over a quick loss of performance. A prime example is with quick compiling programs. If you happen to run a monitoring tool around the same time that a programmer is running a compile, it might appear that the system is being taxed when, in fact, it is not under a sustained load. Most likely you already realize that systems will occasionally face a quick burst load that really does not harm the overall performance of the system. However, do all users or staff members realize this? Most likely they do not—remember, a little user education never hurts.

All-Purpose Tools

Unix provides many tools for the system administrator to monitor systems. However, it is worth noting at this point that what you read here about these utilities might be different, depending on your Linux distribution.

The top Utility

Arguably one of the most popular tools for performance monitoring on Unix systems in general is the top utility. As its name might suggest, this tool displays the top CPU-intensive processes in close to real time. The top display is refreshed every 5 seconds by default, but it can be modified with the -s option for longer or shorter intervals. The top utility also provides an interactive mode for modifying process behavior. The following is the syntax for starting top:

```
$ top
```

Figure 3.1 shows an example of top output to a standard terminal screen.

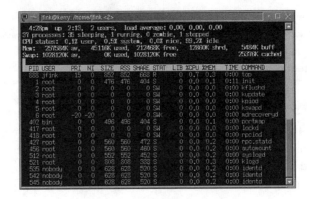

FIGURE 3.1

An example of the top process monitor.

Table 3.1 explains the monitor fields in top.

TABLE 3.1 top Monitor Fields

Field	Description
up	How long the system has been running since the last time it was rebooted. The load averages are displayed as well.
processes	Total number of processes running since the last time the top monitor checked. This measurement includes all processes on the system.
CPU States	An average percent of CPU time. This field examines all aspects of CPU time, including user, idle, and niced tasks. Because niced tasks are included, the total can go over 100%, so do not be alarmed if this is the case (unless it is an outrageous value, such as 160%).
Mem	All the memory statistics, such as total memory, available memory for nonkernel processes, memory in use, and memory that is shared and buffered.
Swap	Swap statistics, including total allocated swap space, available swap space, and used swap space.

Table 3.2 explains the process fields in top.

TABLE 3.2 top Process Fields

Field	Description
PID	Process ID of each task.
USER	Username of each task.

TABLE 3.2   Continued

Field	Description
PRI	Priority of each task.
NI	Nice value of each task.
SIZE	Total size of a task, including code and data, plus the stack space in kilobytes.
RSS	Amount of physical memory used by the task.
SHARE	Amount of shared memory used by a task.
STATE	Current CPU state of a task. The states can be S for sleeping, D for uninterrupted, R for running, T for stopped/traced, and Z for zombied.
TIME	The CPU time that a task has used since it started.
%CPU	The CPU time that a task has used since the last update.
%MEM	A task's share of physical memory.
COMMAND	The task's command name.

NOTE

A task's command name is truncated if the tasks have only the program name in parentheses.

In addition to just watching the top display, you can manipulate the top display in interactive mode and modify running processes. The interactive mode is invoked by pressing H while the display is running.

What about understanding what top tells you and knowing how to filter? A good example is simple filtering. In this example, a process is intermittently jumping to the top of the monitor. It might help to stop the monitor and start it with a few filtering options to get rid of information that you do not want:

```
$ top -i
```

Still, you cannot catch the culprit in action. Next you can disable some of the information that you want by toggling on or off displays such as the memory summary.

The great thing about top is that it provides a lot of different information quickly, and it updates periodically. For example, a process might be at the top, but why? Is it because it requires more processor time? Or is it eating memory? With the additional fields shown, more information is displayed in one location.

3

Unix
Performance-
Monitoring Tools

vmstat

The name vmstat comes from "report virtual memory statistics." The vmstat utility does a bit more than this, though. In addition to reporting virtual memory, vmstat reports certain kernel statistics about processes, disk, trap, and CPU activity.

The syntax for vmstat is as follows:

```
$ vmstat interval [count]
```

A sample syntax with an interval of 5 seconds and five counts would look like this:

```
$ vmstat 5 5
   procs                      memory      swap        io     system        cpu
 r  b  w   swpd   free   buff   cache  si  so   bi    bo   in    cs  us  sy  id
 0  0  0    380   3760  71616 944176   0   0   24    13   40    45   0   0  32
 0  0  0    380   3760  71616 944176   0   0    0     4  105     5   0   1  99
 0  0  0    380   3760  71616 944176   0   0    0     1  105     4   0   0 100
 0  0  0    380   3760  71616 944176   0   0    0     0  103     4   0   0 100
 0  0  0    380   3760  71616 944176   0   0    0     0  103     5   0   0 100
```

The very first line of output by vmstat is the average values for statistics since boot time, so do not be alarmed by high values.

The vmstat output is actually broken up into five sections: procs, memory, swap, io, and cpu.

Each section is outlined in the following table.

TABLE 3.3 The procs Section

Field	Description
r	Number of processes that are in a wait state and basically not doing anything but waiting to run
b	Number of processes that were in sleep mode and were interrupted since the last update
w	Number of processes that have been swapped out by mm and vm subsystems and have yet to run

TABLE 3.4 The Memory Section

Field	Description
swpd	The total amount of physical virtual memory in use
free	The amount of physical memory that is free or available
buff	Memory that was being buffered when the measurement was taken
cache	Cache that is in use

TABLE 3.5   The Swap Section

Field	Description
si	Amount of memory transferred from swap space back into memory
so	Amount of memory swapped to disk

TABLE 3.6   The IO Section

Field	Description
bi	Disk blocks sent to disk devices in blocks per second

TABLE 3.7   The System Section

Field	Description
in	Interrupts per second, including the CPU clocks
cs	Context switches per second within the kernel

TABLE 3.8   The CPU Section

Field	Description
us	Percentage of CPU cycles spent on user processes
sy	Percentage of CPU cycles spent on system processes
id	Percentage of unused CPU cycles or idle time when the CPU is basically doing nothing

Interpreting the output of these measurements tells you that there is some outbound disk activity (as shown by the bo field). Also note the increase in the in field of the system section once vmstat was started. This implies that vmstat increases the number of interrupts. Here you return to the idea of properly reading output. It is a good idea to look at the tools covered in this chapter when the system is idling so that you know what effect a performance-monitoring tool can have on the system.

xload and xosview

Along with many command-line–driven tools for Unix systems are X11-based tools. This section covers two of them, xload and xosview. Both distinctly different graphical monitoring tools, they provide a very quick glance method of watching your systems run.

3

Unix Performance-Monitoring Tools

xload

The first of the two is xload. In a nutshell, xload displays the system load average. It also has an alarm bar that shows when the load average is high. Figure 3.2 shows what xload typically looks like.

FIGURE 3.2

An example of xload.

To start xload, simply open an xterminal on the system and type the following:

```
$ xload &
```

The system knows to which display to go, so it automatically pops up. If you are running xload from a remote system to your X Window System, you can do one of two things:

1. Set a permanent DISPLAY variable in your .profile by entering this:

   ```
   DISPLAY=<your_ip_address>:0
   export DISPLAY
   ```

2. Simply direct it to your system with this syntax:

   ```
   $ xload -display <your_ip_address> &
   ```

The xload utility displays a histogram (chart) of the system load average. It updates this information periodically. The default is every 10 seconds, but this can be changed with the –update option.

xosview

The xosview utility can display a much more detailed collection of histograms about the system's performance in close to real time.

Of course, you easily can filter what you want to see in xosview using command-line options by specifying the subsystem with + or - (true and false, respectively). For example, to not see the CPU histogram, the syntax would be this:

```
$ xosview -cpu &
```

The xosview utility can be started from remote systems to a local X server in the same manner as xload. The colors, font, and other properties can be controlled by Xresource settings.

FIGURE 3.3
xosview, with all subsystems being monitored.

One interesting aspect of xosview is that it combines certain histograms into one horizontal bar. This requires some explanation.

- **LOAD**—This field has two colors. The first color is the load average of processes, and the second color (the background color) is idle processes relative to the load average. When the load average goes above 1.0, the bar will change colors.

- **CPU**—The CPU field has four colors related to process type usage: usr, nice, sys, and free.

- **MEM**—In this field, the full amount of real memory in use is shown. There are four colors in this field: user-allocated memory, shared memory, buffers, and free memory.

- **SWAP**—Swap has two colors; the first indicates the swap in use, and the second indicates what is free.

- **PAGE**—This field has three colors: in, for paging in; out, for paging out; and idle.

- **DISK**—This field has three colors: in, for transfers to disk; out for transfers from disk; and idle.

- **INTS**—This field is a set of indicators that correspond to IRQ usage. They are numbered starting at 0 from the left.

uptime

The uptime command displays the current time, the length of time that the system has been up, the number of users, and the load average of the system over the last 1, 5, and 15 minutes. It looks something like this:

```
6:51PM  up 2 days, 22:50, 6 users, load averages: 0.18, 0.30, 0.34
```

Benchmarking Your Disks with Bonnie

Most disk performance-monitoring tools are built into other performance-monitoring tools (take vmstat, for example). However, there is another approach to take. Benchmarking tools can help ascertain a performance bottleneck, even though the one that will be discussed in this section actually can cause somewhat of a bottleneck itself. At the least, it is a good way to test systems before they are put into production.

The particular tool that this section addresses is called bonnie. The bonnie utility runs a performance test of filesystem I/O; it uses standard C library calls. Bonnie writes 8KB blocks in an attempt to discover the maximum sustained rate of transfer. As an added bonus, it cycles through rereading and rewriting to accurately simulate filesystem usage.

To use bonnie, the syntax is pretty simple:

```
bonnie -d <scratch_directory> -s <size_in_MB_of_testfiles> -m
➥<machine_label>
```

If no directory is specified, bonnie writes to the current working directory. If no size is given, 10MB is used. The machine label generally does not matter.

The following is some sample output of bonnie on a Sun SparcSTATION5:

```
$ bonnie
File './Bonnie.2831', size: 104857600
Writing with putc()...done
Rewriting...done
Writing intelligently...done
Reading with getc()...done
Reading intelligently...done
Seeker 1...Seeker 2...Seeker 3...start 'em...done...done...done...
              -------Sequential Output-------- ---Sequential Input-- --Random--
              -Per Char- --Block--- -Rewrite-- -Per Char- --Block--- --Seeks---
Machine    MB K/sec %CPU K/sec %CPU K/sec %CPU K/sec %CPU K/sec %CPU  /sec %CPU
          100 1650 65.0  1791 12.2  1141 14.1  2379 88.3  3285 20.4  62.5  4.9
$
```

As you can see, the fields of the final output are very self-explanatory. Now here are the results of bonnie on an x86 platform:

```
$ bonnie
File './Bonnie.22239', size: 104857600
Writing with putc()...done
Rewriting...done
Writing intelligently...done
Reading with getc()...done
Reading intelligently...done
Seeker 1...Seeker 2...Seeker 3...start 'em...done...done...done...
              -------Sequential Output-------- ---Sequential Input-- --Random--
              -Per Char- --Block--- -Rewrite-- -Per Char- --Block--- --Seeks---
Machine    MB K/sec %CPU K/sec %CPU K/sec %CPU K/sec %CPU K/sec %CPU  /sec %CPU
          100 2204 12.5  2244  4.3   925  3.1  2356 11.4  2375  6.3  43.0  1.1
$
```

Just a little different?

Tools like bonnie really help illustrate the difference between an untuned system and a tuned one, or an older (in this case, the sparc system) and a new one (and x86 box).

Other Tools

In addition to the general tools and subsystem-specific ones, you have a variety of mixed and other performance-monitoring tools at your disposal. The next sections look at these in more detail.

ps

The ps command is another highly used tool where performance is concerned. Most often it is used to isolate a particular process. However, it also has numerous options that can help you get more out of ps and perhaps save some time while trying to isolate a particular process.

The ps command basically reports process status. When invoked without any options, the output looks something like this:

```
$ ps
  PID TTY          TIME CMD
 3220 pts/0    00:00:00 bash
 3251 pts/0    00:00:00 ps
```

This basically tells you everything that the current session of the user who invoked it is doing.

Obviously, just seeing what you are doing in your current session is not always all that helpful—unless, of course, you are doing something very detrimental in the background!

To look at other users or the system as a whole, ps requires some further options. The ps command's options on Linux are actually grouped into sections based on selection criteria.

Let's look at these sections and what they can do.

Simple Process Selection

Using simple process selection, you can be a little selective about what you see. For example, if you want to see only processes that are attached to your current terminal, you would use the -T option:

```
[jfink@kerry jfink]$ ps -T
  PID TTY      STAT    TIME COMMAND
 1668 pts/0    S       0:00 login -- jfink
 1669 pts/0    S       0:00 -bash
 1708 pts/0    R       0:00 ps -T
```

Process Selection by List

Another way to control what you see with ps is to view by a list type. As an example, if you want to see all the identd processes running, you would use the -C option from this group that displays a given command:

```
[jfink@kerry jfink]$ ps -C identd
  PID TTY          TIME CMD
  535 ?        00:00:00 identd
  542 ?        00:00:00 identd
  545 ?        00:00:00 identd
  546 ?        00:00:00 identd
  550 ?        00:00:00 identd
```

Output Format Control

Following process selection is output control. This is helpful when you want to see information in a particular format. A good example is using the jobs format with the -j option:

```
[jfink@kerry jfink]$ ps -j
  PID  PGID   SID TTY          TIME CMD
 1669  1669  1668 pts/0    00:00:00 bash
 1729  1729  1668 pts/0    00:00:00 ps
```

Output Modifiers

Output modifiers can apply high-level changes to the output. The following is the output using the -e option to show the environment after running ps:

```
[jfink@kerry jfink]$ ps ae
  PID TTY      STAT   TIME COMMAND
 1668 pts/0    S      0:00 login -- jfink
 1669 pts/0    S      0:00 -bash TERM=ansi REMOTEHOST=172.16.14.102
HOME=/home/j
 1754 pts/0    R      0:00 ps ae LESSOPEN=|/usr/bin/lesspipe.sh %s
```

The remaining sections are INFORMATION, which provides versioning information and help, and OBSOLETE options. The next three sections give some specific cases of using ps with certain options.

Some Sample ps Output

Of course, reading the man page helps, but a few practical applied examples always light the way a little better.

The most commonly used ps switch on Linux and BSD systems is this:

```
$ ps aux
USER       PID %CPU %MEM   VSZ  RSS TTY      STAT START   TIME COMMAND
root         1  0.0  0.0  1116  380 ?        S    Jan27   0:01 init [3]
```

```
root         2   0.0   0.0      0      0 ?       SW   Jan27   0:03 [kflushd]
root         3   0.0   0.0      0      0 ?       SW   Jan27   0:18 [kupdate]
root         4   0.0   0.0      0      0 ?       SW   Jan27   0:00 [kpiod]
root         5   0.0   0.0      0      0 ?       SW   Jan27   0:38 [kswapd]
bin        260   0.0   0.0   1112    452 ?       S    Jan27   0:00 portmap
root       283   0.0   0.0   1292    564 ?       S    Jan27   0:00 syslogd -m 0
root       294   0.0   0.0   1480    700 ?       S    Jan27   0:00 klogd
daemon     308   0.0   0.0   1132    460 ?       S    Jan27   0:00 /usr/sbin/atd
root       322   0.0   0.0   1316    460 ?       S    Jan27   0:00 crond
root       322   0.0   0.0   1316    460 ?       S    Jan27   0:00 crond
root       336   0.0   0.0   1260    412 ?       S    Jan27   0:00 inetd
root       371   0.0   0.0   1096    408 ?       S    Jan27   0:00 rpc.rquotad
root       382   0.0   0.0   1464    160 ?       S    Jan27   0:00 [rpc.mountd]
root       393   0.0   0.0      0      0 ?       SW   Jan27   2:15 [nfsd]
root       394   0.0   0.0      0      0 ?       SW   Jan27   2:13 [nfsd]
root       395   0.0   0.0      0      0 ?       SW   Jan27   2:13 [nfsd]
root       396   0.0   0.0      0      0 ?       SW   Jan27   2:12 [nfsd]
root       397   0.0   0.0      0      0 ?       SW   Jan27   2:12 [nfsd]
root       398   0.0   0.0      0      0 ?       SW   Jan27   2:12 [nfsd]
root       399   0.0   0.0      0      0 ?       SW   Jan27   2:11 [nfsd]
root       400   0.0   0.0      0      0 ?       SW   Jan27   2:14 [nfsd]
root       428   0.0   0.0   1144    488 ?       S    Jan27   0:00 gpm -t ps/2
root       466   0.0   0.0   1080    408 tty1    S    Jan27   0:00 /sbin/mingetty
➥tt
root       467   0.0   0.0   1080    408 tty2    S    Jan27   0:00 /sbin/mingetty
➥tt
root       468   0.0   0.0   1080    408 tty3    S    Jan27   0:00 /sbin/mingetty
➥tt
root       469   0.0   0.0   1080    408 tty4    S    Jan27   0:00 /sbin/mingetty
➥tt
root       470   0.0   0.0   1080    408 tty5    S    Jan27   0:00 /sbin/mingetty
➥tt
root       471   0.0   0.0   1080    408 tty6    S    Jan27   0:00 /sbin/mingetty
➥tt
root      3326   0.0   0.0   1708    892 ?       R    Jan30   0:00 in.telnetd
root      3327   0.0   0.1   2196   1096 pts/0   S    Jan30   0:00 login -- jfink
jfink     3328   0.0   0.0   1764   1012 pts/0   S    Jan30   0:00 -bash
jfink     3372   0.0   0.0   2692   1008 pts/0   R    Jan30   0:00 ps aux
```

The output implies that this system's main job is to serve files via NFS, and indeed it is. It also doubles as an FTP server, but no connections were active when this output was captured.

The output of ps can tell you a lot more—sometimes just simple things that can improve performance. Looking at this NFS server again, you can see that it is not too busy; actually, it gets used only a few times a day. So what are some simple things that could be done to make it run even faster? Well, for starters, you could reduce the number of virtual consoles that are accessible via the system console. I like to have a minimum of three running (in case I lock one or two). A total of six are shown in the output (the mingetty processes). There are also nine available nfsd processes; if the system is not used very often and only by a few users, that number can be reduced to something a little more reasonable.

Now you can see where tuning can be applied outside the kernel. Sometimes just entire processes do not need to be running, but those that require multiple instances (such as NFS, MySQL, or HTTP, for example) can be minimized to what is required for good operations.

The Process Forest

The process forest is a great way of seeing exactly how processes and their parents are related. The following output is a portion of the same system used in the previous section:

```
...
root       336  0.0  0.0  1260   412 ?      S    Jan27  0:00 inetd
root      3326  0.0  0.0  1708   892 ?      S    Jan30  0:00  \_ in.telnetd
root      3327  0.0  0.1  2196  1096 pts/0  S    Jan30  0:00       \_ login --
jfink     3328  0.0  0.0  1768  1016 pts/0  S    Jan30  0:00            \_ -
bash
jfink     3384  0.0  0.0  2680   976 pts/0  R    Jan30  0:00                 \_
p
s
...
```

Based on that output, you easily can see how the system call fork got its name.

The application here is great. Sometimes a process itself is not to blame—and what if you kill an offending process only to find it respawned? The tree view can help track down the original process and kill it.

Singling Out a User

Last but definitely not least, you might need (or want) to look at a particular user's activities. On this particular system, my user account is the only userland account that does anything. I have chosen root to be the user to look at:

```
$ ps u --User root
USER       PID %CPU %MEM   VSZ  RSS TTY      STAT START   TIME COMMAND
root         1  0.0  0.0  1116  380 ?        S    Jan27  0:01 init [3]
root         2  0.0  0.0     0    0 ?        SW   Jan27  0:03 [kflushd]
root         3  0.0  0.0     0    0 ?        SW   Jan27  0:18 [kupdate]
root         4  0.0  0.0     0    0 ?        SW   Jan27  0:00 [kpiod]
root         5  0.0  0.0     0    0 ?        SW   Jan27  0:38 [kswapd]
root       283  0.0  0.0  1292  564 ?        S    Jan27  0:00 syslogd -m 0
root       294  0.0  0.0  1480  700 ?        S    Jan27  0:00 klogd
daemon     308  0.0  0.0  1132  460 ?        S    Jan27  0:00 /usr/sbin/atd
root       322  0.0  0.0  1316  460 ?        S    Jan27  0:00 crond
root       336  0.0  0.0  1260  412 ?        S    Jan27  0:00 inetd
```

root	350	0.0	0.0	1312	512	?	S	Jan27	0:00 lpd
root	371	0.0	0.0	1096	408	?	S	Jan27	0:00 rpc.rquotad
root	382	0.0	0.0	1464	160	?	S	Jan27	0:00 [rpc.mountd]
root	393	0.0	0.0	0	0	?	SW	Jan27	2:15 [nfsd]
root	394	0.0	0.0	0	0	?	SW	Jan27	2:13 [nfsd]
root	395	0.0	0.0	0	0	?	SW	Jan27	2:13 [nfsd]
root	396	0.0	0.0	0	0	?	SW	Jan27	2:12 [nfsd]
root	397	0.0	0.0	0	0	?	SW	Jan27	2:12 [nfsd]
root	398	0.0	0.0	0	0	?	SW	Jan27	2:12 [nfsd]
root	399	0.0	0.0	0	0	?	SW	Jan27	2:11 [nfsd]
root	400	0.0	0.0	0	0	?	SW	Jan27	2:14 [nfsd]
root	428	0.0	0.0	1144	488	?	S	Jan27	0:00 gpm -t ps/2
root tty	466	0.0	0.0	1080	408	tty1	S	Jan27	0:00 /sbin/mingetty
root tty	467	0.0	0.0	1080	408	tty2	S	Jan27	0:00 /sbin/mingetty
root tty	468	0.0	0.0	1080	408	tty3	S	Jan27	0:00 /sbin/mingetty
root tty	469	0.0	0.0	1080	408	tty4	S	Jan27	0:00 /sbin/mingetty
root tty	470	0.0	0.0	1080	408	tty5	S	Jan27	0:00 /sbin/mingetty
root tty	471	0.0	0.0	1080	408	tty6	S	Jan27	0:00 /sbin/mingetty
root	3326	0.0	0.0	1708	892	?	R	Jan30	0:00 in.telnetd
root	3327	0.0	0.1	2196	1096	pts/0	S	Jan30	0:00 login - jfink

Applying only a single user's process is helpful when a user might have a runaway. Here's a quick example: A particular piece of software used by the company for which I work did not properly die when an attached terminal disappeared (it has been cleaned up since then). It collected error messages into memory until it was killed. To make matters worse, these error message went into shared memory queues.

The only solution was for the system administrator to log in and kill the offending process. Of course, after a period of time, a script was written that would allow users to do this in a safe manner. On this particular system, there were thousands of concurrent processes. Only by filtering based on the user or doing a grep from the whole process table was it possible to figure out which process it was and any other processes that it might be affecting.

free

The free command rapidly snags information about the state of memory on your Linux system. The syntax for free is pretty straightforward:

```
$ free
```

The following is an example of free's output:

```
$ free
              total       used       free     shared    buffers     cached
Mem:        1036152    1033560       2592       8596      84848     932080
-/+ buffers/cache:        16632    1019520
Swap:        265064        380     264684
```

The first line of output shows the physical memory, and the last line shows similar information about swap. Table 3.9 explains the output of free.

TABLE 3.9   free Command Output Fields

Field	Description
total	Total amount of user available memory, excluding the kernel memory. (Don't be alarmed when this is lower than the memory on the machine.)
used	Total amount of used memory.
free	Total amount of memory that is free.
shared	Total amount of shared memory that is in use.
buffers	Current size of the disk buffer cache.
cached	Amount of memory that has been cached off onto disk.

An analysis of the sample output shows that this system seems to be pretty healthy. Of course, this is only one measurement. What if you want to watch the memory usage over time? The free command provides an option to do just that: the -s option. The -s option activates polling at a specified interval. The following is an example:

```
[jfink@kerry jfink]$ free -s 60
total       used       free     shared    buffers     cached
Mem:         257584      65244     192340      12132      40064       4576
-/+ buffers/cache:      20604     236980
Swap:       1028120          0    1028120


              total       used       free     shared    buffers     cached
Mem:         257584      66424     191160      12200      40084       5728
-/+ buffers/cache:      20612     236972
```

```
Swap:        1028120        0    1028120

                total     used       free   shared   buffers   cached
Mem:           257584    66528     191056    12200     40084     5812
-/+ buffers/cache:        20632     236952
Swap:        1028120        0    1028120
...
```

To stop `free` from polling, hit an interrupt key.

These measurements show a pretty quiet system, but the `free` command can come in handy if you want to see the effect of one particular command on the system. Run the command when the system is idling, and poll memory with `free`. `free` is well suited for this because of the granularity that you get in the output.

time

One very simple tool for examining the system is the `time` command. The `time` command comes in handy for relatively quick checks of how the system performs when a certain command is invoked. The way this works is simple: `time` returns a string value with information about the process and is launched with process like this:

```
$ time <command_name> [options]
```

Here is an example:

```
$ time cc hello.c -o hello
```

The output from the `time` command looks like this:

```
$ time cc hello.c -o hello
0.08user 0.04system 0:00.11elapsed 107%CPU (0avgtext+0avgdata 0maxresident)k
0inputs+0outputs (985major+522minor)pagefaults 0swaps
```

Even though this output is quite low-level, the `time` command can return very enlightening information about a particular command or program. It becomes very helpful in large environments in which operations normally take a long time. An example of this is comparing kernel compile times between different machines.

Some Network-Monitoring Tools

Many times system performance can be relative to external factors such as the network. Unix has a vast array of tools to examine network performance, from single host-monitoring software to applications than can monitor and manage vast WANs. This section looks at four relatively low-key applications for monitoring network activity:

- ping
- traceroute
- tcpdump
- ntop

ping

The ping utility is a very simple program that is most often used to simply see if a host is alive on the network. However, the return information from ping can often tell you how well a particular host-to-host connection is performing. The following is a sample of a ping session:

```
$ ping tesla
PING tesla.dp.asi (192.187.226.6): 56 data bytes
64 bytes from 192.187.226.6: icmp_seq=0 ttl=255 time=6.119 ms
64 bytes from 192.187.226.6: icmp_seq=1 ttl=255 time=0.620 ms
64 bytes from 192.187.226.6: icmp_seq=2 ttl=255 time=3.483 ms
64 bytes from 192.187.226.6: icmp_seq=3 ttl=255 time=1.340 ms
64 bytes from 192.187.226.6: icmp_seq=4 ttl=255 time=0.633 ms
64 bytes from 192.187.226.6: icmp_seq=5 ttl=255 time=7.803 ms
64 bytes from 192.187.226.6: icmp_seq=6 ttl=255 time=5.475 ms
--- tesla.dp.asi ping statistics ---
7 packets transmitted, 7 packets received, 0% packet loss
round-trip min/avg/max/std-dev = 0.620/3.639/7.803/2.681 ms
```

Not too bad at all. Now I have purposely saturated the interface on host tesla (with several other pings running with the -f option to flood it at once, of course). Look at the results:

```
$ ping tesla
PING tesla.dp.asi (192.187.226.6): 56 data bytes
64 bytes from 192.187.226.6: icmp_seq=0 ttl=255 time=3.805 ms
64 bytes from 192.187.226.6: icmp_seq=1 ttl=255 time=1.804 ms
64 bytes from 192.187.226.6: icmp_seq=2 ttl=255 time=8.672 ms
64 bytes from 192.187.226.6: icmp_seq=3 ttl=255 time=1.616 ms
64 bytes from 192.187.226.6: icmp_seq=4 ttl=255 time=6.793 ms
64 bytes from 192.187.226.6: icmp_seq=5 ttl=255 time=1.607 ms
64 bytes from 192.187.226.6: icmp_seq=6 ttl=255 time=2.393 ms
64 bytes from 192.187.226.6: icmp_seq=7 ttl=255 time=1.601 ms
64 bytes from 192.187.226.6: icmp_seq=8 ttl=255 time=6.073 ms
64 bytes from 192.187.226.6: icmp_seq=9 ttl=255 time=1.615 ms
64 bytes from 192.187.226.6: icmp_seq=10 ttl=255 time=9.402 ms
64 bytes from 192.187.226.6: icmp_seq=11 ttl=255 time=1.875 ms
64 bytes from 192.187.226.6: icmp_seq=12 ttl=255 time=1.815 ms
--- tesla.dp.asi ping statistics ---
13 packets transmitted, 13 packets received, 0% packet loss
round-trip min/avg/max/std-dev = 0.601/2.774/8.402/2.802 ms
```

As you can see, there is a slightly higher time lapse, on average.

ping has a number of useful options. Table 3.10 lists some of them with example usage ideas:

TABLE 3.10   ping Options

-c	This option means that ping will ping a node only *c* times. This is especially useful for noninteractive scripts or if you are not interested in watching ping for more than a quick test to determine whether it is alive.
-f	The flood option sends requests as fast as the host you are pinging from can. This is a good way to measure just how well a host can send them. As mentioned in a previous example, it's also an easy way to load down a system for testing.
-r	This option bypasses routing tables and helps if a new node is on the network but the system you are pinging from either is not aware of it or is not in the same subnet.
-s	This option can modify the packet size and is useful for seeing whether the node that is being pinged is having issues with the size of packets being sent to it from other nodes.

traceroute

The traceroute utility is invaluable for discovering where a problem on a network might be located. It also is of great use in ensuring that your host is talking to the network just fine and that any problems might lie elsewhere. On this particular network, I show two traceroutes, one to a host that is local to the network and one to a remote host on a network in another city. The difference between these is astounding.

Here's the local traceroute:

```
$ traceroute andy
traceroute to strider.diverge.org (192.168.1.1), 64 hops max, 40 byte packets
 1  strider.diverge.org (192.168.1.1)  0.547 ms  0.469 ms  3.383 ms
$
```

And here's the remote traceroute:

```
$ traceroute www.diverge.org
traceroute to www.diverge.org (192.168.2.2), 64 hops max, 40 byte packets
 1  strider.diverge.org (192.168.1.1)  7.791 ms  7.182 ms  6.457 ms
 2  gandalf.diverge.org (192.168.2.1)  43.978 ms  41.325 ms  43.904 ms
 3  www.diverge.org (192.168.2.2)  41.293 ms  41.366 ms  41.683 ms
$
```

3

Unix Performance-Monitoring Tools

In this output, you easily can see the routers between my localhost and the remote host www.diverge.org—they are strider.diverge.org and gandalf.diverge.org. The fields are hop-number hostname IPaddress times.

Using the Sniffer tcpdump

A sniffer is a network-monitoring system that captures a great deal of information about the real content of a given network. Sniffers are particularly powerful because they allow for the storage of several layers of TCP information, which, of course, can be used for performing malicious attacks as well as monitoring.

On the upside, a sniffer can provide detailed information for troubleshooting efforts. Figure 3.4 is a snapshot of tcpdump.

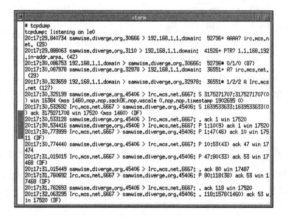

FIGURE 3.4

tcpdump *output.*

The output when tcpdump is started with no options is dizzying. The tcpdump sniffer has an immense amount of command-line switches and options.

Some Practical Applications for tcpdump

Obviously, the output of tcpdump is rather intense. After reviewing some of the options, you have probably surmised that there are ways to focus the tcpdump utility to look for particular information. Table 3.11 describes some options and shows what particular problem they can be used to address.

TABLE 3.11

Command String	Application
tcpdump tcp host <ip_address>	SYN floods
tcpdump dst host <ip_address>	Network stack overflows (a.k.a. Ping of Death)
tcpdump icmp dst host <broadcast_address>	Smurf attacks
tcpdump -e host <ip_address>	Duplicate IP addresses
tcpdump arp	ARP misconfiguration
tcpdump icmp	Routing issues

As an example, let's say that you want to look at ICMP traffic on the local network:

```
#
[root@kerry /root]# tcpdump icmp
Kernel filter, protocol ALL, datagram packet socket
tcpdump: listening on all devices
11:48:30.214757 eth1 M 172.16.141.99 > 192.187.225.50: icmp: echo request
11:48:30.215135 eth1 M 172.16.141.99 > arouter.local.net: icmp: echo request
11:48:32.277764 eth1 M 172.16.141.99 > frame.local.net: icmp: echo request
. . .
```

This output tells you that there are a lot of echo requests from the node at 172.16.141.99. In fact, this is a new router being installed, and the administrator is probing the network from the router.

ntop

One particularly interesting tool for constant network monitoring is the ntop utility. Basically, ntop displays the top network users. Figure 3.5 shows ntop running in an xterminal.

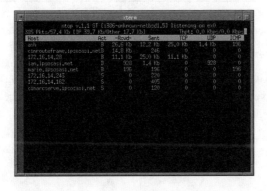

FIGURE 3.5

ntop *in action.*

The `ntop` utility has a vast array of command-line options and interactive commands. Table 3.12 gives a few examples of the more interesting ones.

TABLE 3.12   ntop Options

-r	Changes the rate that `ntop` updates the screen display. This is very helpful for determining time ranges in which a problem may be occurring.
-p	Specifies the IP protocol to monitor. Because the default is `all`, this option can act as a filter.
-l	Logs information captured by `ntop` into `ntop.log`. An application here is post-analysis of `ntop` results.

Interpreting `ntop` is pretty straightforward. The Host field contains either a hostname (if it can be resolved) or an IP address.

TABLE 3.13   ntop Output Fields

Field	Description
Host	Contains either a hostname (if it can be resolved) or an IP address
Act	Gives more information about the host:
	B indicates that a host has received and sent data.
	R indicates that a host has received data.
	S indicates that a host has sent data.
	I indicates that a host is idle.
Rcvd	Shows the amount of traffic that a host received between updates.
Sent	Shows the amount of traffic that a host sent between updates.
<protocol>	Gives three columns (TCP, UDP, and ICMP) that show the changes of the protocol type.

To make a little more sense of this, consider the following line as an example:

```
cingwise.ipsosasi.net   S   2.2 Kb  4.8 MB  1.8 Kb    420    0  0
```

The hostname is cingwise.ipsosasi.net, and the last thing the host did was send traffic. During the last update, it received 2.2Kb and sent 4.8MB; there was a difference of 420 bytes between updates in traffic with the TCP protocol.

The `ntop` utility is very useful for watching network activity in general.

Summary

This chapter examined popular Unix tools that have been ported to or rewritten for use on Linux. It also covered analyzing the output of these tools. The next chapter moves forward to tools that were specifically designed on Linux for performance monitoring.

3

Unix
Performance-
Monitoring Tools

Linux-Specific Tools

Performance monitoring and tuning are not the easiest of tasks. Both require a large toolbox and the expertise to understand exactly what many of those tools are conveying. Chapter 3, "Popular Unix Performance-Monitoring Tools for Linux," discussed how to interpret generic tools for Unix operating systems.

Coupled with the normal complexities of understanding generic tools, operating systems have their own eccentricities or differences. All Unix or Unix-like operating systems have their own differences. In some cases these differences are seen only in system administration commands; in other cases, the performance analyst faces a myriad of differences in the underlying subsystems and architecture.

Because of these underlying differences among operating systems and even revisions within those systems, performance-monitoring tools must be tailored to the OS. Many tools (such as the generic Unix tools) are portable or can be emulated easily for use on Linux (vmstat is one example). Not all tools are easily ported, though, and sometimes it is easier to design a tool specifically for a particular operating system.

The Linux kernel has inspired a great deal of software writers to write tools just for the Linux kernel and subsystems. This is due partly to the efforts of ibiblio.org (formerly metalab, which was formerly sunsite). Authors can write their tools, package them, and upload them to the ibiblio.org FTP server for the rest of the Linux world to use at no cost.

This chapter examines tools designed to be used specifically with Linux, as well as some tools that originally were used for Linux and that have been ported to other Unix-like and Unix operating systems.

The sysstat for Linux Distribution

In 1999, a bright software writer named Sebastien Godard wrote a set of utilities for Linux called sysstat. In sysstat the entire collection of tools includes mpstat, iostat, sar, isag, and sa tools. These tools exist on other systems, but Godard wrote versions of them for Linux. This section looks at iostat and mpstat.

> **NOTE**
>
> The sysstat package can be downloaded in a variety of formats from `ftp://ftp.ibiblio.org/pub/Linux/system/status/`, or from the sysstat Web site at `http://perso.wanadoo.fr/sebastien.godard/`.

iostat for Linux

The iostat utility is a common Unix utility.

As you might have guessed, the iostat utility monitors system I/O. It can generate two types of reports:

- CPU utilization
- Device utilization

The general syntax of iostat is as follows:

```
iostat iostat [ -c | -d ] [ -t ] [ -V ] [  -x  [  device  ]  ] [interval [
►count ] ]
```

In the most generic form, iostat can be run like this:

```
iostat
```

The following is an example of iostat running:

```
# iostat 10 2
Linux 2.2.14-5.0smp (kerry)     03/09/01
avg-cpu:  %user   %nice   %sys   %idle
0.27    0.00    0.44   99.29
avg-cpu:  %user   %nice   %sys   %idle
          0.40    0.00    1.10   98.50
Device:        tps   Blk_read/s   Blk_wrtn/s   Blk_read   Blk_wrtn
hdisk0        1.90       0.00        15.20         0        152
hdisk1        0.00       0.00         0.00         0          0
hdisk2        0.00       0.00         0.00         0          0
hdisk3        0.00       0.00         0.00         0          0

avg-cpu:  %user   %nice   %sys   %idle
          0.70    0.40    0.40   98.90
Device:        tps   Blk_read/s   Blk_wrtn/s   Blk_read   Blk_wrtn
hdisk0        1.90       0.00        15.20         0        152
hdisk1        0.00       0.00         0.00         0          0
hdisk2        0.00       0.00         0.00         0          0
hdisk3        0.00       0.00         0.00         0          0
```

NOTE

The first report contains information about the system since system startup. Do not be alarmed.

4

LINUX-SPECIFIC
TOOLS

The CPU utilization report is the first of the two reports generated. It has the following data fields:

- %user
- %nice
- %sys
- %idle

Table 4.1 illustrates each field.

TABLE 4.1   iostat CPU Utilization Fields

%user	The CPU utilization percentage measurement, for user processes only or those in nonprivileged mode
%nice	Percentage of CPU utilization that occurred at a modified nice level
%sys	Percentage of CPU utilization that was executed in system or privileged mode
%idle	Percentage that the CPU was idling or rather doing nothing

It is worth noting some terminology here: The %user and %nice fields occur at the application level, or, as many people (especially in the BSD communities) refer to it, in "userland." The %sys field occurs at the kernel level, or in privileged mode. The terms *application*, *nonprivileged*, and *userland* all mean the same thing—they're processes that do not have direct access to the kernel. By the same token, *system*, *privileged*, and *kernel* (within this context) all refer to processes that can talk directly to the kernel.

The next portion of the report contains the device utilization fields. Table 4.2 explains what each field represents.

TABLE 4.2   iostat Default Device Utilization Fields

tps	A verbose listing of the number of transfers per second that were sent to a device.
Blk_reads/s	The amount of data read from the device. In the case of these disks, this is expressed in the number of blocks per second.
Blk_wrtn/s	Data written to a device. Again, this is expressed in the number of blocks per second.
Blk_read	Blocks read from the device per second.
Blk_wrtn	Blocks written to the device per second.

Now let's interpret the output of the example output shown previously. According to the fields of the output, this system was doing a lot of writing to disk when the measurements were taken. If you look at the second set of the report, you will notice that the nice field is 0.40. In reality, a large binary file was being written during both measurements. When the first set ran, it was running with default priority; when it was run again, the nice value was modified.

Additional `iostat` Options

The output and information can be modified for `iostat` with a few options.

Here is some sample output using the `-c` option to show only the CPU utilization report and the `-d` modifier to show the device report:

```
[jfink@kerry jfink]$ iostat -c 2 2
Linux 2.2.14-5.0smp (kerry)      03/09/01


avg-cpu:  %user   %nice    %sys    %idle
           0.01    0.00    0.01     9.73
avg-cpu:  %user   %nice    %sys    %idle
           0.00    0.00    0.00   100.00
[jfink@kerry jfink]$ iostat -d
Linux 2.2.14-5.0smp (kerry)      03/09/01


Device:         tps   Blk_read/s   Blk_wrtn/s   Blk_read   Blk_wrtn
hdisk0         0.05         0.12         0.24     236966     460096
hdisk1         0.00         0.00         0.00          0          0
hdisk2         0.00         0.00         0.00          0          0
hdisk3         0.00         0.00         0.00          0          0
```

The mpstat utility gives the performance analyst another way to view processor statistics. It should be obvious by now that Sebastien Godard has illustrated a very old Unix saying, as much of the entire Linux community has: There is definitely more than one way to do something.

To quote the manual page, mpstat "reports processor-related statistics." This means that, by default, mpstat reports information pertaining to each processor on SMP-capable systems in averages. On single uniprocessor (or UP) machines, the information is always the average.

In the simplest form, mpstat can be invoked like this:

```
mpstat
```

The following is an example of mpstat in use with an interval and count specified:

```
[jfink@kerry sysstat-3.3.6]$ mpstat 10 2
Linux 2.2.14-5.0smp (kerry)      05/21/01


09:04:36 AM  CPU   %user   %nice  %system   %idle    intr/s
09:04:46 AM  all    0.50    0.00     1.20   98.30    157.60
09:04:56 AM  all    0.50    0.00     0.20   99.30    162.00
Average:     all    0.50    0.00     0.70   98.80    159.80
```

4

Table 4.3 describes the different fields in mpstat:

TABLE 4.3   mpstat Fields

CPU	Which processor is being looked at. This is specified by the -P option. However, the -P option is not available on uniprocessor machines.
%user	Utilization that occurred from userland processes.
%nice	Utilization from userland process that occurred with a modified nice priority.
%system	Utilization that took place in privileged mode.
intr/s	Total number of interrupts that were received by the CPU per second.

ktop and gtop

Along with the vast array of command-line tools developed for or initially on Linux operating systems are GUI-driven utilities. This section briefly looks at two of these tools:

- ktop, or KDE top
- gtop, or GNOME top

The figures that follow are a variety of snapshots of ktop and gtop in action. Figure 4.1 shows the current user's running processes.

FIGURE 4.1

A ktop single user process list.

The fields of `ktop` are similar to those of top. From left to right, the fields are shown in Table 4.4.

TABLE 4.4   `ktop` Fields

Name	Name of the program that is running
PID	The process ID
Username	The username that is running the process
CPU%	How much of the CPU in a percentage the process is using
Time	The CPU time the process has used
Priority	The process priority
State	The current state of the process
Memory	How much memory the process is using
Resident	How much resident memory the process is using
Shared	How much shared memory the process is using
Command Line	The command line that called the process

Figure 4.2 shows all running processes on the system.

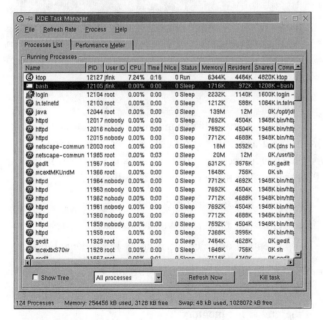

4

FIGURE 4.2
The ktop *all users process list.*

This is much more information and has one very big benefit over the console-based top: You can scroll up and down the entire list.

The tab in Figure 4.3 is a performance meter showing a variety of information about how the system is doing in a set of graphs.

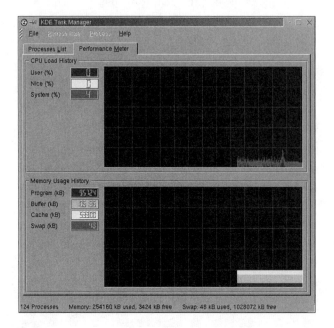

FIGURE 4.3
The ktop *performance meters.*

The performance meters are pretty self-explanatory. On the left is a legend with exact numerical representations of the graph. The top half of the meter shows the CPU load history. On the left are three bars that show percentages of the values being measured; on the right is a histogram of the CPU activity. The three values are as follows:

- **User%**—The percentage of userland processes
- **Nice%**—The percentage of processes with a modified niceness
- **System%**—The percentage of processes running in privileged mode

The lower half of the meter shows a memory histogram. It has the same fields as most memory monitors, but the values in the bars on the left are in kilobytes. The fields are as follows:

- **Program**—Programs using memory
- **Buffer**—Buffer usage

- **Cache**—Cache usage
- **Swap**—Swap usage

This particular graph shows a pretty quiet system that is not overly taxed while using a lot of memory. At one point, however, a spike in system activity went up; this was actually caused by a user running `ls -1R` on a large filesystem.

The `gtop` view in Figure 4.4 shows all running processes.

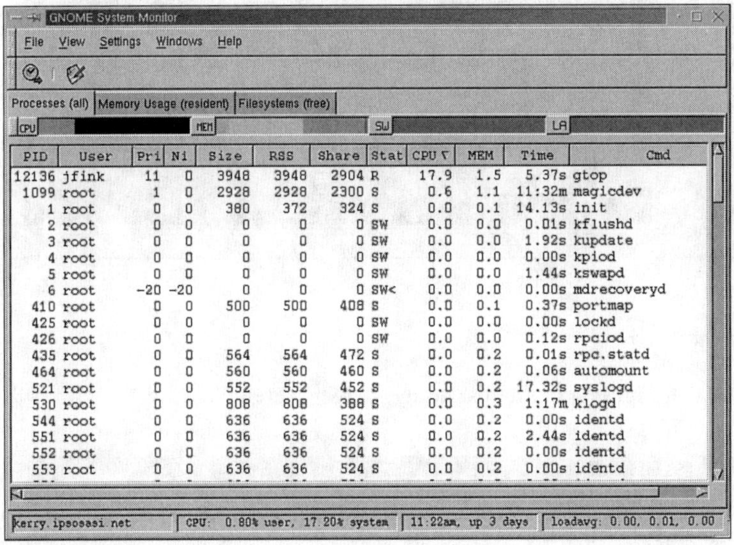

FIGURE 4.4
The `gtop` all user processes.

The `gtop` utility is functionally similar to that of `ktop`. The GUI is somewhat different, though. The fields of `gtop`'s process monitor are self-explanatory and are similar to those of `ktop`. However, just above the actual process list are four bar graphs. These show miniature histograms about general system information such as the CPU, memory, swap space, and latency.

Figure 4.5 shows a graph of resident memory usage.

The bar on the left is a graphic representation that compares how much memory is being used by processes. This spans out to the right with colored lines, which, in turn, are represented by the name of the process on the far right, the number of instances a particular process has, and the resident size it is taking up.

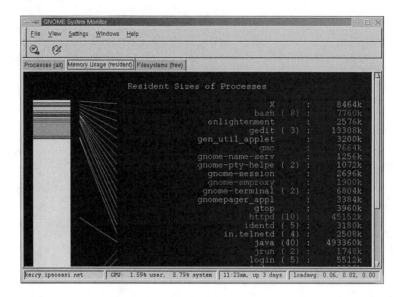

FIGURE 4.5

The gtop *performance meters.*

In the gtop view in Figure 4.6, the disk usage statistics are displayed.

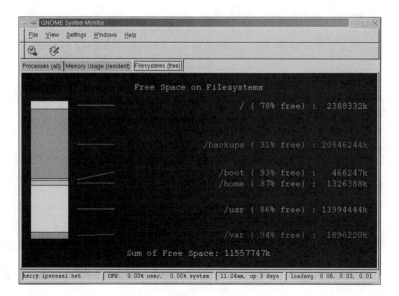

FIGURE 4.6

The gtop *disk usage graph.*

The next tab shows filesystem usage information. Again, there is a relative graph on the left and colored lines that match the name going to the right. However, the filesystems are represented in this case. It is important to note that this graph does not distinguish local and NFS-mounted filesystems.

With both `ktop` and `gtop`, the performance analyst has the ability to change the status of processes to which he has access. Obviously, as root this would be all of them. With both of them, the mouse can be used to select and modify processes that the user has rights to alter. For example, with `ktop`, highlight the process name and then hit the right mouse key to produce a list of options.

Using the `/proc` Filesystem to Monitor System Activities

Earlier, it was mentioned that in Unix (and especially Linux) a vast array of tools essentially gather similar information and output it in very different ways. Getting this information is relatively easy under Linux. Most software writers who make performance-monitoring tools for Linux make use of the `/proc` filesystem, and the performance analyst certainly can make use of it as well. Developers like to use `/proc` because the interface from a programming perspective is much simpler than using system subroutines. As an example, to access information without using `/proc`, the developer must use the C programming language (at some point, even if it is linked into another language) to access the applicable subroutine for information. Within the `/proc` interface, the information is treated almost like any other normal file operation, so a variety of languages are now at the developer's disposal.

In the most rudimentary form, reading information in `/proc` consists of nothing more than periodically concatenating (cat) files. This hardly seems prudent, however. A better solution might be to write a script or program (in whatever language the analyst prefers) to do this work. There is also the quite valid argument regarding why anyone would want to do so, with so many tools available. The answer is simple: because you can.

Without going into too much detail about `/proc`, a simple example is useful.

In this example, the goal is to create a command-line tool that mimics some of the capability of the free utility but is a little easier to read. The actual data source is `/proc/meminfo`, which, when examined, looks something like this:

```
         total:     used:     free:  shared: buffers:  cached:
Mem:  263766016 110858240 152907776 12779520 70127616 18976768
Swap: 1052794880         0 1052794880
MemTotal:     257584 kB
MemFree:      149324 kB
MemShared:     12480 kB
```

```
Buffers:        68484 kB
Cached:         18532 kB
BigTotal:           0 kB
BigFree:            0 kB
SwapTotal:    1028120 kB
SwapFree:     1028120 kB
```

Obviously, running cat on the file periodically would achieve a similar result, but it would not be quickly readable. The simple answer is to write a script. In this case, the data source is a constant format, so any language can be used. For prototyping purposes, Perl will be used. The easiest way to reparse the file is to load it into an array in Perl and then reparse it to match the desired result. For brevity, only the first two lines will be used; however, with judicious use of the chomp() or chop() functions, every line in the /proc/meminfo file could be put to good use. It also should be noted that this is a local script, not a program that would be released to the public or another server. When you're releasing programs to the public, many other considerations must be taken into account (such as the different file formats for /proc/meminfo between kernel revisions).

The name of the script is get_mem; the following is the code:

```perl
#!/usr/bin/perl
# get_mem:       loads the /proc/meminfo file into an array and
#                prints out the first 2 lines once by default or
#                periodically based on arguments
#
# this is a hack job AT BEST, I am shocked that it even has one function

# load /proc/meminfo into an array and return the array to the caller
sub loadfile {
        if ( -e "/proc/meminfo") {
                $MEMINFO = "/proc/meminfo";
                open(MEMINFO);
                @local_mem_array = <MEMINFO>;
                close(MEMINFO);
                return @local_mem_array;
        } else {
                print "hmmm . . . no /proc/meminfo? what did YOU DO!\n";
                exit 1;
        }
        return "blah!";
}


# main ####
```

```
# check for too much input
if(@ARGV >= 3) {
        print "oops, too many parameters specified\n";
        print "get_mem usage: get_mem <interval> <count>\n";
}

# check for interval and count; otherwise, just do it once
if(@ARGV >= 1) {
        $sec = @ARGV[0];
        $int = @ARGV[1];

    # read and print what we want until the counts are 0
        until($int == 0) {
                @mem_array = loadfile(@mem_array);
                print "@mem_array[0...2]";
                $int--;

        # unless we are on the last count, sleep
                if($int) >= 1) {
                        sleep($sec);
                }
        }

} else {
        @mem_array = loadfile(@mem_array);
        print "@mem_array[0...2]";
}

# end get_mem
```

The default output looks like this:

```
[jfink@kerry jfink]$ ./get_mem
        total:    used:    free:  shared: buffers:  cached:
 Mem:  263766016 111575040 152190976 13373440 70152192 19509248
 Swap: 1052794880        0 1052794880
```

When supplied with an interval and count arguments, it looks like this:

```
[jfink@kerry jfink]$ ./get_mem 5 5
        total:    used:    free:  shared: buffers:  cached:
 Mem:  263766016 112812032 150953984 16613376 70152192 19513344
 Swap: 1052794880        0 1052794880
        total:    used:    free:  shared: buffers:  cached:
 Mem:  263766016 112828416 150937600 16637952 70152192 19513344
 Swap: 1052794880        0 1052794880
        total:    used:    free:  shared: buffers:  cached:
```

```
Mem:  263766016 112836608 150929408 16642048 70152192 19513344
Swap: 1052794880         0 1052794880
        total:    used:    free: shared: buffers:  cached:
Mem:  263766016 112840704 150925312 16642048 70152192 19513344
Swap: 1052794880         0 1052794880
        total:    used:    free: shared: buffers:  cached:
Mem:  263766016 112840704 150925312 16642048 70152192 19513344
Swap: 1052794880         0 1052794880
```

As noted in the source code, get_mem is a hack job, at best. However, it should be easy to see how safe and prudent use of the /proc filesystem can be of benefit to the performance analyst.

It is also of interest that when get_mem is run without any arguments, the output is the same as:

```
[jfink@kerry jfink]$ head -3 /proc/meminfo
        total:    used:    free: shared: buffers:  cached:
Mem:  263766016 111427584 152338432 12787712 70152192 19521536
Swap: 1052794880         0 1052794880
```

That's just food for thought to budding scripters.

Additional information about /proc can be found in online documentation for the kernel at /usr/src/linux/Documentation/filesystems/proc.txt.

Other Free Utilities

The ibiblio FTP server has a plethora of utilities available for Linux performance monitoring and tuning. Additionally, other Web sites have host or list utilities, including these:

Freshmeat: http://www.freshmeat.net/

Appwatch: http://www.appwatch.com/

In addition to all the command-line tools, many of the ibiblio.org utilities are GUI-driven.

Summary

Although traditional Unix tools are a great addition to the kit for the performance analyst and system administrator, sometimes it is best to use a tool that is designed specifically for the Linux kernel. Additionally, the filesystem interface to /proc provides an easy way for the sysadmin to write his own scripts and programs to analyze the kernel.

Performance Monitoring Techniques

PART

III

IN THIS PART

5 Apparent and Nonapparent Bottlenecks   85

6 X Window Performance   99

7 Network Performance   119

Apparent and Nonapparent Bottlenecks

There Is Always a Bottleneck

One thing to keep in mind is that there is always a bottleneck in the system. If there wasn't, the work of the system would be done as soon as it was initiated. Whether it's the CPU, the network, the drive interface, memory fragmentation, or various combinations among them, some subsystem undoubtedly will be slowing the overall speed of the system. All of these subsystems have their limitations and applicability in your situation, so the best that you can do is find a balance among them. If you can find a point at which the system is operating as fast as possible with the given hardware and software allotments, you can consider the problem of tuning to be solved.

User Expectations

In the end, your tuning success relies on what the end users say about the system. As long as they are reporting performance issues, the tuning process goes on. But it is important to consider the fact that some user complaints are not resolvable, given the hardware or the software architecture in place. As development and rollouts occur, users tend to want more from the system as they see the uses inherent in it. But there comes a point at which expectations exceed reality. Hopefully the system was constructed with future growth in mind, but that can't cover all the bases. To make room for increased demands, new software needs to be written or a major infrastructure upgrade is in order.

As an administrator or an architect, it is important to know when this point has been reached and when further tuning efforts will not likely introduce the needed performance gains. Likewise, it is important to realize when the system is being used improperly—such as when inefficient database queries are being used, which can have disastrous effects on the system as a whole. Finding these abuses often can have a greater impact on overall utilization than any tuning operation.

Performance Agreements

Depending on your system, you might be bound to or bound by different types of performance agreements. Chapter 7, "Network Performance," covers quality-of-service agreements that generally apply to network service levels, but this is only one specific type of agreement. If you are a provider, you will be bound to different contractual obligations, whether they are network coverage guarantees, system uptimes, processing rates, or something else. If you are the receiver of one of these services, you might be promised certain transfer rates at given times, certain data received within a given turnaround time, and so on.

These agreements could have a significant impact on your system's bottom line. If you are promised data within a certain time range and promise analysis to your customers within a range beyond that, a bad link farther up could put you in a bad situation very quickly. A performance agreement to cover liability with everyone you deal with in these situations is highly recommended because your customers have essentially hired you with a contract, which can be viewed as its own performance agreement. Liability also must be defined between your systems and the ones on which they depend. If you don't get the data ready by the time specified in your contract, the data might be useless. The same situation might occur if the system experiences an unusual load, causing normal users to have to deal with unreasonable delays in their data.

Either way, safeguards need to be in place to cover these agreements, along with solid insurance to cover the worst case. This can include redundancy of network links, servers, application failovers, and duplication of the data involved. The system needs to be capable of suffering the worst imaginable tragedy and still maintaining a given quality-of-service level; without that failover, your business could go down with that server or network uplink.

Tuning CPU Bottlenecks

Depending on your architecture, you might have a CPU-bound load. In this case, no matter how much you tweak the systems, no noticeable gain will occur until you either fix the CPU usage or throw more hardware at the problem.

Hardware Solutions

Chances are, getting around CPU bottlenecks will depend on your application. For starters, let's assume that your application is running on a single-processor machine. By monitoring system usage over time, you find that the CPU specifically is being overworked in comparison to the rest of the system. You have a couple of options. One should be fairly obvious: Get a faster processor. This will reduce the strain that your application is placing on the system.

What if you are already using the fastest CPU you can get, and there's still a bottleneck? In this case, you probably need an SMP machine. Depending on the application, different numbers of CPUs might be appropriate. Another factor is whether your application will benefit from this hardware. If it works by forking itself into separate processes, it can probably benefit. A preferred method is a threading model that would allow it to spread its computations across the CPUs present, but this could require more in-depth knowledge of your application than you have.

Check with your vendor about what benefits would be gained by going with an SMP machine. Linux can scale to many CPUs, depending on the architecture. On 32-bit systems, it can handle 32 processors, and it can manage 64 on a 64-bit architecture. But gains might not be as apparent as you approach this limit. In reality, on a 32-bit system, Linux should scale fairly cleanly to 2-, 4-, and 8-CPU systems, with some performance drop-off at 16 CPUs and above. Also keep in mind that by the time you hit these limits, there is a high probability that the system is overloading other subsystems present, such as the memory bus, and that your CPU bottleneck has shifted elsewhere. If your requirements have been met, that's all well and good, but you might just have easily opened up a performance-tuning problem in another area.

We discussed threading briefly in Chapter 2, "Aspects of Performance Tuning," but some additional grounding of this knowledge is probably in order. Consider the case in which your application is performing many calculations, most of which can be done independently from each other. If your application is written in a threaded manner, having multiple CPUs present will allow the kernel scheduler to run some of those computations on other CPUs, balancing the load nicely. This is true only if the application was written with POSIX threads, though. If it was written with user-space threads, it cannot take advantage of the other CPUs present, except by virtue of the fact that the system can use the extra hardware for other general work that it needs to do, such as handling interactive logins and disk interaction.

If your load is high enough, you might be stretching the capabilities of the architecture. The Intel architecture has been upgraded constantly over the years, but it does have its limits. Some applications might be better suited to another architecture, such as Compaq's Alpha processor, which is a 64-bit architecture known for its speed. Many scientific clustering systems have been built around this architecture for its capabilities in this arena. This is just one example, of course—Linux has been ported to many other architectures.

Another architecture that might be of interest is Non-Uniform Memory Access (NUMA). With this system, CPU nodes maintain local memory, and the system tries to keep the local code's data in that local memory bank because it is more expensive to coordinate access to memory on other nodes in the system. Although this is generally assumed to be a memory bandwidth saver, it also helps in CPU scalability because the local node is free to fully utilize the CPUs present. SGI has contributed to Linux's support for the NUMA model, although this is not a very common option. Rumors have it that various chipmakers are moving toward a NUMA architecture for future systems, but the effects of this research remain to be seen.

Software Solutions

Hardware problems are tough to work around because you are generally locked into your system's physical architecture. You might be running the absolute latest in hardware, but it still might not be enough. In this case, you need to look at exactly what software you are running and how it is configured. Although this requires extensive knowledge of your problem domain (which you should already have), solutions are much cheaper and easier to deploy on the software side than in hardware.

General Application Tuning

Before you start throwing hardware at the problem, make sure that your application is correctly configured. Be sure to turn off components or capabilities of the app that you aren't using. For example, if it is an audio-streaming tool that is taking in a feed and streaming it to some clients, you might not need the content after it is finished with the data. Make sure that it is doing only the streaming conversion, not trying also to save the contents by converting it to another codec locally. This might sound obvious, but most gains can be made by analyzing your system and making sure that it is doing exactly what you need—and nothing more. Because it is highly dependent on the needs of the system, this task must be done on a case-by-case basis.

As mentioned in the earlier section "Hardware Solutions," it might also be a good idea to know more about the capabilities of your application. If you find that your application cannot benefit from more CPUs and you already have the fastest hardware possible, it is probably time to look for another solution—which probably means a more capable piece of software.

Specific Clustering Solutions

If you are truly running up against the capabilities of a single machine, clustering is probably the next best bet. In the realm of scientific applications, large performance gains and scalability can be achieved by writing your code to be cluster-aware or by selecting products that can take advantage of a cluster, if present.

Beowulf

When most people think of clustering and Linux, Beowulf clusters are the first systems that come to mind. By writing code to take advantage of these clustering capabilities, calculations can be distributed across a group of machines relatively easily. There are a few prerequisites, though. One is that your problem must be capable of being made inherently parallel. If it relies on serial calculations and cannot be broken up into independent operations, having a cluster present will not help. Also, the code needs to be explicitly written to use the cluster, which might not be the case. In general, clustering applications are custom-built to the problem at hand, although a few general applications can be run off the shelf and can use a local cluster.

Third, the networking infrastructure needs to be very solid. Because a great deal of message passing is going on in the system, the interconnection needs to be as fast and as capable as possible. This means using many switching fabrics and, most likely, the network bonding described in Chapter 7. Although this places a lot of preconditions on the application, it is generally thought to be the most capable and scalable solution. Refer to `http://www.scyld.com` for more information on deploying and using a Beowulf cluster.

MOSIX

Although it's not as well known as Beowulf, the Multicomputer Operating System for Unix (MOSIX) can give you clustering capabilities without requiring that your applications be written explicitly for a cluster. MOSIX transparently migrates processes to other nodes in a cluster, all from within the kernel. It can balance your load by migrating processes off a machine that might be swapping over to a machine that has some free memory. By using Direct File System Access (DFSA), processes that have migrated away from their home node can still perform I/O operations without being forced back to the home node. Currently, the GFS and MFS filesystems are DFSA-compliant, allowing this capability.

Because the migration is handled from inside the kernel, the operation is hidden from the application's view. This way, your application doesn't need to have any idea that it is being run inside a cluster, and it doesn't need any specific alterations to its configuration or code base. It takes a small amount of planning to make sure that the machines involved are correctly balanced for the application and that the network is up to the load. However, when compared to applying normal clustering technologies, MOSIX is very easy to deploy.

Some caveats to MOSIX clusters might prevent them from being applicable in your specific system. One is that shared memory cannot be migrated between the nodes, and processes using mmap calls cannot be moved. Other restrictions also exist, but, in general, if your application doesn't rely on these methods, MOSIX might be the right path for you. For the cost of a set of new systems, you essentially have a large SMP machine that communicates over the network and doesn't require any modification to the application you are running. Compared to systems that require specific code rewrites to utilize clusters, this can be a very cost-effective solution that is easy to test and deploy.

Clustering is a scalable technology that, when applied correctly, can make a CPU-bound system almost indefinitely scalable. But this requires you to have specific knowledge of your problem domain, and it might require specific code to be written to take advantage of the cluster. Both techniques described here have been used in production environments for years, though, and have worked on very difficult problems; if you can't scale your system via the normal routes, a Linux cluster might be what you need. In general, MOSIX is helpful when you can't directly parallelize the code yourself, and Beowulf can yield gains if you can write code to take advantage of the system.

Tuning CPU-Related Parameters in the Kernel

When it comes to getting extra performance out of your existing CPU, there isn't much you can do to the kernel to squeeze out those extra few cycles. About the only thing that is tunable via the kernel is CPU defined in your kernel build. When selecting the processor type and features, make sure to select the specific type of processor you have. This way, the kernel can take advantage of hardware-specific extensions present in the chip. There is a slight price to pay for this, though: If you build the kernel for an advanced architecture rather than the base 386 chipset, you cannot expect the kernel to run on different types of similar chips because they might not all have the same capability set. Most distributions assume a low-end baseline, which is the 386. By rebuilding to utilize your physical hardware, though, you can achieve faster processing. This is in addition to the other capabilities that the processor offers, such as the capability to address different memory ranges, which could be needed to address the large amounts of RAM that today's servers need.

In general, the kernel build will select the most useful GCC optimizations to use in building your image. Most of these optimizations make sense, and you might find them present in other application builds. On the x86 architecture, a couple of common ones can have a significant impact:

- `-fomit-frame-pointer`—For functions that don't need a frame pointer, this prevents the compiler from emitting instructions to deal with it. This saves the overhead of managing it and frees a register in the process. Frame pointers are invaluable for debugging purposes, of course, so this should not be used if you might need to debug work down the road.

- `-funroll-loops`—This looks at code loops whose size can be determined at compile time, and it unrolls the loop if doing so would help performance. This can yield larger executables, but might help speed execution.

- `-ON`—(Here, N is 0, 1, 2, or 3, as in `-O1`.) This is probably the most common optimization. Depending on the level requested, the compiler attempts to perform various levels of optimizations on the code that is generated. It also causes inline functions to be rolled into their callers, which can cause a slight increase in code size but saves the overhead of function calling during runtime.

This is by no means inclusive or even truly indicative of what optimizations are happening within the kernel build. It is only meant to be a view of what is going on and a springboard into other areas, if you are interested. For more information, check the GCC pages or any book on code optimizations. With detailed knowledge of your physical hardware, you can accomplish amazing feats of engineering. These days, when CPUs are fast and memory is cheap, these feats are regarded as almost trivial, unlike in the past, when they were truly needed. Nevertheless, correct utilization of your hardware can reap huge performance rewards if you use the right approach.

Tuning CPU-Related Parameters in Software

Your software often can be configured to take advantage of hardware present nearly the same way that the kernel can. Take video manipulation, for example. Although the application performing this can use the basic Intel instruction set, extensions to the chipset are expressly developed for this kind of work. Making sure that the software is built to use these instructions is of utmost importance. If you run the application out of the box without making sure that it uses something like MMX, SSE, or other technologies, you most likely won't get nearly the performance that you should get out of the machine.

Depending on the application, there might be different ways to tell what was and wasn't built into the application. If you are building and installing it from source, pay close attention to what it detects and builds for. In some cases, if you build it on a system that doesn't have support for these extensions, the build won't detect it and will assume that it doesn't exist. When you move the application to a box that has this capability, the code might not be built to use it. This depends on how you received the application and how it was built. It is impossible to overstress the importance of making sure that your applications are doing the right thing in your environment.

Another mechanism to get speed gains across the board is to use a distribution that assumes a higher baseline when building packages. This way, everything on the system is built to assume a higher standard, and you don't have to explicitly recompile code to make sure that it is optimized for your processor. Although this does have some merit, the actual gains of doing this across your system are debatable. In reality, most of the system doesn't spend much time doing processor-centric work, and the biggest gains from using specific CPU extensions come from the application that you are using most. As a result, that is where you should generally focus.

Processor bottlenecks can be very difficult to work around, depending on your needs. If you are living on the edge of modern hardware, there might not be much you can do. In general, though, you can take many paths to sidestep the issue, whether it is doing application tuning, using processor extensions, performing clustering, or using more efficient threading. Be sure to choose what is right for your environment and what will most likely scale your problem in the future.

Memory Bottlenecks

Recently, memory speeds have greatly increased, although there is still a disparity between the processor's speed and the speed of the memory subsystem. Hardware caches are growing constantly to help sidestep this problem, but calculation speed throttles down when dealing with standard system memory.

Hardware Factors

A large portion of memory bottlenecking issues comes from inherent hardware limitations. When building your system, make sure that you use the fastest memory and system busses you can get, along with ample cache on the processors involved.

In general, hardware caches provide good speed gains, but growing them too large can actually cause longer cache lookups than it would take to get the data directly from the normal memory banks. Passing this crossover point can give you a system that costs more to build and works less efficiently. Caches have grown larger over the years, well past what used to be considered good sizes to prevent the crossover point. Along with them, however, have come speed improvements when searching that cache.

For the memory itself, getting the fastest for the bus and the processor makes for a much speedier system, especially if the system is mainly CPU- and memory-bound. This way, the data that the processor needs to keep running at high rates can be fed as fast as the processor requests it. As usual, this requires a good understanding of your problem domain. Some interesting developments coming in the industry will yield even better performance. One of the most recent advancements has resulted in doubling clock speed by allowing synching on both sides of the clock pulse. But this is a fast-moving market, and it helps to see what's out and what's coming in relation to the system you are trying to build.

Virtual Address Space

In general, Linux will handle managing your process's address space transparently, as it should. As you or your applications kick off new processes, the kernel will take care of creating a new process space for it to run in. If the process outgrows this area by using the entire stack allocated to it, the kernel might decide to allow it more program space. Likewise, the kernel handles allocations of areas outside the stack, or on the heap, and traps faults that occur involving these areas.

Signs of trouble involving your process's address space usually are indicative of bad coding by the developer, unless it is a simple problem of the machine not having enough memory. Stack problems should never be visible to the user. One thing to keep in mind is that user-level threads implement all threads in the same address space as the parent process, carving out portions of the stack space for each individual thread's stack. So, if a certain thread is exceedingly heavy on its stack portion, it is more likely to cause a crash of the process than a program threaded with POSIX threads.

PAE

One aspect of process space management that you might have to deal with occurs on Intel systems with large amounts of memory. Because Intel's current family of chips is a 32-bit architecture, these chips can address only 4GB of memory. (2^{32} works out to about four billion, or 4GB of RAM.) But systems are being built that need to address more than this amount of memory, and Intel's 64-bit chip isn't out yet. So what can you do to get your machine to address large amounts of physical RAM?

Introduced with the Pentium Pro, the Processor Address Extension (PAE) provides a means of performing 36-bit addressing on a 32-bit machine, with some hardware changes and a kernel that knows how to make use of it. This causes a bit more work in the kernel's VM tables, but it allows addressing of up to 64GB of RAM without jumping to a 64-bit architecture, which can yield large cost savings. Without unnecessarily going into the details of how this works, the kernel breaks up the memory above the 4GB mark into 3GB chunks. These 3GB chunks can be allocated as address spaces for applications, although this still limits a single process to 3GB within its address space.

If you need an application to use up to 64GB of RAM as one solid address space, you should look into using a 64-bit architecture. Linux already runs on several and is well established, especially on the Alpha architecture. This will make sure that your requirements are fulfilled, and you will get the other benefits of using a 64-bit architecture. PAE will cease to be applicable on Intel systems with the introduction of Intel's 64-bit offering.

Contiguous Memory Spaces

Occasionally, your application might need to have a large portion of data in one contiguous area. Although this is generally limited to imaging drivers that need to have large buffers ready for video capture to memory, you might need it for another reason. The concept is fairly simple: At boot, a large portion of memory is set aside in a contiguous block for later use. If this isn't done, general memory use by normal applications could result in fragmentation so that when the buffer is needed, a chunk that large cannot be found. This capability resides outside the normal kernel tree in a bigmem patch, although it might be an integrated capability with the kernel that ships with your vendor's distribution. Check with your vendor about this, or get the newest kernel along with the bigmem patch to roll your own.

Dynamic Buffers Cache

As described throughout the book, Linux makes heavy use of caching whenever it can. Because of this, it will appear at most times that all your memory is in use—and, in a way, it is. But as applications need the memory set aside for buffers, the kernel releases its buffers to make room for allocations made by applications. Don't be alarmed if, as a result of this, the system swaps out a little bit of data. This is normal. If the kernel decides that some programs don't need to be in memory, such as the gettys attached to your other virtual terminals that haven't been used in two months, it swaps them out. This way, unused code leaves main memory, the application requesting more memory gets its request filled, and the kernel continues to use all or most of the buffers it had previously. Refer to Chapter 9, "The Linux Kernel," for information on how to manipulate this cache.

Shared Libraries

These days, a program rarely needs to be statistically linked with all its libraries when it is built. Historically, code libraries were built to be static, which meant that when you built an executable image with your library, everything was linked back together into the image. Although this can remove any missing dependency problems, it results in larger binaries and wastes disk space because the library code is replicated in all binaries that need it.

Shared libraries handle this problem. When you build or run an application involving shared libraries, the executable is built with the library names that it needs in the file. Then, when the executable is run, the appropriate libraries are found and linked so that the program can run. All applications that depend on this library will link against it at runtime, saving all the duplication work that would be involved in the static build.

Another advantage of shared libraries is that they reduce the load on main memory. With file mapping, the linking process links the image to the appropriate page frames where the library lives. The page frames used by the library can be shared by all programs that are using it. If you have a lot of processes running that all use the same shared library, this can save the overhead of duplicating the shared library code dozens of times in the system's RAM. When the code is configured to be a shared library and applications are linked against it, all management of this is controlled behind the scenes. No interaction from the user should be required, except for maybe the LD_PRELOAD hooks described in Chapter 2.

Factors to Keep in Mind

When you are watching memory usage, keep in mind that looking at the output of top might not be the best way of getting a handle on the real memory usage. Although it will give you a nice ballpark figure, the actual memory in use can differ greatly from this. This is how the various fields presented in system usage utilities should be interpreted:

- **SIZE**—This is the address space seen by the process. It can include mmap calls, which can grow the apparent size of the application without really allocating any more memory. For example, X servers generally use map against the memory present in your video card. If you have a video card with 32MB of RAM, the size of the X server will grow by 32MB, even though no extra memory was allocated from normal physical RAM. This is generally viewed as the real size of the program when, in reality, it is usually very far off.

- **RSS**—Resident Stack Size, or RSS, is the actual amount of memory that the process is using in RAM. When you're looking for a basic metric, this is the path to take. Chunks of code that have been swapped out of the process's memory space to disk are not counted in this set. Thus, if you have a process using 1MB of RAM but the system has swapped out 300KB to disk, the RSS should be roughly 700KB.

Also figured into this number is the space used by shared libraries. Because the memory used by shared libraries is shared across processes, this might shift the value higher than what is accurate. At a minimum, the C libraries are usually added to this, which can make the process look larger than it is; in reality, the shared instance of the C libraries, which could be in use by dozens of other processes on the system, is using only one copy of itself in memory.

• **SHARE**—This is the portion of the memory in the RSS that is shared data, such as shared libraries.

Overall, a good estimate can be achieved by subtracting the SHARE value from the RSS value. This turns out to be a little low because there is an instance of the libraries that ends up not being counted. For most purposes, though, this is sufficient.

Also be sure to look into how processes are sharing data. Depending on the configuration, an application might resort to different types of sockets to transfer data, which can be resource-intensive compared to using SysV shared segments. Making sure that SysV is used when possible can result in much more efficient use of the system's memory.

Paging and Swapping

In general, the mechanics of paging and swapping are hidden behind the scenes and require interaction only when your machine runs out of physical memory and starts moving chunks of data into swap.

Originally, historical Unix systems performed swapping by moving the entire address space of a process to disk. Linux uses a more fine-grained approach, in which swapping is done on a per-page basis. Because Linux uses a 4KB page, this is the most granular chunk that can be moved to disk. With some hardware hooks and use of some spare room in the page table, requests for data that is swapped out are quickly detected and handled.

As mentioned before, swapping can result in chunks of code being placed in swap and left there for a long period of time. If you have memory free and there is still swap in use, don't be alarmed: The kernel just hasn't found a reason to bring that data back into memory yet. This is for the benefit of the in-memory kernel buffers and general memory access for applications that require it.

Again, swapping is handled transparently by the kernel and should require help only when the system is running out of resources. If you think that the system is not handling swap pressure as it should, refer to Chapter 9 for information on how to force it to shift behavior as swap levels are met.

Checking for System Integrity

You can check for system integrity in a variety of ways. Depending on your needs, these ways can range from simplistic to complex. You even can check processor usage in many ways, from using vmstat or top, to doing SNMP polling from across the network. You can check memory bottlenecks and swap usage the same way. But under very heavy load, you might need to make sure that processes aren't dying because of failed memory allocations, resource starvation, and the like. These factors might not be readily visible when looking at memory usage, but failed processes could be causing users to lose access to their data.

If you want a more in-depth look at what is going on, it will likely involve custom approaches, depending on the applications involved. With high loads, the kernel might begin dumping messages to the log files, giving valuable clues in the hunt for the bottleneck. If not, watch your individual application log for signs of what could be going on and whether the system's integrity is still valid. Consider the case in which your Web servers are running Apache under a very heavy load. A new product is up and running and is applying a new set of stress factors to the system. When Apache's children get to the point that they can't allocate more memory, you will begin to see signs of this behavior in the Apache log, and possibly in the kernel's log, if the stress has caused problems within the VM. In this case, it is a simple matter of adding more memory, shutting down other services, or reconfiguring Apache to use a different configuration that requires less memory overhead.

Custom tools for custom products exist and could be appropriate to help you see the exact health of individual applications and components on your system. Although this is not as highly recommended because it usually results in a limited set of vendor-supplied details, sometimes it is the only way to go. Preferable to this is SNMP support, which many vendors support. With this support, you can calculate statistical usage over time and you can look at general system parameters and application-specific values. If this is deployed over a secondary management network, the impact of this approach is minimal on the production systems.

Conclusion

Whenever you are tracing a problem, you might go running down the wrong track in looking for a solution. Sometimes this is the nature of the game—if everything required a simple path to solve, all our lives would be easier. But in reality, there always will be ambiguities in the equation to make the process difficult.

As with most anything else, knowledge of your system will usually prevent you from running down the wrong road. If there is a memory problem and you have 256 forked instances of some code, it is helpful to know that if each instance is a tiny binary linking against a shared library, it isn't necessarily the culprit in this situation. In the end, this could be the problem, but at least knowing how to interpret the memory usage enables you to initially discard some factors that might have confused someone with lesser knowledge of the environment. So, it might be said that the moral of the chapter is that knowledge will take you farther than just about anything else.

X Window Performance

The speed and responsiveness of the X Window System, particularly on desktop and workstation computers, heavily influences the perception of a Linux system's overall speed and responsiveness. This chapter discusses methods for improving X Window performance. In addition to describing methods for tuning the X server, it offers suggestions for improving the performance of X clients, explains how to create a baseline performance profile, and shows you how to measure the effect of performance modifications.

Analyzing the X Server's Performance

Before exploring how to tune X servers and clients, it is important to evaluate the server's current performance. Doing so establishes a starting point of objective metrics against which to measure the results of your tuning efforts. It also might identify specific problems, permitting you to focus your efforts. To measure X's performance, use the x11perf program, a standard part of the XFree86 distribution and usually installed by default. After you have established the baseline, the basic tuning procedure is to apply one of the tweaks discussed the later section "Tuning the X Server for Local Use," rerun x11perf, and then use x11perfcomp to measure the tweak's impact. x11perfcomp, another standard program in the XFree86 distribution, is a handy utility for comparing the results of several x11perf runs and displaying the results.

In the process of running tests and applying tuning enhancements, keep in mind that X servers and clients do not run in isolation. Rather, they run on loaded systems—that is, systems running other servers and programs. As a result, tests run on unloaded, relatively quiescent systems will vary sometimes dramatically from tests on loaded systems. Likewise, tweaks that work on unloaded systems might not work as well—or at all—on loaded systems. Finally, an enhancement that works on one system might not work as well on another otherwise identical system because of each system's *usage profile*, the mix of programs running and how each system is normally used.

Consider, for example, the difference between the usage profile of a computer used for standard office duties, such as email, Web browsing, and document preparation, and an identically configured computer used primarily as a computer-aided design (CAD) workstation. The office workstation makes considerably lighter demands on the CPU, graphics hardware, kernel, and X server than does the CAD station, so performance enhancements sufficient for the office computer could be inadequate for the CAD workstation.

Understanding x11perf

x11perf tests the performance of the X server. It tests both basic graphic functions, such as drawing circles, polygons, and lines, and the server's speed while performing window-management functions, such as drawing windows, scrolling, and resizing windows. Although basic graphics operations are important, the window-management functions are arguably more important for the user typing an email, starting and stopping applications, or minimizing windows.

Before running your tests, restart the X server. Doing so ensures the most consistent results. In fact, for both testing and tuning, it might be easiest to start X from the command line (run level 3) rather than endure the long shutdown and restart procedure of the X login (run level 5). Depending on your situation and needs, you might want to restart the entire system.

x11perf accepts more than 280 command-line arguments, most of which specify the tests to perform. Its basic syntax is this:

```
x11perf [-option1 [-option2 […]]]
```

Table 6.1 lists useful options that do not specify tests.

TABLE 6.1   x11perf Nontest Command-Line Options

Option	Description
-display *host:display*	Connects to the X server running on *host:display*.
-repeat *n*	Performs each test *n* times. The default is 5.
-time *s*	Performs each test for *s* seconds. The default is 5.
-all	Performs all tests.
-range *test1[,test2]*	Performs all tests from *test1* to *test2*, inclusive.
-labels *[test1[,test2[...]]*	Displays the descriptive labels for each listed test. If a test is not specified, all labels are displayed.
-fg *color*	Uses the foreground color *color* when performing tests. The default is black.
-bg *color*	Uses the background color *color* when performing tests. The default is white.
-depth *n*	Sets the color depth to *n* bits per pixel during the test session. The default is the server's current depth.

As each test completes, the results are written to stdout, so you must redirect them to a file to save them. In most situations, the default values for options accepting arguments will be sufficient. Be careful using the -all option because running over 260 tests can take a long time. On the system described earlier, running all tests only once (using -repeat 1) took more than 35 minutes. The -labels option displays the descriptive text for each test. The column on the right in Listing 6.1 shows some of these labels. When using the -range option, if *test2* is not specified, the range of tests will start with *test1* and continue to the end.

To see the list of tests and their execution order, execute an unadorned x11perf command, as shown in Listing 6.1 (output was trimmed for readability):

LISTING 6.1   An Abbreviated List of x11perf Tests

```
$ x11perf
usage: x11perf [-options ...]
where options include:
...
        -dot                    Dot
        -rect1                  1x1 rectangle
        -rect10                 10x10 rectangle
        -rect100                100x100 rectangle
        -rect500                500x500 rectangle

...
        -move                   Move window
        -umove                  Moved unmapped window
        -movetree               Move window via parent
        -resize                 Resize window
        -uresize                Resize unmapped window
        -circulate              Circulate window
        -ucirculate             Circulate Unmapped window
```

The complete test sequence begins with -dot and ends with -ucirculate. It tests graphics operations first, followed by window-management operations. If you are pressed for time or are interested only in a specific type of test, consider using the -range option to select a subset of the tests.

NOTE

The tests and the results described in this chapter were performed on a computer with an Intel Pentium II 266MHz CPU, 128Mb RAM, and an ATI XPERT@PLAY 98 graphics card with 8Mb RAM. The Linux version used was a freshly installed Red Hat Linux 7.1 system running basic system services, such as the system logger and cron, and key Internet services, including the BIND name server, the sendmail mail server, and the Apache Web server. The X server was XFree86 4.0.3, and the kernel was 2.4.2. Obviously, the test results that you get will vary.

So much for the theory of using x11perf. The next section shows how to use x11perf to test performance.

Using x11perf

So, how does x11perf work? The following x11perf run tested the server's speed to move windows of increasing size. The command used was this:

```
$ x11perf -movetree > movetest
```

This test moved 100 squares, the child windows, around the parent window. Listing 6.2 is an excerpt of the test results that x11perf generated. The listing wraps because of the book's page design requirements.

LISTING 6.2   Test Results from an x11perf Test

```
x11perf - X11 performance program, version 1.5
The XFree86 Project, Inc server version 4003 on :0.0
from localhost.localdomain
Fri Apr 27 22:37:27 2001

Sync time adjustment is 0.1980 msecs.

 240000 reps @   0.0215 msec ( 46600.0/sec): Move window via
➥parent (4 kids)
 240000 reps @   0.0214 msec ( 46700.0/sec): Move window via
➥parent (4 kids)
 240000 reps @   0.0214 msec ( 46700.0/sec): Move window via
➥parent (4 kids)
 240000 reps @   0.0215 msec ( 46600.0/sec): Move window via
➥parent (4 kids)
 240000 reps @   0.0227 msec ( 44100.0/sec): Move window via
➥parent (4 kids)
1200000 trep @   0.0217 msec ( 46100.0/sec): Move window via
➥parent (4 kids)
```

The first few lines identify the x11perf version, release information about the server tested, the system tested, and the time the test started. The *sync time adjustment* is the amount of time that the monitor spends resynching and is subtracted from each test result. The next five lines show the test results. Each line lists the total number of reps, or operations, performed and also the time per rep, the number of reps per second, a brief description of the test, and how many objects were used. For example, on the fifth pass, a total of 240,000 move operations moved 4 child windows across the parent window. Each rep took 0.0227 milliseconds, which equates to a rate of 44,100 per second. The sixth line shows summary data: the total number of reps (1,200,000), the average speed per rep (0.0217), and the average speed per second (46,100).

When you have established the baseline of the server's performance, apply one of the suggestions discussed in this chapter for improving its performance. Rerun the same test, compare the results as explained in the next section, and decide whether the tweak made a significant difference.

Measuring the Results

After implementing a possible enhancement, you will want to see if it worked. x11perfcomp makes this task easy. First, retest using the same test, saving the output to a file. Next, use x11perfcomp to compare the results. The good news is the x11perfcomp is much simpler to use than x11perf. Its syntax is this:

```
x11perfcomp [-r|-ro] [-l label_file] file1 file2 [...]
```

Here, file1 and file2 store the results of the tests of the first and second tests. You can specify additional files, too. -r indicates that the output should include a column showing the performance of the second and subsequent tests relative to the first. -ro means to show only the relative performance of retests. Use -l label_file to restrict the tests selected for comparison (use x11perf's -labels option to determine the proper labels to use). file1 must contain results for all tests in the retests, or the program will fail. Listing 6.3 illustrates a typical x11perfcomp session.

LISTING 6.3   Output from x11perfcomp

```
$ x11perfcomp -r movetree.1 movetree.2
1: movetree.1
2: movetree.2

      1                 2           Operation
  --------      -----------------   -----------------
   46100.0       43100.0 (  0.93)   Move window via parent (4 kids)
  105000.0       92300.0 (  0.88)   Move window via parent (16 kids)
   94700.0      123000.0 (  1.30)   Move window via parent (25 kids)
  112000.0      174000.0 (  1.55)   Move window via parent (50 kids)
  115000.0      180000.0 (  1.57)   Move window via parent (75 kids)
  104000.0      184000.0 (  1.77)   Move window via parent (100 kids)
  121000.0      185000.0 (  1.53)   Move window via parent (200 kids)
```

The first two columns show the test results being compared. Because the example used -r, the third column expresses the relative performance of the second test as a percentage of the first. The final column shows the test performed. This example generally suggests that whatever tweak was applied worsened the performance of the server on this particular test because all but two of the tests were slower in the retest.

Tuning the X Server for Local Use

This section offers a number of suggestions for improving the performance of an X server used locally—that is, for a server running on the same machine as its clients.

> **TIP**
>
> To save some time while testing and tuning the server, if your system boots to run level 5, the X login window, change the default run level to 3, the text login. Then use the `startx` script (or its equivalent on your system) to start the server.

Increase the Server's Priority

As a rule, the X server is one of the most CPU-intensive processes on a Linux system. However, few Linux vendors or Linux users take advantage of the capability to increase the server's priority in relation to other processes. As a result, the X server runs at the same priority as a simple text editor. In many situations, simply increasing the X server's priority will eliminate sluggish performance. Home computers, office workstations, and computers used primarily for Internet access generally respond very well to this straightforward technique.

To increase the X server's priority, give it a lower nice value. A process's *nice value* is a number that the kernel uses to modify how much CPU time the kernel will give it relative to other processes. Nice values range from –20 to 20. The lower a process's nice value, the less "nice" it will be to other processes—that is, the less often the kernel will interrupt it to give CPU time to other processes. The default value is 0, meaning that the kernel will not modify the process's priority based on the nice value. So, given two processes, A and B, both running with the default nice value of 0, changing A's nice value to –20 gives it greater priority over B. Changing B's priority to 20 gives it less priority than A.

> **NOTE**
>
> The Linux kernel's algorithms and heuristics for process scheduling are more complicated than explained here. Nevertheless, for this chapter's purposes, this simplified explanation will do.

To start the X server with a specific nice value, use the `nice` command. To adjust a running X server's nice value, use the `renice` command. Mortal users can decrease the priority of their own processes, but only the root user can change other users' processes or increase a process's priority.

The syntax of the nice command is as follows:

```
nice [option] [command [arguments]]
```

Here, *command* and *arguments* specify the program to run and any options that it requires, respectively. *option* can be *-value* or *-n value*, where *value* is the nice value that you want. If *option* is not specified, nice starts the program and increments its nice value by 10. For example, to start the X server with a nice value of –5, either of the following commands would work:

```
# nice --5 /usr/X11R6/bin/X
# nice --n -5 /usr/X11R6/bin/X
```

Of course, the command shown starts only the server itself, not the window manager, the desktop environment (GNOME or KDE, for example), or any clients.

Keep in mind that increasing the X server's priority, especially if it is heavily used, can adversely affect other programs, particularly those that are sensitive to CPU scheduling, such as CD-burning programs.

TIP

The XFree86 documentation recommends a nice value of –10.

If the server is already running, use renice to modify its nice value. The syntax is as follows:

```
renice pri pid
```

pri is the new priority, and *pid* denotes the process ID of the process to change. Remember that only root can increase a process nice value. For example, the following commands adjust the nice value of the X server (running with a PID of 786) to –10 and use ps to show the changed priority:

```
# renice -10 786
786: old priority 0, new priority -10
# ps -o pid,nice,pri,opri,stat 786
  PID  NI PRI PRI STAT
  786 -10  34  65 S<
```

As the output of ps shows, the new nice value, listed in the second column, is –10. The < in the STAT column indicates that the process is a high-priority one.

NOTE

The calling syntax of renice is actually more complex than shown. See the renice man or info page for complete details.

Verify the Server Configuration File

Making sure that the configuration file, /etc/X11/XF86Config-4 on most Linux systems running XFree86 4.x, correctly describes the host system's hardware configuration is another simple step to take. XFree86 servers do a good job of detecting most graphics hardware, but values in the configuration file override detected values. Thus, if the values are wrong, the server's performance suffers. Pay particular attention to the Device section, making sure that the driver that it loads (using the Driver keyword) corresponds to the graphics chipset. If it's present, ensure that the VideoRAM directive correctly states the amount of RAM (in kilobytes) on the card.

Along similar lines, browse the server's log file, often stored in /var/log, looking for signs of misconfiguration. Any entry in the log prefixed with (EE) denotes an error that should be investigated and solved, whether it affects performance or not. Warnings in the log are prefixed with (WW) and might or might not represent a current or potential problem. For example, the following entry from the X server log indicates that one of ATI X server's built-in video modes cannot be used:

```
(WW) ATI(0): Default mode "1792x1344" deleted (insufficient memory for mode)
```

Discrepancies between detected information, prefixed in the log with (--), and actual values, such as the graphics chipset, the amount of RAM, or the keyboard or mouse type, should be corrected.

Decrease Color Depth or Display Resolution

The higher you set the server's color depth (that is, the number of bytes used to color a pixel on the screen), the more memory, CPU cycles, and time the server and the graphics card need to refresh the screen. Accordingly, the server and graphics card have less memory and CPU cycles for graphics and window-management operations. The same applies to the display resolution, the number of pixels displayed on the screen.

The memory requirements for a given combination of color depth and display resolution are easy to calculate. Simply multiply the resolution times the number of bytes required to color a single dot on the screen. Then divide the resulting value by 1024 to obtain the value in kilobytes rather than bytes. The basic formula is this:

(Hres × Vres × Bytes) / 1024 = Memory in Kilobytes

Keep in mind that 24 bits per pixel (bpp) equates to 3 bytes per pixel, 16bpp equates to 2 bytes, and 8bpp equates to 1 byte. Also, there are 1024 bytes in a kilobyte, not 1000, as many people erroneously believe. So, for a resolution of 1024 × 768 at 24bpp, the calculation would be this:

(1024 × 768 × 3) / 1024 = 2304KB

Memory requirements for a resolution of 1280×1024 at 24bpp would be as follows:

$$(1280 \times 1024 \times 3) / 1024 = 3840KB$$

Fortunately, you can often trade image clarity for color richness, or vice versa. Experimentation and testing will determine the best combination for your situation.

> **Tip**
>
> To convert kilobyte values to megabyte values, divide the kilobyte value by 1024. For example, 3840KB equates to 3.75MB. That is,
>
> 3840 / 1024 = 3.75.

The `x11perfcomp` output shown in Listing 6.4 illustrates the impact of richer color depths (8, 16, and 24bpp) at the same display resolution on the X server's performance.

Listing 6.4 Comparing Different Color Depths at the Same Resolution

```
1: 8bit
2: 16bit
3: 32bit


      1         2         3      Operation
 --------  --------  --------  ----------
  45800.0   46300.0   41100.0  Fill 10x10 64-gon (Convex)
  13900.0   10600.0    2530.0  Fill 100x100 64-gon (Convex)
  33200.0   33400.0   31600.0  Fill 10x10 64-gon (Complex)
  13500.0   10600.0    2530.0  Fill 100x100 64-gon (Complex)
```

The four tests measured the server's performance drawing 64-sided polygons, either 10×10 pixels or 100×100 pixels in size, at a constant display resolution of 1280×1024 pixels and progressively higher color depths of 8, 16, and 24bpp. Although the results are not entirely uniform, especially at the 16bpp color depth, the general trend is evident: At the same display resolution, higher color depths resulted in lower performance results, particularly when moving from 16bpp to 24bpp.

Disable Unused Modules and Server Extensions

If you do not use an X module or server extension, do not load it. This will speed up the server's startup time and reduce the server's memory footprint. The default configuration that most Linux vendors provide might not be ideal for your installation. To see what modules and extensions your server loads, look for the section Module directive in the configuration file. Listing 6.5 shows an example section.

Listing 6.5   The Module Section Specifies X Modules and Extensions to Load

```
Section "Module"
        Load    "GLcore"
        Load    "dbe"
        Load    "extmod"
        Load    "fbdevhw"
        Load    "dri"
        Load    "glx"
EndSection
```

The functionality that these modules provide is summarized in the following list:

- **GLCore**—Provides basic 3D rendering capability
- **dbe**—Enables support for double buffering
- **extmod**—Loads a variety of X server extensions
- **fbdevhw**—Provides server support for accessing hardware frame-buffer devices
- **dri**—Implements the Direct Rendering Infrastructure, a method for sending 3D data directly to graphics hardware
- **glx**—Implements an interface for connecting core 3D rendering to the X11 windowing system

If you do not need 3D rendering capabilities, disable the GLCore and glx modules by commenting the lines that load these modules using the hash sign (#), or delete the lines from the configuration file. Doing so will speed up the server's startup time and free the memory for other uses.

The good news is that XFree86 4 uses a dynamic module-loading scheme that works much like the Linux kernel's. Modules, even those providing essential functionality, are loaded as needed. The bad news, though, is that many modules are also built into the server. Some, however, are used only at startup and then are unloaded. To identify built-in modules, look for entries in the server's log file that resemble the following:

```
(II) Initializing built-in extension MIT-SHM
(II) Initializing built-in extension XInputExtension
(II) Initializing built-in extension XTEST
```

The XFree86 log file records modules loaded at startup. To determine what modules are loaded when the server starts, look for entries in the log file that resemble the following:

```
(II) LoadModule: "bitmap"
(II) Loading /usr/X11R6/lib/modules/fonts/libbitmap.a
(II) Module bitmap: vendor="The XFree86 Project"
        compiled for 4.0.3, module version = 1.0.0
        Module class: XFree86 Font Renderer
        ABI class: XFree86 Font Renderer, version 0.2
```

Before ruthlessly disabling a particular module, though, make sure that the server does not automatically unload it. For example, the scanpci module is unloaded during startup. Look for entries similar to the following:

```
(II) UnloadModule: "scanpci"
(II) Unloading /usr/X11R6/lib/modules/libscanpci.a
```

Use Chipset-Specific Configuration Options

Using configuration options specific to a given graphics chipset, card, or driver could improve the X server's performance. For example, the mga driver, which supports a number of Matrox chips, understands 15 options; the generic vesa driver recognizes 1. These options are documented in text files named README.*foo* and can be found in the XFree86 directory hierarchy, usually under /usr/X11R6/lib/X11/doc. Some of this documentation has been converted to man page format in XFree86 version 4. So, for example, you can either read /usr/X11R6/lib/ X11/doc/README.mga or execute man mga to get details specific to the mga driver.

The default option settings are ideal in many instances, but not all cases. Several graphics chipset vendors, such as NVIDIA and Cirrus, do not make graphics cards. Instead, they make graphics chipsets that they license to card vendors, who then build graphic cards based on the chipsets. The cards might not use all of a given chipset's features, or they might use these features improperly, so using a different option value could improve performance. A notable example of this involves cards based on older Cirrus chipsets. Many of these cards incorrectly used the hardware cursor. The default setting, Option "hw_cursor" in XFree86 version 3 or Option "HWCursor" "yes" in version 4, caused performance problems and unsightly video artifacts. This problem was solved by using Option "sw_cursor" (version 3) or Option "HWCursor" "no" (version 4).

After reading the man page appropriate for your driver, experiment with the various settings to determine whether settings other than the defaults improve the server's performance in your situation.

Rebuild the Server

Compiling the X server to match the host system's CPU, using optimizations and options intended to take advantage of that CPU's features, might make a significant difference in server performance. Although recompiling an X server seems dramatic, Linux vendors often use the most generic compiler settings, particularly with respect to CPU-specific settings and optimizations, to enable their products to run on the widest possible variety of hardware. For example, the GNU C compiler's -mcpu=i386 option generates code that will run on any Intel x86 CPU, from the 386 through at least the Pentium III. To run on a 386, Pentium III-specific optimizations and instructions are left out. The compiler's -march=i686 option, however, does emit code that utilizes Pentium III-specific features, albeit at the cost of creating code that will not run on a 386.

Moreover, some X servers might have experimental code or compile time configuration options, disabled by default, that take advantage of chipset or server features. This could result in a significant difference in the server's performance. Keep in mind, though, that these options are disabled for a reason: Such code might result in instability, server crashes, file corruption, and other undesirable behavior. So, before putting such a server into production, test it thoroughly and be sure to read and understand all of the documentation, READMEs, and warnings before you proceed.

Load Fewer Fonts

As with other tips in this chapter, you can reduce the server's memory consumption and its startup time by loading fewer fonts, especially fonts that are rarely used or not used at all. The fonts loaded depend on the configuration file's FontPath statements, which typically resemble the following:

```
FontPath      "/usr/X11R6/lib/X11/fonts/misc/"
FontPath      "/usr/X11R6/lib/X11/fonts/75dpi/:unscaled"
FontPath      "/usr/X11R6/lib/X11/fonts/100dpi/:unscaled"
FontPath      "/usr/X11R6/lib/X11/fonts/Type1/"
FontPath      "/usr/X11R6/lib/X11/fonts/Speedo/"
FontPath      "/usr/X11R6/lib/X11/fonts/75dpi/"
FontPath      "/usr/X11R6/lib/X11/fonts/100dpi/"
```

If you do not use Type1 or Speedo fonts, for example, keep them from loading by commenting out the appropriate line with the hash sign (#), or delete the line entirely. Scaled fonts are prime candidates for disabling because they require CPU-intensive floating-point operations to build when the server starts.

To modify the fonts available in a running X server, use the xset command and its q and fp options. The q option simply shows the server's current configuration. The fp option enables you to manipulate the X server's font path on the fly. xset's syntax is atypical of ordinary Linux command syntax, so only usage of the fp option is covered in the following summary:

- **xset fp default**—Resets the font path to the server's compiled in default
- **xset fp=*fontpath1*[,*fontpath2*[...]]**—Sets the server's font path to the path(s) specified in the *fontpathN*
- **xset -fp *fontpath1*[,*fontpath2*[...]]**—Deletes *fontpathN* from the front of the server's current font path
- **xset fp- *fontpath1*[,*fontpath2*[...]]**—Deletes *fontpathN* from the end of the server's current font path
- **xset +fp *fontpath1*[,*fontpath2*[...]]**—Adds *fontpathN* to the front of the server's current font path

- **xset fp+** *fontpath1*[,*fontpath2*[...]]—Adds *fontpathN* to the end of the server's current font path

- **xset fp rehash**—Instructs the server to reread its font database, based on the current font path

After changing a running X server's font path, you must force the server to rebuild its in-core font database, or the change will not take effect. To do so, you need to execute the command `xset fp rehash`. Follow up with `xset q` to confirm the results. Listing 6.6 demonstrates how to delete a font path using `xset`. The output has been trimmed to conserve space and reduce clutter.

LISTING 6.6   Deleting a Font Path Using `xset`

```
$ xset q
...
Font Path:
/usr/X11R6/lib/X11/fonts/local/,
➥/usr/X11R6/lib/X11/fonts/misc/,
➥/usr/X11R6/lib/X11/fonts/75dpi/:unscaled,
➥/usr/X11R6/lib/X11/fonts/100dpi/:unscaled,
➥/usr/X11R6/lib/X11/fonts/CID/,
➥/usr/X11R6/lib/X11/fonts/75dpi/,
➥/usr/X11R6/lib/X11/fonts/100dpi/
...
$ xset -fp /usr/X11R6/lib/X11/fonts/local/
$ xset fp rehash
$ xset q
...
Font Path:

/usr/X11R6/lib/X11/fonts/misc/,
➥/usr/X11R6/lib/X11/fonts/75dpi/:unscaled,
➥/usr/X11R6/lib/X11/fonts/100dpi/:unscaled,
➥/usr/X11R6/lib/X11/fonts/CID/,
➥/usr/X11R6/lib/X11/fonts/75dpi/,
➥/usr/X11R6/lib/X11/fonts/100dpi/
```

The first `xset` command shows the existing font path. The second `xset` invocation uses `-fp` to remove `/usr/X11R6/lib/X11/fonts/local/` from the server's font path. Note that the `xset` requires the terminating / to properly specify a directory path. If it is missing, `xset` issues a warning that the font path was not changed. After using the `rehash` option to refresh the server's font database, the final `xset` call confirms that `/usr/X11R6/lib/X11/fonts/local` is no longer part of the X server's font path.

As usual, after altering the set of loaded fonts, be sure to test the server's performance and evaluate the results. In this case, the tests to perform should include x11perf's character drawing tests, or at least some subset of them. A complete test can be invoked using the command x11perf -range ftext,rgbftext.

Use a Font Server

Use a font server rather than loading a specific set of fonts. A font server transfers font rendering and management from the X server to another process, the font server, which has been designed and (hopefully) optimized for font management. Offloading font rendering to a separate service independent of the X server prevents font management from bogging down the X server. Fortunately, XFree86 version 4 includes a sophisticated font server that is capable of managing standard X fonts and the popular TrueType fonts. So, rather than specifying a particular set of fonts to load in the configuration file, as illustrated in the previous section, the configuration file contains a single FontPath directive pointing at a font server, as shown:

```
FontPath    "unix/:7100"
```

This entry directs X programs connecting to the server to communicate with port 7100, the font server's default port, on the local system for font services. The entry could just as well be this:

```
FontPath    "fontbeast:7101"
```

This directive tells X clients to connect to port 7101 on the host named fontbeast for font-rendering information and services.

The font server itself can be configured to limit the number of clients that it will service, to specify alternate font servers, to enforce the default font sizes and resolutions available to X clients, and to offer only a limited selection of fonts to X programs. Individual users can also run font servers on their workstations, a measure that offloads font rendering to the users' systems. This again reduces server loads, but still permits users to use as many fonts as desired.

Upgrade the Server

Installing the latest and greatest XFree86 version might have more of an impact on your X server's performance than any other single tip suggested so far, short of upgrading the computer's underlying hardware. This is particularly true if you are still using XFree86 version 3.

Most importantly, version 4.0 introduced dramatic changes in XFree86's basic design and architecture. It has a more modular design, resulting in more efficient performance because unrelated functionality has been split into separate modules loaded on demand rather than monolithically. The X server itself, the component that implements core X protocol functionality, has been stripped down to bare essentials. Noncore functionality is loaded on demand from modules and extensions.

Similarly, the drivers have been modularized and optimized. Across the board, drivers are faster. A core driver might implement functionality common across a chipset family, supplemented by one or more modules specific to a particular chip or chip revision loaded dynamically. Support for X extensions, features not present in the original X protocol specifications but added later, have also been broken down into functional units, implemented as modules, and loaded on an as-needed basis. Examples include the font drivers, support for input devices (keyboards, mouse devices, graphics tablets, joysticks, and so on), and features such as support for 3D graphics, video, multihead, and video.

> **NOTE**
>
> When this book went to press, XFree86 4.0.3, the most current release, supported fewer graphics adapters than version 3.3.6, but the number of unsupported cards had declined dramatically from the initial 4.0 release.

Other improvements include better support for PCI and AGP video adapters; a more consistent and extended configuration file syntax; the Xinerama extension, which enables a single screen to be spread across multiple monitors; much better support for 3D graphics, particularly SGI's OpenGL standard; native support for TrueType fonts; and support for VESA's DDC standard, which enables graphics adapters and monitors to communicate. (The benefit here is that you are much less likely to blow out your monitor if the video card attempts to run the monitor beyond its capabilities.)

To give credit where it is due, some of XFree86's improvements are the result of markedly better support from vendors of video cards, manufacturers of graphics chips, and suppliers of commercial X servers. After Linux burst upon the scene in 1999, information and assistance from previously uncooperative sources became much easier to obtain.

In short, if you are still using XFree86 version 3, you should upgrade to version 4. In addition to offering an improved design and a richer feature set, it is the base upon which further server enhancements will be built.

Upgrade the Hardware

For the sake of completeness, the last tip is to upgrade the system on which the X server runs. In some cases, all of the software tweaks and refinements that you can apply will have less cumulative effect than more system RAM, large disk drives, a faster CPU, or a 3D video adapter with all the latest whistles and bells. Recognizing that hardware upgrades might not be an option in many circumstances and that the recommendation itself is often an excuse used to avoid doing the hard work of solving difficult problems, nothing else remains to be said on the subject.

Before moving on to tuning X clients, consider this final note: The performance improvement resulting from any single tweak discussed in this section might prove relatively small. However, the cumulative effect of multiple tweaks could be significant. Finding the best mix of improvements is up to you. Good luck, and happy tuning!

Tuning X Desktop Performance

The tips in this section focus on coaxing better performance from X client programs and from the desktop environment in general. The following is a general observation related to desktop environments and window managers; it offers ideas to improve overall desktop X program performance.

About Those "Desktop Environments..."

GNOME and KDE, arguably the two most popular Linux GUI interfaces, provide rich functionality and stunning visuals. They also make heavy demands on the host system and the X server because they are more than mere window managers. Instead, they are—or attempt to be—complete desktop environments.

What is the difference between a window manager and a desktop environment? Why does it matter? Keep in mind that the X specification defines the core services that a windowing system should provide, not what a window looks like. It is the job of a *window manager* to define a window's appearance and how it responds to keystrokes or mouse clicks. Window managers largely disregard the underlying operating system, providing instead the user interface to the X Window System.

Desktop environments, on the other hand, provide much more than a convenient interface for the X protocol. In addition to implementing the standard window-management functions, desktop environments are keenly aware of the underlying OS. In fact, they attempt to hide and extend the OS by encapsulating OS features and services, such as file management and Internet access, beneath an attractive, user-friendly interface for manipulating those OS services. Desktop environments also layer additional capabilities on top of basic window management, including but not limited to these:

- A consistent interface and appearance, enforced on compliant and noncompliant applications
- A complete application-programming framework
- A unified help system incorporating the environment's own documentation and the standard man and info pages, the LDP FAQs and HOWTOs, and application documentation stored in the /usr/doc directory tree (/usr/share/doc on LSB-compliant systems)

- Integrated utilities such as graphics viewers, file managers, Web browsers, text editors, and, in many cases, complete office productivity suites

- A horde of applications and applets built around the desktop environment's APIs

What's the point? The functionality and alleged convenience that desktop environments provide require substantially more system resources than mere window managers do. If you or your users do not need this additional functionality, consider a simpler alternative: a window manager that decorates windows, translates keyboard and mouse input, and uses menus to enable easy access to your favorite programs but that otherwise stays out of your way and eschews the overhead of omnipresent desktop environments. The range and variety of window managers precludes coverage in this chapter, so take a look at The Window Managers for X Web site, at `http://xwinman.org/index.html`, to get an idea of the available alternatives to KDE and GNOME.

Improving X Client Performance

A list of tips and hints follows. Not all of them will be relevant to your situation. As with the suggestions for server tuning, find the combination that fits best in your environment. The intent here is to offer as many ideas as possible, enabling you to find one or more that makes a real difference.

- Use a simple solid-color or pattern background on your desktop. Solid and pattern backgrounds load more quickly and require less memory than image-based backgrounds.

- To improve desktop startup time, remove unused or rarely used applications from menus, toolbars, and panels.

- Consider whether you really need to have a mail notification program, such as xbiff, or a clock, such as xclock, running. Most mail clients can be configured to check mail at arbitrary intervals. Your wall clock or wristwatch is surely capable of showing you the current time.

- Evaluate other terminal emulators. A mind-boggling variety of terminal emulators exists that might well suit your needs without exacting unnecessary performance overhead. A (surely incomplete) short list of alternatives includes nxterm, rxvt, xterm, xvt, konsole, kvt, color-xterm, ansi-xterm, dtterm, emu, eterm, mterm, mxterm, and xiterm. No doubt more exist.

- On a system with little memory, reduce the size of the terminal emulator's history or scrollback feature. Instead, learn how to exploit the shell's history and command-recall capabilities.

- Using xset (introduced in the section titled "Load Fewer Fonts"), adjust the speed of your mouse cursor. The option to use is m. The proper syntax is this:

```
xset m accel limit
```

accel and *limit* work together, so they need to be explained together. The mouse cursor moves across the screen *accel* times faster than the mouse driver is compiled in default when it moves more than *limit* pixels in a short time. That is, if you flick your wrist quickly to move the mouse cursor across the screen (while playing a game, for example), it will move much faster than it would under normal circumstances (while moving one window out of the way of another, for example). Specifying m by itself applies compiled in defaults. Specifying only one argument to m sets only *accel*.

Naturally, the mouse's speed heavily affects the user. Almost any adjustment will seem awkward at first. Over time, your kinesthetic sense will help you adjust to the mouse cursor's reaction time. Allow yourself time to adjust before discarding the change.

- Disable window manager options resembling Show Window Contents While Moving. On an underpowered client system, the screen refreshes necessary to maintain the appearance of a moving window bog down the system and the X server. How vital is it, after all, to see the 17 directories on 4 files in that window if you are simply moving it out of the way so that you can look at another window?

- Reduce the number of applications that start when you log in. Many window managers and desktop environments enable you to define a set of applications (a mail client, a Web browser, two or three terminals, the CD player, a sticky notes program, and so forth) to start each time you log in. Honestly evaluate whether you really need them started automatically.

- Configure your most commonly used programs to use the same fonts. If the five applications that you use most often use the same fonts, they will start more quickly because they do not need to wait while the X server loads extra fonts.

- Similarly, run a font server and store the fonts that you use most often locally. As a separate process and with the needed fonts stored locally (provided that you do not use many different fonts), program startup will be faster because you do not have to wait for the X server or a remote font server to load or process the fonts you need. Be careful not to overload the local system.

- Evaluate your screensaver, if you use one. Admittedly attractive, xscreensaver loads a daemon program to detect keyboard and screen inactivity and kick off the screensaver. KDE and GNOME do the same. Screen blanking (see xset's s option in the xset man page), albeit far less entertaining than other alternatives, is implemented in the X server and is much less hungry for system resources.

Any list of tips, hints, suggestions, and tweaks to enhance X client performance could continue for pages. The ideas behind any such list, though, are surprisingly simple. Desktop eye candy, such as impressive wallpaper or terminal emulators with transparent backgrounds shadowing that wallpaper, consume memory and CPU cycles, as do admittedly convenient utilities such as mail notifiers and clocks. If the performance of X clients is unsatisfactory, you must decide whether appearance and convenience are more important than speed and responsiveness.

Summary

No precise formula exists to produce an exquisitely tuned X server or client running at peak efficiency. Instead, to squeeze the best possible performance out of the X Window System, a few general principles apply: Reduce memory consumption, minimize CPU usage, and eliminate unused features. It is also important to experiment, test, and evaluate the results of performance improvements to find the combination of tweaks on both the server and the client side that is most appropriate to your needs.

Network Performance

Overview of Network-Performance Issues

In these days when nearly everything you do depends on your network, you need to make sure that the network you are deploying will be physically capable of handling the load and that your machines on the network are correctly configured to maximize usage of the physical wiring. Generally there are many ways to increase performance, through modifications to the network hardware, the protocols used over the network, the machines and applications that use those protocols, and good policy on utilization of that bandwidth, either physically imposed or just through general usage procedures.

Always take into account all activity happening on your network, your current architecture, the planned architecture, and planned usage. Ensure that decent knowledge is present on both the operating system and application side and on the networking side. Decent knowledge should be enough to cover your current needs, but also enough for you to know that you won't be held back in the future because of a lack of expertise. If you're just doing basic application work, a decent knowledge of TCP/IP and maybe DNS is probably appropriate; whereas if you are looking for extreme performance, you might need someone who knows the IP stack of the kernel by heart. All the Linux tuning experts in the world won't help a bit if your network isn't laid out correctly.

Poor network performance can effectively bring a system to a halt, as dependent as we are on being able to communicate between systems in real time. A mismanaged network is probably the worst thing that can happen to your business because nearly everything will come to a dead stop without it. This chapter is as much about making sure that your physical network is prepared as it is about making sure that your software is using it correctly.

Hardware Methods

Described here are some methods you can use to improve your physical network to help your system's efficiency. No book can cover everything involved, but this section presents some decent low-order changes you can make to your network.

First, determine the correct underlying transport architecture, at the lowest level. Raw 10MB Ethernet simply isn't going to cut it anymore for many applications, and although 100MB switches do the job in many situations, in demanding environments even gigabit Ethernet still won't provide the throughput you need. In some situations, you need to raise the bar to something like ATM, although usually you can pull some tricks out of your sleeve to avoid that route—this is a management nightmare when compared to traditional technologies like Ethernet. Other systems out there, such as Frame Relay and ISDN, generally aren't contenders these days when laying out a system. If they are, you will face special considerations in utilizing that bandwidth; some of the Linux bandwidth-management techniques described here might help you keep that pipe behaving correctly. Likewise, wireless protocols aren't favored for the most part, but they are beginning to take hold in some environments, especially for desktop use.

Another quick win in the performance arena can be had by duplicating hardware. If you can justify the bandwidth need, deploying multiple switch fabrics (multiple segments or paths by which network traffic can travel) can greatly increase speed. With multiple switches, you can join each machine to multiple segments, giving them more links to the network fabric and increasing their effective bandwidth. With a four port network card in a machine, each connected to different physical networks, your bottleneck starts to move from the network to other subsystems. Otherwise, the links between the switches can be the bottleneck. As described in Chapter 5, "Apparent and Nonapparent Bottlenecks," there is always a bottleneck, but if you can be sure that your network fabric is up to the job, the problem of tuning becomes simpler because fewer variables are involved.

Getting the most out of your network depends on finding the right hardware to suit your needs. As with general tuning of a Linux box, you can go only as fast as the underlying hardware. Choosing the right framework is important and requires up-front thinking; rolling out large network modifications down the road can be very disruptive. Because networking is extremely complicated, the best thing to do to make sure that you are prepared is to bring in an expert and explain the raw data needs of the system. Then build the system around that. This forces a separation of the network design requirements because the networking hardware is concerned only with transporting raw data and has explicitly defined limits. Do the math on what raw throughput you anticipate needing, and build the network around that. This doesn't have to be an exact calculation, of course, because of variances in user demand and other factors, but at least some simple predictions should be made. This is nearly always going to be an environment-specific measurement. This doesn't have to be that difficult for the most part because a simple guess can be made by simply figuring out average request sizes and multiplying that by the number of requests predicted over a given period of time. This can become difficult in some environments, but operations such as Web serving is very simple. Find the size of the average HTTP request made (by writing a bit of server-side code to keep the values or just by saving the response and looking at the file size) and multiply that size by the number of users per second. This should give you a decent idea of how much raw bandwidth you need. Figure on allowing a lot of room for growth in your network, and always assume that congestion will prevent you from ever getting the full bandwidth rate out of your hardware. For example, a decent value to assume on an unswitched 10MB network is actually about 3.3MB/sec because every card on the network backs off its transfers significantly in the face of a network collision. Then when you are sure that the network fabric is up to the job, you can worry about tuning the individual machines to correctly utilize the network.

Application Network Tuning

Depending on what application you are using, tuning its usage of the network probably will give you more of a performance jump than tuning the kernel. Specific applications that depend on their own protocols generally support different implementations of the protocols and different configurations for each protocol, resulting in vastly different performance yields. What follows are a few simple examples of the normal means of ensuring that applications make the best possible use of the resources presented to them.

Examples: Database Work

Although this example blurs the lines of pure network utilization and performance, it's a good way to demonstrate how many factors might be involved when looking to tune your operations. When you're using code written in Java with Oracle's JDBC drivers, you can configure the JDBC driver to use the SQL*Net protocol in a few ways.

The "thin" driver provided is a pure Java implementation of the protocol—that is, it doesn't need to use any underlying system libraries to talk to the database. The code might also be capable of having Java hook to the native drivers and interact with the database through the C-based OCI interface. In this case, both types are using the same protocol. However, you should get better performance with the native drivers, especially for high-bandwidth database requests which may stress a Java environment that isn't optimized enough to handle the work effectively. Therefore, switching the application to hook through the native drivers could avoid the bottleneck.

This case wasn't necessarily a matter of network tuning, but it shows that what might appear to be a network issue could just as easily be a matter of application configuration. At first glance, though, the problem was probably diagnosed as a slowdown of data transfer, and investigating both the processing server and the database server might not have shown anything out of the ordinary. Your first guess in this case might be to look at your network usage, when it's more important to reconfigure the drivers for the application.

Along that same vein, another general application-tuning issue when dealing with database servers is the use of connection pooling. (Although it is not the exclusive domain of the database realm, this is a well-known method of speeding processing.) When applications use and discard database connections, it might not make sense in most situations to really close the connection to the database. Because the database needs to perform initialization and shut down work on each connection, and because both machines involved need to perform socket creation and destruction, it is generally a good idea to keep the connection to the database open. When one thread or section of code finishes with its connection, it can simply throw it back into the pool. Then when another thread needs a connection, rather than opening and initializing a whole new connection (which causes network overhead and extra traffic), it can simply pull out the old one back from the pool. This raises the requirements on the database and application server slightly because they each need to handle more simultaneous connections, but the speed gains greatly outweigh the cost.

HTTP Speed-ups

A lot of work these days revolves around Web interaction and HTTP transfers, so you might have software whose performance depends on its interaction with various HTTP servers, such as Apache. A simple way of speeding up transfers is to make sure that all parts of the transfer are using HTTP 1.1. The original HTTP 1.0 specification had no mechanism for allowing multiple files to be transferred over the same HTTP request. To pull a page with multiple components, such as frames, images, scripts, and so on, the client had to make individual socket requests for each piece. Under HTTP 1.1, the specification was updated to allow multiple files to be transferred within the same socket session, saving the costs of repeated socket negotiations and HTTP overhead. By making sure that everyone involved in the transfer is using HTTP 1.1, you might find a speed-up by a factor of 10 in your processing.

Different content encodings can also help. By configuring your Web server to use gzip encoding (Apache has a module written to do this), the content that comes out of your Web server, which is generally textual HTML, can be automatically compressed before it hits the wire. On the client end, if it can understand the "Content-encoding: gzip" response in the HTTP headers, it will receive the compressed version of the content, decompress it, and display it. In addition to getting the content to the client quicker, this also makes much better use of your network. Text, such as HTML, compresses very well. What's more, if your network is congested due to thousands of HTTP requests for HTML, it could reduce your network load to a trickle. There is a penalty on both the Web server and the client because extra work is involved with the compression and subsequent decompression. However, if you can afford to handle that in return for better network performance, it is probably a path that you will want to consider.

The Value of Knowing Your Domain

This might seem complicated, but it is a good example of knowing your application domain and making good use of the technology you have. The usability of the GNOME desktop system relies on this capability. GNOME is founded on the principles of CORBA, a system that forces the application designer to write out all interfaces beforehand and then implement the client and server ends of the code based on the calls specified in the interface. There are CORBA mappings for many different languages, enabling you to implement the client and server in different languages.

7

**NETWORK
PERFORMANCE**

Also built in is the idea of network transparency, so you can run the server on one machine in one language, such as C, and the client on another machine in another language, such as Java. CORBA will handle all the translations in the background, allowing the developer to work on the problem at hand and not have to worry about where the server is running or what protocol to use to reach it. (This is only a small subset of what CORBA does—refer to the GNOME project documentation or a CORBA book for more details.)

GNOME uses this to cleanly define system components, among other reasons. But the average GNOME desktop user is running code solely on his machine: At the moment, at least, it is rare for someone to be using components that are being served off remote machines. The problem is that even though CORBA implementations have become much faster over the years, CORBA still will be slower than an application that is simply linking against a local shared library. Inherent in CORBA calls is the process of taking server-bound calls, preparing the parameters for network transfer (marshalling), talking to the remote object to make the call, reconstructing the passed values on the other side (demarshalling), and optionally returning data the same way. No matter how fast you write your code, this process always will be slower than a direct hop to a function resident in your process's memory space as a result of the linking process.

So, to get a speed advantage in the common case, the designers made a modification to ORBit, which is the CORBA implementation that GNOME uses. When you make a CORBA call, ORBit tries first to make the call via a shared library as a normal application would, and then it resorts to the CORBA transport, if it needs to. For the average case, the "short circuit" to a normal linking saves a lot of time, both for the machine and for the user. This results in a very responsive desktop system.

Does this sound complicated to you? It should—this is not as simple as looking at your system and playing with a configuration file. But in the end, it results in a huge performance gain, without which the system might not be usable for most people. This is a very good example of making sure that you use every bit of technology available—and how sometimes intelligent use of this knowledge is what makes the system work.

Tuning Samba

Knowing your application and domain is all well and good, but sometimes you just want to make sure that you are getting the most out of your file server. You don't have time to go into the depths of the documentation to find every last bit of information on every technology involved. Here are some hints on getting more out of your Samba server.

As the SMB protocol changes, there will undoubtedly be other minor modifications that you can do to make your version faster. At the time of this writing, Samba 2.2 has just come out, and, understandably, it doesn't have as much field use as the 2.0 series. As 2.2 begins widespread deployment, more information will appear on how to tune it, but here the primary focus with respect to specific configuration directives will be on the 2.0 series. What is described here should translate to 2.2 also, but if you are using 2.2, it is probably worth checking around for any other tips that users have found to be useful with that version. For instance, some options make Samba faster with Windows NT clients. You likely will find some hints that you can give to Samba to make it work better with Windows 2000 clients.

First off, let's look at what Samba does for you and the differences between the versions, to help you determine which one is right for you. At the core of it all is the SMB protocol, which you can use to manage facilities on your network such as printers and file shares. With authentication, you can use Samba to replace your existing Windows servers, and you can save the licensing costs involved with using Microsoft's version. Although Samba 2.0 had limited usability when it came to managing users (restricted to Windows 9x and NT clients), 2.2 can handle Windows 2000 clients, emulate DFS servers (a Windows 2000 distributed file server), manage domains, and also perform the normal file and print services. In addition, there is a unification of the NFS and Samba file-locking mechanisms in 2.2. Now, if you are serving the same data via Samba and NFS, file locking is coordinated between the two rather than having two different sets of locks, which could result in unsafe operations. ACLs, which have always been different between Windows and Unix, have joined together, so you can have the same set of permissions on both the Windows clients and the Unix users. Samba is heavily used in the field: Most of the largest machines serving data to Windows clients aren't running Windows on the server—they are running a Unix flavor with Samba installed.

One more note before we get started: With 2.2, a profiling mechanism is now present that you can enable in your build of the suite. If it is built with profiling on, you can send signals to the server daemon at runtime to turn profiling on and off. By looking at the data generated by this profiling operation, you might have more insight into what your server is spending most of its time on. This will probably help you quickly zero in on the right tuning operation.

Filesystem Buffers

Most of what Samba is doing depends on the caches used on the system. If a large portion of the data requested is the same files, making sure that they live in the filesystem buffers will help performance. That way, the server doesn't have to spin the disk to repeatedly get the files for clients. So, the first priority is to make sure that your machine is making proper use of its memory for filesystem buffers. In most environments, the machine running Samba is a standalone file server and isn't taxed heavily by other applications running on the machine. In this case, most of the system memory can be used to buffer filesystem requests. Refer to Chapter 9 on tuning the kernel for specifics on how to do this. Trying the buffer system configuration presented as an example in Chapter 2, "Aspects of Performance Tuning," might help you get better performance for your clients. In the end, tweaking these values might suit your environment.

Fake Oplocks

Oplocks (opportunistic locks) are grants made by the Samba server to clients. If the server decides that the machine is the only one using a file, it grants an oplock to it, letting that client assume that it can cache file locks locally. Caching the operation on the local machine is obviously much faster because the machine doesn't have to keep generating traffic to the server to coordinate what it is doing. By setting fake oplocks on for the server, Samba grants oplocks to all clients, whether or not they are the only one working on the file. This can give large performance gains, particularly on read-only filesystems that will only ever have one concurrent user anyway, such as a shared CD-ROM. However, this can cause corruption if users are allowed to step on each other's work. Samba turns this off value by default. If you know your environment can survive the possible usage ambiguity, this can help speed performance, but shouldn't be used in a multiuser environment.

If needed, individual files can be selected to not allow oplocks. Refer to the documentation on the `veto_oplock_files` parameter for more information. Note that this applies only in older versions of Samba (before 1.9.18); although it still works, this is now a deprecated behavior.

```
fake oplocks = yes # no by default
```

Caching `getwd` Calls

You can cache `getwd()` calls, which return the current working directory, with the use of the `'getwd cache=yes'` setting. Samba turns this on by default, especially when combined with the `wide links` parameter set to `no`. The `wide links` parameter controls whether a user can get to a file outside the shared directory tree via a symbolic link. With `wide links = yes`, the server allows users to get anywhere they can in the filesystem, if a symbolic link allows them to go outside the default tree.

With a badly placed symbolic link, users might be able to get to directories to which they shouldn't otherwise have access. With `wide links` set to `no`, there is significant overhead involved for the server to make sure that the user isn't going outside the normal tree; making sure that `getwd()` calls are cached helps this process. So, what follows is the configuration recommended if you want to make sure that users cannot leave their tree. Even if you do allow them to go outside their tree, the `getwd` cache can help performance in other areas, so it is always good to leave it on.

```
getwd cache = yes
wide links = no
```

Hiding/Vetoing Files

If you are noticing performance slowdown and you have file hiding enabled, this could be the cause. The mechanics of hiding files is not discussed here because it is assumed that this was explicitly enabled by the administrator. Keep in mind that doing the work to make sure that the file is not in a hidden set when serving will slow the process of serving the said file. The reason this slows is fairly straightforward—if the server is just serving any file it sees, assuming that the user has access, the process is straightforward and quick. The more complex the hiding mechanism is (the hiding expressions can become fairly complex), checking every file against this pattern can place a significant load on the server. With a lot of complex patterns and a lot of users running directory listings of the shares in question, the server can experience a significant load. It is for this reason that hiding be enabled only when needed; and if files should be hidden, it is better to store them somewhere else in the system where they will not be seen.

Level 2 Oplocks

This is the preferred method of handling oplocks, as of Samba 2.0.5. This allows read-only locks, which can greatly help with files that don't generally get written to. Essentially, clients get an oplock allowing a read-write oplock while they are the only handler of a file. If another client comes into the picture, the oplock is downgraded to read-only. At this point, it can still serve to cache reads until another client comes into the picture and performs a write. At that point, the clients holding the (read-only) oplock are told to delete their read-ahead caches. The main difference between this type of oplock and fake oplocks is that fake oplocks hand off full control to multiple clients and might allow users to mishandle concurrent access to a file, whereas this type coordinates the concurrent work more safely. Level 2 oplocks are a much better option in nearly all cases, and should always be preferred over fake oplocks unless you know your environment very well. This option is allowable on a share only if the share also has oplocks set to true.

```
level2 oplocks = yes
```

Log Level

Using a log level above 2 is not recommended because it causes constant flushing of the log file, blocking the system. The higher the log level is, the slower the system will be. Try to find a trade-off point where you get the information you need, but not so much that the accounting of the operations impacts performance.

Considering Packet Transmit Size

Tweaking this parameter might yield small increases in performance, but probably nothing really substantial. max xmit controls the largest packet size (in bytes) that the Samba server will transmit over the network. The default is 65536, but lowering this forces data to be written to the wire in smaller bursts. Lowering it below 2048 is not recommended. This causes many more packets to be written, and the overhead of this might not be beneficial.

```
max xmit = 16384
```

Raw Reads and Writes

Raw reads and writes allow the server to do exactly what it says: perform low-latency optimized reads and writes of data to and from clients. This enables large reads and writes to the network, up to 64KB in size. The presence of this option can greatly speed operations, as long as you have clients that can handle it. In some environments, clients don't handle the raw operations well, although these days problem clients are rare. Depending on the types of clients reading and writing data to the server, the negotiation of the process might not be performed correctly, so this depends on your environment. Test this thoroughly with your specific clients before deploying.

```
read raw = yes
write raw = yes
```

Read Prediction

This is a simple parameter that enables Samba to do explicit read-aheads on files while waiting for new requests. Because the file was opened and read from, chances are good that the remote application will want more of the file eventually. Although this works only on files that were opened as read-only, it can help greatly if you have an application that does a lot of small reads on a file. This parameter is disabled by default.

```
read prediction = yes
```

Read Size

If your disk speed is roughly the same as your network speed and a transfer that is larger than the read size is being read (or written) (in bytes), the data will begin writing the data before the entire set has been assembled, say, from the network stack. This is dependent on hardware present, meaning that your machine's network hardware (and wiring) and disk hardware need to be similar in read and write throughput, and involves some testing to find out if the two match up well. The default value is 16384 bytes, meaning that if the network is requesting more than that amount of data, Samba will begin writing out some of the data to the network before the entire data set is collected from disk. If your disk can keep up with the network transfer, the first 16384 bytes will be written to the network, while the rest of the data is streamed from disk. This data will get written to the wire as if it had been assembled completely before the transfer had started. The closer your network and disk performance is, the lower this value can go because the disk will be able to keep up easier with a network transfer that has already started. Larger values, such as anything over 65536, will only result in wasted memory allocations.

```
read size = 8192
```

Socket Options

Samba can handle many socket options to tweak usage of the operating system's underlying socket system. Described here are the ones most relevant to tuning, but their applicability might vary depending on attributes present in your specific needs. Some might even cause Samba to fail completely. Each option has an explanation of how it applies to the network stack, but it also helps to have an already solid understanding of TCP to know which options are right for your environment.

- **SO_KEEPALIVE**—Keeps sockets alive over time. The length of time depends on the value specified via `sysctl`, as described later. This can help initialization overhead by already having sockets open for transfer.
- **TCP_NODELAY**—Doesn't delay on TCP packet sends. Otherwise, it waits to coalesce packets before pushing them out. This is the most influential option, usually giving up to a 40% speed gain in most environments.
- **IPTOS_LOWDELAY**—Is similar to `TCP_NODELAY`. This is helpful if you are on a local network. This option is generally used in conjunction with `TCP_NODELAY`.
- **IPTOS_THROUGHPUT**—Is most helpful in wide area network environments, to make better use of the available bandwidth. You can use these options on a single line, as in `socket options = TCP_NODELAY IPTOS_LOWDELAY`.

Write Cache Size

With this enabled, Samba creates an extra cache for every oplocked file. Both reads and writes are served from this cache, but the gains aren't received from this. This is meant more as a means of forcing reasonable writes for RAID drives. If the write cache size corresponds with the RAID stripe size, it can result in better handling of writes.

```
Write cache size = 131072  # value for per file cache in bytes
```

As you can see, Samba offers many angles from which to tune. Some of the options work against each other, so use only what is appropriate in your environment. Some options, such as `TCP_NODELAY`, seem to be appropriate in any environment. Keep in mind what clients you have, and plan your tuning process accordingly.

Because 2.2 is out and offers tighter integration with Windows 2000 networks, widespread acceptance probably isn't too far off. The options presented here apply to 2.2, but keep in mind that there will probably be other ways to tweak 2.2 down the road as more people test with Windows 2000. Check for updates on the Samba Web page, at `www.samba.org`.

7

NETWORK PERFORMANCE

Tuning NFS

Chapter 2 discussed options concerning NFS performance. The `rsize` and `wsize` parameters are the best way to directly affect how your NFS server behaves. Some people have found 4096 to be a good value to use when sharing between Linux boxes, although that might change in your environment, depending on the types of network cards you use. Generally, when dealing with other implementations of NFS, such as when mounts on a Solaris machine are involved, it takes more testing to get those values right for each NFS implementation.

A few options can help beyond the previous example, though. One is the number of NFS daemons that you run on your server. The default number is eight, mainly because that is simply what it has always been. If you are heavily using NFS services, you might need to raise that number. Having more servers available will help serve large numbers of requests efficiently. This is because there are more processes that might be available to handle a request, rather than blocking and waiting for an already busy process to finish up. Keep in mind that the number of processes shouldn't be set too high because eventually it will outstrip the number of requests, and only end up wasting system memory. It should be defined in your distribution's NFS startup script, something like the following:

```
daemon rpc.nfsd $RPCNFSDCOUNT
```

Packet sizing can also affect your performance if you are using NFS over UDP. TCP should autodiscover the correct packet size for the network, but UDP will not. Tracepath can be used to find the base MTU over a network path, if there is any doubt. (Tracepath generally isn't installed by default, so check with your vendor for a package including it.) If you are using this on a local network and there are no routers involved, this likely isn't a problem.

> **TIP**
>
> For more information, visit `http://nfs.sourceforge.net/nfs-howto/performance.html`.

In high-volume situations, you might need to make some changes to kernel resources as they affect NFS performance. One is the input queue, which buffers requests until they can be handled. If you have a large number of daemons running, each instance will get only a small portion of the overall input queue to use for its client's pending requests. To fix this, use the following commands:

```
# echo 262144 > /proc/sys/net/core/rmem_default
# echo 262144 > /proc/sys/net/core/rmem_max
(start/restart your nfs server)
# echo 65536 > /proc/sys/net/core/rmem_default
# echo 65536 > /proc/sys/net/core/rmem_max
```

This raises the size of the input queue (bytes available for socket handling during requests) for the NFS daemons (among other things), but puts it back to the normal settings afterward. The socket queue by default is at 64KB, which, if you are running 8 instances of the NFS server daemon, limits each one to having only 8KB of space to buffer pending requests. This example raises the size of the input queue to 256KB, which, with 8 servers, raises the space for each server to 32KB. (If you have a different default, use that. Be sure to check the original value before replacing it at the end.) This is a bit of a hack, and it shouldn't be done unless you are really pushing a lot of data. If this is the case it should be done by your startup scripts rather than doing it by hand after everything has started up. Even then, it might make more sense to raise the values marginally and leave them as set. Before doing this, make sure that you really are having problems with failed connects on the box. Run a port scanner across it at high load, and see if it fails the connects. (Nmap or xnmap will do the job perfectly, by just targeting it at port 111, the sunrpc port. It might be beneficial to run a full scan, just to see if all services are getting the network resources they need.) If the scan does fail, this approach might be needed; otherwise, you're better off looking somewhere else.

Another possible source of problems is packet fragmentation overflow. Like the input queue problem, this is not really specific to NFS, and problems might be evident elsewhere on the box if this is occurring. Essentially, the network stack is attempting to track fragmented packets by keeping them in memory until they can be reassembled. Fragmentation occurs when transmitted packets are broken up and need to be reassembled at the destination point, but need to be tracked in the meantime until the entire set has been received and can be put back together. But because of the volume, it doesn't have enough space to keep all the balls in the air until enough packets come in and complete the set.

If you need to modify how much is considered allowable fragmentation thresholds, look under `/proc/sys/net/ipv4/`, in `ipfrag_high_thresh` and `ipfrag_low_thresh`. Here's how they work: If the number of fragmented packets goes above the high value, new ones are dropped until the number of incomplete packets drops below the low value. To see if this is happening, watch `/proc/net/snmp` under high load, with careful attention to the ReasmFails field.

Other than these tweaks, not much can be done with NFS other than raising the hardware bar, either the network, the drive hardware, or the machine's components, such as memory. NFS is an old protocol, and although it has been updated, it isn't as flexible as schemes such as Samba. NFS and NIS are fairly easy to deploy side by side, and that might make sense for your environment. Still, Samba will work as well as or better than NFS as a file server because it is more flexible in its options. It also fits better in a heterogeneous environment. Choose what is right for the environment, keeping in mind current needs and what might need to be integrated down the road.

Tuning NIS

If you have deployed NFS, you most likely use NIS to provide login and other centralized services. Fortunately, NIS is very easy to tune for performance. The best way to do this is to add slave servers. The method for doing this is relatively simple: NIS needs to be configured to run as a slave server, preferably on subnets that are physically removed from the central server. This process is nearly the same as the original NIS configuration on the central server. On the slaves, however, you run `ypinit -s master` to cause the node to be initialized as a server slave rather than a master. NIS authentication over slow links with timeouts can be painful, so it's recommended that you set up a slave at any remote subnet without quick access to the server.

The next operation on the slave is the addition of the updates to the root crontab. Recommended settings are as follows:

```
20 *     * * *    /usr/lib/yp/ypxfr_1perhour
40 6     * * *    /usr/lib/yp/ypxfr_1perday
55 6,18 * * *    /usr/lib/yp/ypxfr_2perday
```

Depending on the usage patterns on the link and the size of the user maps, you might want to go in by hand and reconfigure how the transfers are done and when. If it is an extremely slow link, schedule updates once per day during off-peak hours. If you are unlucky enough to have a remote network with dial-up–only access, this is probably your best bet. This way, you reduce the load on the central server, replicate your information, and make the lives of the users on the other end of the link much better.

There is another option to speed NIS operations. With the GNU C library, a daemon called nscd can cache NIS operations locally, greatly speeding lookups. In general, though, NIS with slave servers on a local net is generally pretty quick. The most that you really need to tune it is to add new slave servers, although the nscd daemon can come in handy if you have an application that requires many local lookups.

Making Kernel Changes to Improve Performance

There generally isn't much on the kernel side in terms of driver control to get better performance. Sometimes multiple driver versions are available on the net: One might be focused on getting extreme performance out of the card, whereas another might be focused on maintaining a generic driver for a whole family of cards. Sometimes drivers don't take full advantage of the card by default. To be safe, sometimes options will be turned off. Full-duplex mode can be turned off by default for some drivers, and it is a good idea to check your log files to make sure that the driver is initializing the card the way you want it to. If it isn't, usually an option can be passed to the kernel or to the module to modify the behavior of the driver.

Some options that can be done via `sysctl` in the `/proc/sys` interface to the kernel. Under `/proc/sys/net` is a slew of configuration options that you can use to customize behavior to suit your needs. As explained earlier in the section "Tuning NFS," `rmem_max` and `rmem_default` can be modified to lengthen the pending queue. A few others might help you out as well. Listed here are some configuration options that can help tune the IP layer. Speedups with other protocols are possible, but, these days, if you are doing heavy networking, chances are good that it is IP-based. Remember that the options listed here are not all-inclusive. Other options exist that are the most relevant to the work at hand.

Device Backlogs

If you are severely pressuring the network subsystem with many connections and the machine is doing other work as well, raising the value in `/proc/sys/net/core/netdev_max_backlog` might help. This will allow a larger buffer to be used in dealing with the hardware device while the kernel is working on other issues. This can help especially with usage patterns that involve large spikes of heavy usage, and prevent requests from being dropped.

Disabling ICMP

Although this is more for prevention of a denial-of-service attack, the `/proc/sys/net/ipv4` values `icmp_echo_ignore_all` and `icmp_echo_ignore_broadcasts` can be used to disable responses to ICMP requests and broadcasts. This will prevent the kernel from wasting time responding to these messages and will prevent work overloads during an attack. This also makes better use of your network because ICMP broadcasts result in massive amounts of back-talk on your network. Although the congestion is not damaging to your servers directly, it can bring your network to a halt. Turning both of these off is not recommended as a precautionary measure, though, because it might make network management more difficult. If you don't need ICMP ECHO for your management, then it might be safe to turn off.

Local Port Range

An important one for large systems is `/proc/sys/net/ipv4/ip_local_port_range`. When an incoming connection is made to your machine, such as an HTTP request, it initially is made on the default port for that service. But as the socket negotiations take place, the server effectively moves this socket's port to a higher range for the rest of its lifetime. Another example that is more visible to the end user if done through a browser is FTP. Connections are made on the standard FTP data port, but for the actual transmission, it is renegotiated on a higher port for the duration of that file's transfer. The default value for this used to be 1024–4999 but is now 32768–61000. It is rare to need more than this, and if you are stretching this limit, the box is probably also in extreme duress in general. Still, it might be helpful to try. You should have at least 128MB of ram to use the 32768–61000 range.

7

NETWORK PERFORMANCE

Path Discovery

As discussed earlier with NFS packet sizing, sockets attempt to discover the MTU for the path they will be taking and coordinate packet sizes accordingly. This should be fine in nearly all cases, but you can turn off the capability by setting a 1 in /proc/sys/net/ipv4/ip_no_pmtu_disc. If you know to whom your machine is going to be talking, and if it never involves paths that might fluctuate, this can be turned off safely. You should take steps to ensure that large packets are still in use, though, and haven't dropped back to a small default such as 512 bytes, which would severely impair performance. Also, if you are working over a network segment that has ICMP disabled to prevent flood attacks, path discovery will fail, and trying to work with it is a complete waste of time. (ICMP ECHO is used for pinging and the like, but ICMP generally has many useful and nondestructive uses on a network, such as path discovery. In many cases, ICMP is turned off only when ECHO requests should be disabled.)

Fragmentation Thresholds

Again, as described with NFS tuning, /proc/sys/net/ipv4's ipfrag_high_thresh and ipfrag_low_thresh values can be helpful in preventing lost packets during periods of high fragmentation. These values can be raised to make sure that the stack keeps attempting to reassemble packets during these times. Otherwise, it will silently drop fragmented packets when it sees the high threshold until the low threshold is reached.

Keep in mind that you shouldn't raise this too high because it will raise the kernel's memory requirements. In that case, fragmentation could work as an attack against your system by forcing large amounts of memory to be used for fragment handling while the rest of the system suffers. Knowing your underlying network architecture can help greatly. If you plan your architecture so that fragmentation should not be an issue (by making sure that all network paths are correct for your needs), this shouldn't be a problem. In reality, though, you might not have complete control over your network, or you might need to leave your network to get some data; in this case, fragmentation is a likely possibility.

ECN

If you are working with data that is sensitive to packet loss, such as video streaming, /proc/sys/net/ipv4/tcp_ecn is probably worth investigating for the sake of your system's performance. ECN is a congestion-notification system specified in RFC 2481. Although normal TCP sessions can handle packet loss, recovery of the lost data is generally done after the fact. If a router somewhere in the path experiences an overload and drops some packets, the transport will ensure that the lost packet is re-requested.

But some data, such as our example of video streams, doesn't react well to waiting for the machines at either end to figure out that some data was dropped and must be resent. In the case of a temporally compressed format such as MPEG2, each frame can depend on what was present in a previous frame. If you lose part of a frame, it might take several frames for the algorithm to fully recover the image.

Loss of content is one side effect, but performance also is slowed. By using ECN, routers can set the Congestion Experienced bit in the packet so that the machines involved know that packet loss likely happened. This can save the TCP stack on each end from just extending its window until it determines that loss did occur, and then it can take immediate action on the problem.

The issue with ECN at this stage is that some routers will block it, and some operating system stacks don't understand it yet. If this is the case with your system or the network path you are using, you probably want to disable ECN. But if you can convince everyone on your path to enable ECN, both in network hardware and in systems, it can provide a much better method of recovering from congestion.

Keepalive Times

The `Ttcp_keepalive_time` value, specified in seconds (the default is 7200), controls how long sockets are left open when `SO_KEEPALIVE` is specified on the socket. This depends greatly on your needs. However, if you have applications that specify that keepalive should be used but they really don't need it for most cases, you could end up with large numbers of old sockets being left open for two hours. Reducing this value might help lower the impact of having all these leftover sockets open.

As described earlier, Samba allows the specification of `SO_KEEPALIVE`, but two hours might be a long time to keep a socket open in the hopes that it might be used for SMB traffic. If the machine is doing other work and would benefit from having those resources elsewhere, shrinking the time and overhead of keeping that socket in a good state will save resources on the box. Finding a good balance between making sure that sockets are kept open for a while and reducing unused overhead may help you manage your system load better.

tcp_sack

When multiple packets of data are lost from a single window of data during a TCP transfer, performance can drop significantly. The sender can learn about only one lost packet per round-trip time. There are ways around this, but it generally results in retransmission of already handled data, wasting network bandwidth and processing overhead. Selective acknowledgement, as turned on in `/proc/sys/net/ipv4/tcp_sack`, allows the receiver to send immediate SACK packets back to the sender about what set of packets were lost during the window. Because this can be done immediately and in full, it saves the overhead of waiting multiple round-trip times, and the sender can retransmit all lost packets in one burst. Quicker recovery from data loss is experienced.

By default, this value is turned on in the interface. Some people have gotten better results with it off, but this might require absolute control over your local network by disabling it to give you any advantage.

Urgent Pointers

The `tcp_stdurg` value is a setting that, although disabled by default, might offer gains if your environment supports it. As specified in the TCP functional specification, control bits in the TCP header can specify urgency, along with an urgent pointer to data that the receiving end might not have gotten yet. By using the urgent pointers, the receiver will know that urgent data of some type is coming down the wire and that it should take appropriate action to make sure that the data is handled quickly.

This is disabled by default because it can cause interoperability problems with other systems. However, if you have control over the systems you are using, know that it is supported, and know that your patterns can make use of the capability, you might want to enable it.

Window Scaling

Another example of a value that should be left on is `tcp_window_scaling`. This is a capability specified in RFC 1323, which was a suite of performance enhancements to TCP. TCP packets need to be transmitted over the network and received with a sliding window algorithm because reassembly is likely to be done, and the system needs to know when some packets need to be resent. Scaling allows the transmission to use a wider window, allowing for a greater range in what data can be in transit at any point in time. The kernel defaults this value to 1, and it should be left this way unless you have a strange local implementation on your network that doesn't support it.

Large Windows

Unless you have a small amount of memory in your system, it is a good idea to make sure that large window support is enabled in your kernel build. Without it, the available window of what can be in transit is smaller, resulting in slower performance. This should be enabled on nearly all systems by default.

TCP Timestamps

By default, this option is off, although it can be enabled with a value of 1. As specified in RFC 1323, TCP timestamps are used to determine round-trip time measurements, but a slight performance hit is incurred in generating them.

As always, with kernel tuning parameters, be sure to check for any new capabilities that have worked their way into the kernel. Given the large number of uses that people have for their networking systems, anything that might need to be tuned is generally written to be tunable via sysctl. As time goes on and more standards are written, more capabilities will be added.

Bonding

Different vendors call this by different names, but the core concept remains the same. The idea is that to add raw bandwidth to your machine, you add multiple interface cards to the machine and bind them together as one single interface. This should be done in conjunction with network infrastructure layout because its usefulness is limited to certain network configurations. This can be used to give a single machine a 200Mb interface to a 100Mb network, or it can be used for failover situations in a redundant environment. Its applicability varies, though, so be sure to check that you really have a network bottleneck before looking into applying bonding over your network.

Originally, bonding was used in relation to the Beowulf project. Beowulf is a system that allows massively parallel computers to be constructed by interconnecting many Linux boxes over standard network interfaces. Because message passing in a cluster is directly related to the speed at which it can work through data, raising the number of interconnects and bandwidth has a huge impact on the cluster's usefulness. Since it was written, though, the bonding driver has undergone some significant changes. It now exists separately from the Beowulf project and ships with the kernel. (Kernel 2.2.18 at least is recommended.)

Bonding is enabled in the kernel build under Network Device Support. It can be built as a module or can be built directly into the kernel. If you are doing this in a live environment (which is possible but not recommended), you can enable support for bonding, bind devices to it, and have a large bandwidth interface without an interruption in service, if your hardware is present. If you want to use bonding as a failover safety, you need to build it as a module because you need to send explicit options to the module when loading. In reality, it is best to test your network configuration and bonding approach on a test network, and to schedule a time to add bonding to the production side. Alterations might need to be made to the network to handle the bonding, so this is the preferred method.

Some description of what happens is in order. If you know how the transport is handled, you know that the transport is dependent on your network card's hardware address. If you add a new network card, it will cause traffic to use its separate hardware address, right? You would think so. But, in reality, the hardware address of a network card is a configurable option in the hardware. By specifying the hardware address with ifconfig's ether parameter, you can easily rewrite the value that is burned into the hardware, at least for the current boot. At first guess, this might sound like a trick that would be used in attacks against the network, but it comes in handy when doing failover and load balancing between devices. By making sure that all devices in a bonding set are using the same hardware address, the kernel can selectively load-balance throughput with the set. As it hits the wire, it appears that all data transferred came from the same hardware address. The bonding set gets its hardware address from the first card that is added to the slave set.

In a load-balancing situation, the kernel uses a round-robin method to balance output between cards in the set. If you are looking to use bonding as failover, only one card will be used at a time, but the others in the set will be used if one fails.

At this point, bonding sounds like a good idea, but how do you actually do it? First, as mentioned, make sure that you are running a compatible kernel, or add support to your kernel with a patch, if it is old. You will need a userspace tool called ifenslave, which controls the bonding set. This is available at `www-miaif.lip6.fi/willy/pub/bonding/`. (Willy Tarreau and Constantine Gavrilov are the current maintainers of the bonding driver.) Your vendor might have its own way of getting the tools you need. Check with the vendor channels for possible information on this. If you need to do it by hand, don't be alarmed; it's very simple. After you download the ifenslave.c file, run the following commands to compile and install it on your system:

```
# gcc -O2 -s -o ifenslave ifenslave.c
# cp ifenslave /sbin
```

Now you need to configure your modules to prepare the system for the bonding module. It is assumed that bonding is enabled as a module, so parameters can be passed. If you read through this and determine that you don't need to send parameters to the bonding module on load, feel free to build it into the kernel statically. You will need at least the following line in `/etc/modules.conf`, assuming that you have a single bonding device:

```
alias bond0 bonding
```

If you need more bonding devices, add more lines for each bonding device present, naming them in sequence as bond1, bond2, and so on. Now that the association between the bonding device and the bonding module in the kernel is set, the bonding device itself needs to be configured. This assumes that the machine in question is using a Red Hat–derived distribution, but it can be modified to suit any vendor's method of handling devices. Under Red Hat, files for each network interface are stored under `/etc/sysconfig/network-scripts`. Each `ifcfg-*` file present corresponds to one of your network devices, whether they are Ethernet (eth*), PPP (ppp*), or something else. Add a file to specify the parameters for the new bonding interface as follows:

```
DEVICE=bond0
IPADDR=192.168.1.1
NETMASK=255.255.255.0
NETWORK=192.168.1.0
BROADCAST=192.168.1.255
```

```
ONBOOT=yes
BOOTPROTO=none
USERCTL=no
```

Modify names and parameters as needed, but your first bonding device should be named ifcfg-bond0. If you have multiple devices, create a file for each device. As with other network config-uration files, DEVICE names the device for the system control scripts, USERCTL makes sure that it can't be modified by regular users, and BOOTPROTO means that it doesn't use a boot protocol. ONBOOT should generally be specified because you will want to create the bonding set as the sys-tem comes up. IPADDR is the address of the device, to which all network devices involved will be attached. The other parameters should be set as needed based on your network.

Also present in the scripts directory should be configuration files for your network devices that will be integrated into the bonding set. We will assume ifcfg-eth0 and ifcfg-eth1, although there may be more. This would be the case if you were adding more than two devices to the bonding set or had the machine configured to use other Ethernet interfaces in addition to the two that are bonded. These file should look something like the following:

```
DEVICE=eth0
USERCTL=no
ONBOOT=yes
MASTER=bond0
SLAVE=yes
BOOTPROTO=none
```

As you can see, this is fairly straightforward. The major difference is that now the ifcfg-eth* files don't specify the IP configuration because it is defined in the bond0 device. This file is just enough to make sure that the Ethernet device is configured to use bond0 as its master and is configured to be a slave. This should be replicated for all Ethernet devices involved, modify-ing the DEVICE name and MASTER name as needed. Also, the Ethernet devices present don't have to be of the same type to be bonded; they can be any type of physical Ethernet hardware that Linux supports, although it helps if they understand MII status monitoring so that the bonding driver can cleanly handle situations when a slave link status goes bad. Refer to your hardware vendor's documentation on the card to see if this is supported.

To bring up the device, you need to either use the system-specific restart script or do it by hand with ifconfig and ifenslave, as discussed previously. For Red Hat and derived systems, running /etc/rc.d/init.d/network restart' shuts down the network subsystem and brings it back up with the bonding device configured. If you aren't running a Red Hat–based system or you don't want to shut down the whole network while this is configured, you can easily do it by hand:

```
# /sbin/ifconfig bond0 192.168.0.79 netmask 255.255.255.0 up
# /sbin/ifenslave bond0 eth0
# /sbin/ifenslave bond0 eth1
```

7

NETWORK
PERFORMANCE

```
....
# /sbin/ifconfig
bond0     Link encap:Ethernet   HWaddr 00:50:DA:C8:46:80
              inet addr:192.168.0.79  Bcast:192.168.0.255  Mask:255.255.255.0
          UP BROADCAST RUNNING MASTER MULTICAST  MTU:1500  Metric:1
          RX packets:258235565 errors:0 dropped:0 overruns:0 frame:0
          TX packets:275074186 errors:0 dropped:0 overruns:0 carrier:0
          collisions:0 txqueuelen:0

eth0      Link encap:Ethernet   HWaddr 00:50:DA:C8:46:80
          inet addr:192.168.0.79  Bcast:192.168.0.255  Mask:255.255.255.0
          UP BROADCAST RUNNING SLAVE MULTICAST  MTU:1500  Metric:1
          RX packets:129172364 errors:0 dropped:0 overruns:0 frame:0
          TX packets:137537093 errors:0 dropped:0 overruns:0 carrier:0
          collisions:0 txqueuelen:100
          Interrupt:10 Base address:0xd400

eth1      Link encap:Ethernet   HWaddr 00:50:DA:C8:46:80
          inet addr:192.168.0.79  Bcast:192.168.0.255  Mask:255.255.255.0
          UP BROADCAST RUNNING SLAVE MULTICAST  MTU:1500  Metric:1
          RX packets:129063201 errors:0 dropped:0 overruns:0 frame:0
          TX packets:137537093 errors:0 dropped:0 overruns:0 carrier:0
          collisions:0 txqueuelen:100
          Interrupt:9 Base address:0xd000
```

As before, if multiple bonding devices or more Ethernet devices should be added to the set, a few more commands might be involved. You also might need to specify other networking parameters, and you might want to set eth0's hardware address by hand with ifconfig so that the bonding device has a known Ethernet address.

If you want to use this to increase bandwidth, you probably don't need to set any module parameters. A mode option needs to be set if you are looking to use this as a failover device. In this case, you need to set the following line in /etc/modules.conf:

```
options bond0 mode=1
```

By default, the mode used is 0, which uses round-robin scheduling between the devices in the bonding set, based on the order in which they were inserted with ifenslave. With the failover configuration for high availability, you need to make sure that all cards present understand MII link status monitoring. Otherwise, the driver can't cleanly tell when the current baseline card's link has gone down and won't know when to switch interfaces to the failover device. High availability might need some reconfiguration, such as VLAN trunking, in your network hardware to be fully active. When interfacing with a switch, it should be configured so that the switch doesn't see the same MAC address coming from two separate links. This can cause issues with the switches configuration that can be difficult to track down.

Although this sounds like a nice, simple way of aggregating bandwidth on your local network, it should be approached with care. The underlying network might not be up to the task without adding switches. It is generally good to implement bonding over multiple switches, to ensure better failover in case of a switch failure, but this relies on an interswitch link (ISL), causing a bottleneck between the switches. If you have multiple bonding devices all switching over the same ISL, that becomes a bottleneck.

Take a close look at what you are looking to implement and where bonding fits best. For many situations, it is probably better to configure bonding directly between two machines. This might be the case if you have replicating file servers or database servers that need to negotiate large amounts of data between them and maybe have an extra interface to work with the rest of the network. An interhost bond is best in this case because it doesn't require extra hardware—you can simply connect the two machines to each other. Also, this reduces the load on the rest of the network because the data replication happens over the bonding link, outside the scope of the general network. This gives you better response time on the replication because it has at least double the bandwidth that it had previously, and the rest of the network will behave as if it was upgraded, too. In this case, it might be worth getting a four-port card for each machine. This will save PCI slots in the machine from being used up by all the network cards, leaving them open for other uses.

Another factor to remember is the speed of the storage mechanism that is feeding the network interface. If you have an old IDE disk, hooking a 400Mb link to it won't gain you much. Having a fast disk subsystem is a major prerequisite to going this route, unless you are using it as an interconnect for distributed computation and are more interested in message passing than serving data.

Enforced Bandwidth Limitations

Sometimes the best way to manage your bandwidth is by limiting it. Certain subsystems might need to get the data from a remote network, but that machine might be trying to pull data over a slow link at the same time another box on the network tries to pull some over, too. Eventually, everything will work out because it will just bottleneck at the link for a while. But if one machine's smooth operation is more important to general system health, you might be in trouble.

Say that you need to get analysis of the data at the other end of the link out in two hours. If the other machine is taking bandwidth at the same time, you might not even be done transferring, let alone begun the analysis, by the time the deadline is up. In this case, you probably want to configure your network to achieve a certain amount of guaranteed bandwidth over that link for each party involved. Applying guaranteed bandwidth and rate limitation is one of the first steps in laying out a solid framework for reliable networking.

The implications and work involved in deploying a true QoS (Quality of Service) and rate-limiting architecture are beyond the scope of this book. Large companies make a living by selling these capabilities as a service, so it's really not something that can be summed up easily in a few pages of text. Rather than flood the text with all the possible ways of doing this, here is an overview of the technology involved, some tools that are used in the process, and some pointers on where to look next if this is viable for your situation. Also remember that many of the concepts listed here are generally implemented in hardware and have only in recent years become available for use in standard software packages. Generally, deploying a Linux box will be much cheaper than rolling out expensive hardware, but it depends on your specific needs and whether the tools here will fit them. For some situations, a hardware device is still your best bet.

Limiting bandwidth is a common practice. As explained in the previous example, there are many instances in which limiting bandwidth for certain groups can be beneficial to the network in general. Also, if you are reselling your bandwidth in fragments, this is a clean way of making sure that everyone using a fragment of your bandwidth is only using that fraction and is not stepping on everyone else's. There are implementations on the market that are more capable than Linux for some uses; there are situations in which a customer might be allowed to burst higher rates than what the contract allows.

The Linux traffic shaper might be what you need when working with limitation rules such as these. You will need the shapecfg tool, as presented by your vendor or pulled from the net. The concept is simple: The shaper device attaches to your Ethernet (or other) interface, and you enforce bandwidth limitations on the shaper device with shapercfg. As you need to add more users—say, for another 64Kb pipe through your network—you can add another shaper device with that bandwidth limitation and attach it to your uplink, adding a local route for it. You might need the iproute2 tools to take full advantage of different routing tables.

QoS takes another angle on bandwidth management. Differentiated Services is usually grouped with this term. Generally, though, the concept is that a certain level of quality is ensured by the group managing the network. QoS with Differentiated Services has been available as a patch to the 2.2 kernel for a while and is integrated with the 2.4 kernel as of late in the 2.3 series. As with the shaper, you will need the iproute2+tc package added to your installation to make use of it. These tools enable you to tweak the QoS settings in the kernel. By default, the packet scheduler will use a *first in, first out (FIFO)* mechanism to determine what gets sent first. With QoS enabled, you can choose from a variety of algorithms to determine ordering. QoS and bandwidth limiting are related to each other in general, but are not to be seen as the same thing. QoS guarantees certain types of service in any type of resource load, whereas bandwidth limiting, as the name states, limits the amount of bandwidth that any group can have. Segmenting your bandwidth to ensure a level of QoS can be done by making sure that no one user can use the entire bandwidth, but bandwidth limiting is only a small part of the problem of guaranteeing QoS.

Another set of tools that might be of interest is iptables and ipchains. The ipchains tool can be considered obsolete as of the 2.4 kernel, but it might be useful if you want to play it safe while 2.4 gets more widespread use. However, iptables as present in 2.4 offers many benefits that could be worth the jump. Both tools deal with routing and the kernel, filtering what traffic can and cannot be passed through different routes, and determining what happens to that traffic as it passes through the box. This might not be directly applicable to tuning, but it can be helpful as a preventative measure. If you have a network segment that should not be used except by certain boxes, placing routing rules in front of that segment might help ensure that the segment remains clean for those machines to use.

New and Interesting Capabilities

Because so much of Linux is done by interested parties all over the world, there are always new additions being made to its base set of capabilities. Some of these get worked into general distributions, while others always exist outside the normal development tree and are there only for those interested in that specific set of capabilities. Here are a few of the current additions to the Linux community and how they can help in different situations.

TUX

HTTP servers have been around for a long time, at least by Internet standards. Over time, two major families have developed: those like Apache, which might not be the fastest implementations of HTTP handlers but which are the most flexible and feature-rich, and those that might not have as many features but are designed to be as fast as possible when serving data.

TUX joins the two. It is a kernel-resident HTTP server that may greatly speed the serving of Web data. Originally, in version 1.0, TUX was written to sit in the kernel and answer all HTTP requests. If the request was for static data, such as an HTML file or image data, TUX could serve the request without ever having to pass the data to a userspace Web server such as Apache. This meant much less work for the Web server, which translated into large improvements in overall performance. New records were made with Linux servers using a combination of the kernel and userspace servers. With TUX 1.0, if a request was made for dynamic content, it was handed off to the resident userspace handler.

As of TUX 2.0, even dynamic capabilities have been rolled into the mix. With either userspace or kernelspace modules, TUX can hook to different handlers to generate and cache dynamic content as needed. For requests that involve a mix of new dynamic content and pregenerated content, TUX can merge them from the cache for optimal speeds. The catch is that to use TUX's dynamic cache, existing CGI code must be modified to use the TUX API. But the capability to just push dynamic requests to the userspace server from 1.0 is valid, so this can be done on an as-needed basis for CGI requests that would benefit from the speed increase. Also in 2.0 is the integration of host-based virtual hosting support. By collecting different host roots under the main HTTP root and enabling virtual server support, a machine can serve as any number of hosts without any performance penalty.

TUX can be integrated with any distribution, although the general method of access is with a source RPM. Contact your vendor to see if there is a simpler way to integrate it into your system. After it is built into the kernel and is running, its configuration is done via the /proc interface. Generally, there is a userspace Web server running on an alternate port, to catch requests that TUX can't handle. This Web server should run on an alternate port, and that port number should be piped to TUX's /proc interface as the port to redirect requests to.

If you are running a high-performance Web server, TUX might be capable of helping you get massive performance gains. Even if nearly all of your content is dynamic, adding TUX to serve your image data can reduce the strain on the userspace server. Then it can focus on generating your content.

Zero-Copy Networking

This is a very new addition to the 2.4 series, and it caused a stir when it was integrated into the kernel. Zero-copy networking reaches deep into the networking system, but it has been found to be very stable and yields large performance benefits on fast networks. This will likely raise the bar even higher when it comes to performance test suites.

You might be wondering exactly what it is, though. Essentially, this is a way to ship data to the wire without copying it around the system. If you are using FTP to retrieve a file from a server, that server collects the data (read() calls) and ships it out of the socket (write() calls). Without zero-copy networking, the data in question gets copied several times. The absolute best case is a direct copy to the kernel side of the business, where it is broken down into individual packets to be sent to the wire. The act of doing this takes CPU time and dirties the cache. For most work, checksums also must be computed over the data being transferred, which requires another pass over the data. All this work introduces a bottleneck, keeping the machine from utilizing its hardware correctly.

With the introduction of sendfile() way back in the 2.1 development series, this got a little bit better because the userspace application didn't explicitly have to read the data into its memory space and write it back through to the kernel through the socket. It was even faster than an mmap/write combination because the kernel did all the work of the transfer. All you needed to give the kernel was the outgoing socket file descriptor and the file descriptor of the file to be sent. The kernel handled the rest, keeping all memory management on that side of the wall.

Even with the sendfile call, though, multiple copy operations still were taking place in the kernel. The kernel still had to at least copy from the page cache to the network stack. There the data was handled even further while the CPU did checksumming work over the data before it did the DMA call to push the data to the network card.

Zero-copy networking handles this in a clean manner by allowing DMA directly from the page cache. It also uses the checksumming hardware present in modern cards to save the overhead of copying the data for the checksum pass. This saves CPU overhead and also prevents cache pollution by not replicating the data. The catch is that your network hardware (and driver) needs to be capable of doing the checksumming and also performing the DMA "scatter/gather" operations to piece together the data for transfer.

On systems that rely heavily on network speed, this can yield large performance gains. Informal tests have shown that an average Pentium III machine with zero-copy networking enabled can push enough data onto the network to swamp a gigabit segment and not even utilize the CPU. As this gets more testing in the field, get ready to see some interesting benchmark results.

TUX, mentioned earlier, is a perfect example of a use for zero-copy networking; it is written with the idea that the zero-copy networking patches are also present on the system. Because it is serving data directly from the kernel side, ensuring that the kernel is efficiently getting its files from disk to the network card is of utmost importance. Having zero-copy networking in place means that the kernel is getting the best performance possible from those file send requests that it is handling. The data is going directly from the page cache to the network card via DMA, so the impact of these requests on the rest of the system is minimal.

High Availability/Load Balancing

When you are working with a high-availability network, you have two major goals: making sure that the machines are always available, and making sure that the network and general load are balanced between them. Although this can be a factor of CPU and memory performance, the Linux high-availability projects are also useful in distributing network requests. The work is done by several centralized groups, and several companies are building products on top of their work (Red Hat's Piranha, VALinux's UltraMonkey, and SGI's FailSafe products are a few names close to the project). The project and implementation details of doing high-availability work can become complex, but the general concepts are fairly easy to understand. Described here are some basic concepts and information on how they would apply to distributing your network load over a set of machines.

A couple angles on the approach exist, but two major components are involved: failover and load balancing. Although failover is not directly related to the task of tuning, it does apply to capacity planning: You need to build redundancy into a network of any significant size. Failing to do so results in a design flaw in the network, with possibly disastrous repercussions.

That said, the general approach for failover, as far as the high-availability project is concerned, focuses mainly on having quick IP address failover in case a primary machine fails. Although there are hardware solutions that can emulate failover, they are generally expensive; for most purposes, the approach described here is sufficient.

Failover of a single box to a secondary machine is done by what is known as heartbeat code. The heartbeat runs on the machines involved, so the failover machine will know when to perform IP takeover if a failure occurs. The heartbeat must take place over at least two interfaces by default, such as a serial line and TCP or UDP. This way, one connection can go down without the failover machine trying to take over the address. The primary machine might still be up, but someone in the server room might have disconnected the serial line to move it. In this case, because the Ethernet connection was still valid, the machines could talk over the network and failover did not take place. If the secondary machine determines that the primary is down through all available interfaces, it takes over for the primary box.

Although there is a lot more involved in failover than that short paragraph, our main focus here is on network load distribution, which is the other side of the project. This is handled by the Linux Virtual Server (LVS) project. The LVS allows a single front-end machine to act as a load balancer for a cluster of machines in the back. (Failover should at least be applied to the front server because losing its connection can result in the loss of access to the whole cluster.) If you are doing large volumes of data transfers, it probably doesn't make sense to expect one single machine to handle the load of the entire network. With LVS, you can place as many machines in your cluster as you want, depending on how far you want to distribute the load.

This can be done in a variety of ways, but not all of them apply to our problem of network load. The first is virtual serving via Network Address Translation (NAT). Clients make requests against a central server, which transparently forwards the request to a server in the cluster to handle the response and then ships the given response back to the client as if the NAT server had actually done the work. Although this works, it doesn't scale beyond about 20 servers in the NAT cluster, and it creates a network bottleneck at the NAT box.

The second solution offers much more flexibility. Known as IP tunneling, it requires all responding nodes in the cluster to have public IP addresses, but it may make much better use of the network than the NAT approach. In this system, clients talk to a central server (again, hopefully with failover). However, rather than have the responses all tunnel back through the NAT server, the NAT machine creates an IP tunnel to one of the nodes in the cluster. This node handles the request and then responds directly to the requesting client. This reduces the network strain on the NAT box and also allows the handling server to use another network segment to send the response. The extra network segment advantage might not help in serving Web clients over the Internet because the bandwidth isn't quite as high, but it can be useful in clusters of machines that work close to each other and have high throughput demands.

The second solution is much better, but some improvements can still be made. A third solution, called direct routing, offers even better scalability and performance. In this situation, the same central machine handles the initial request. Rather than tunneling to the handling server, though, the load balancer selects the machine that will handle the request, modifies the Ethernet address of the data frame to match the requesting server, and rebroadcasts it on the local network. At this point, the handling server responds to it, handles the request, and ships the response back to the client. The catch is that all the handling servers need to be on the same physical segment. Although this introduces everything onto one segment, the request for data should be smaller than the data itself and can be configured to leave the network through different paths. This also saves load on the initial server because it doesn't have to tunnel the data—it only needs to select a server, modify the packet, and drop it on the back-channel network. This and the tunneling approach should scale cleanly to more than 100 nodes, still without a bottleneck at the load balancer.

Getting a light overview of high availability and load balancing is probably more dangerous than not knowing anything about it at all. However, you should now have enough information to tell whether this solution is applicable on your network. This is a fairly new technology, but it is being deployed in the field in a very competitive market space. It offers scalability for nearly all needs at a fraction of the cost of similar hardware solutions.

These are only a couple examples of interesting developments in the Linux arena, as applied to networking. Currently dozens of other projects are also looking to make sure that the networking system is the absolute fastest that it can be. As these projects get tested and their ideas worked into the kernel as needed, even more gains will be seen.

Tools

How will you know if there is a bottlenecking problem with your network unless you have the tools to watch for it? Network analysis tools are the most important part of any performance analysis: Without them, the changes you are making might either help or harm operations—but you have no way of knowing. These tools may help make sure that you are using the right protocols, may assist in troubleshooting connectivity problems, and may ensure that the right content is being used within each protocol.

If your application is configured to communicate requests over TCP in a certain format but it's not acting correctly, analyzing the packets being sent might be the best way to track down exactly what is going wrong in the transfer. The next sections discuss a couple of the tools used to examine networks and explain how they might be used in your environment. Although these are very capable tools, you might need to bring in more protocol analyzers to get a good picture of all angles of your network. Depending on your hardware, bringing in a vendor to check your network configuration with its hardware might be worth your time and money.

Ethereal

Ethereal is one of the better tools when it comes to live network analysis. Ethereal itself is meant for graphical analysis of your network, while tethereal is meant for console-based analysis of traffic. Both can read capture files from a host of different sources, such as snoop, Microsoft's Network Monitor, different router debug outputs, nettl, and many others. By capturing live data to a file, you can replay what exact behavior is present on the network repeatedly, giving insight into your application's usage of the network. Ethereal categorizes the traffic into different types and presents collections of data to you as trees of information. Stream following is a capability, meaning that you can pick a session and view all the actions that took place over it. When you're debugging server problems with specific protocols, this can be very helpful.

If you are running a proprietary protocol, it might take more work to piece together what is going on. Using another tool, such as tcpdump configured to capture raw packets, could work better. If you are using any open protocol, though, Ethereal probably has support for it. Direct support is enabled for everything from Telnet to NetBIOS, to many of the protocols used for the various instant-messaging systems prevalent today. Ethereal also supports nearly any type of interface type to which you would need to talk.

Figure 7.1 shows Ethereal from the project's page at www.ethereal.com. It illustrates a basic capture session with the contents of a TCP stream from an HTTP request.

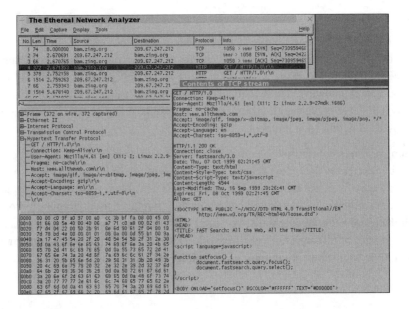

FIGURE 7.1

Ethereal in action.

tcpdump

Although it is one of the more venerable network analysis tools, tcpdump is still very useful in a networked environment. Its purpose is similar to that of Ethereal, although it is more oriented toward live analysis of your network. In addition, tcpdump is very easy to use to get raw dumps of what it sees on the network. tcpdump has a very expressive means of defining what types of traffic you want to see on the command line, and it is very easy to script with. If you want to capture traffic at different times of the day, using different tcpdump calls from cron that fire every hour and quit after a certain packet count might be a good way to automatically get usage patterns over time. Here is the beginning of a sample session that starts capturing everything that it sees on the network, without name resolution (the -n):

```
# tcpdump -n
tcpdump: listening on eth0
19:08:07.467729 192.168.50.4.6000 > 192.168.50.2.2959:
➥ P 811641207:811641239(32) ack 1314660296 win 43800 (DF)
19:08:07.468071 192.168.50.2.2959 > 192.168.50.4.6000: . ack 32 win 62780
➥ (DF)
19:08:07.832771 192.168.50.4.6000 > 192.168.50.2.2959: P 32:64(32) ack 1
➥ win 43800 (DF)
19:08:07.833052 192.168.50.2.2959 > 192.168.50.4.6000: . ack 64 win 62780
➥(DF)
19:08:12.458322 arp who-has 192.168.50.4 tell 192.168.50.2
19:08:12.458348 arp reply 192.168.50.4 is-at 0:50:22:40:3:78
19:08:12.539192 192.168.50.4.6000 > 192.168.50.2.2959: P 64:96(32) ack 1
➥ win 43800 (DF)
19:08:12.539458 192.168.50.2.2959 > 192.168.50.4.6000: . ack 96 win 62780
➥ (DF)
19:08:13.507953 192.168.50.4.6000 > 192.168.50.2.2959: P 96:128(32) ack 1
➥ win 43800 (DF)
19:08:13.508227 192.168.50.2.2959 > 192.168.50.4.6000: . ack 128 win 62780
➥ (DF)
```

As you can see, the data that it gets by default is very detailed. Some switches can be enabled along with simple alterations to the type of information that comes through, such as replacing port 80 data with www. Using these switches and standard Unix pipe filtering, you can find in seconds a detailed view of exactly what you are looking for.

Netwatch

This is an invaluable utility for viewing what is going on at a higher level within your network. Although tcpdump and Ethereal provide good views of your network, the data provided is generally more in-depth than what you are interested in finding. A large portion of your network analysis probably consists more of trying to keep track of who is talking to whom and what the real network load is, rather than what exact byte stream is coming back from your Web server. Netwatch does exactly what you need in this situation: It presents a clear view of what bandwidth is being used by whom. Here's a sample of it in action, with the default view:

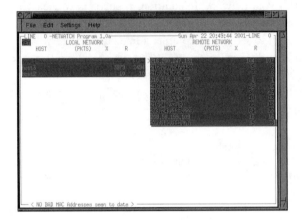

FIGURE 7.2
Netwatch looking at some recent network traffic.

SNMP

SNMP is a simple protocol that allows applications to pull trees of configuration data from remote machines in a standard manner. Embedded in these trees is usage data about various subsystems present on the machine. From this, it becomes very easy to keep track of various utilization rates and to determine exactly what has happened to your machine over time.

Some applications, such as Oracle, have their own extensions to SNMP so that remote tools such as OpenView can look at specific variables concerning the Oracle instance running on that remote machine. With either off-the-shelf software or custom scripts to act on bad conditions, the SNMP suite can get your network management under control quickly. Most distributions ship with an SNMP daemon to run on the machine, along with several tools to poke at the tree to retrieve data. OpenView, already mentioned, performs high-level management of the data, although OpenNMS might provide a viable option to this expensive software in the near future.

Testing Tools

You can use a variety of tools to test your network's performance. Most of them are oriented toward testing a particular application, but if you use them while making sure that the box running the application isn't stressed, you can end up with a good test of your network. Many are commercial applications and can be very expensive. However, there are many companies considering adopting rental licensing so that you can run tests for a week or so with their software. This way, you can use it but don't have to pay a lot to keep it for life, when you only need it temporarily.

If you are looking at testing only minor interfaces, a simple script might be all you need. To test a component of a CGI script, writing a script that performs a typical number of connections, distributed in a manner similar to the normal client base, might offer enough of a real-world strain. As your script is running, watch the status of the server and look for any indications that it is overloaded. If the script can time responses, you should be able to get some usage statistics together without much work.

A few options out there do much of the work for you, such as Apache's JMeter. JMeter can test HTTP, FTP, and database requests. It also offers a threaded model and visualization plug-ins. In addition, it is written in Java, so you can run it anywhere. This is just one example of the suites. Keep in mind that if you are working with custom protocols, you need to either contact the vendor involved or write custom code to test the performance under high loads.

As an example, here's a simple Java program that will run 30 threads against your server and do some work on them as specified by an object that isn't listed. This isn't intended to be directly usable—for one thing, hard-coding your number of connections is generally considered to be bad taste. Instead, it's is a way of showing how simple it is to write some custom code to test your application:

```java
import java.net.*;

public class Test
{
    public static void main(String args[]) {
        Test test = new Test();
        test.runTest();
    }

    public void runTest() {
        Socket s;
        for (int i = 0; i < 30; i++) {
            try {
                s = new Socket("testserver",80);
                Thread t = new Thread(new Handler(s));
                t.start();
            } catch (Exception e) { }
        }
    }
}
```

```
class Handler implements Runnable
{
    Socket s;
    public Handler(Socket s) {
        this.s = s;
    }
    public void run() {
        //do something here that tests the server
    }
}
```

Again, although this isn't usable directly, you could easily build a multithreaded test suite with this code. The important part is testing exactly what you need to. If you're trying to tweak your NFS implementation, write a script that runs on a bunch of machines and forks itself so that it can simulate 400 file copies at the same time, or maybe simulate something that attempts 200 encrypted logins to the same machine. Do whatever is appropriate to your network and tuning task.

Conclusion

It might be tempting to look at what has been done in a benchmark test and instantly apply it to your network, but there are several reasons to hold back. One is that benchmark results are rarely directly applicable in practice because the load type presented by the benchmark suite is hardly ever in line with what goes on in the real world. Second, making those changes implies that several options are changing at once, which can easily introduce unknowns into the system and make the entire process of tracing the original bottleneck impossible. Make sure that you choose options that make sense for your environment and your specific type of workload.

Also make sure that your usage policies make sense. If you have two production systems that share a common segment with your company's default path for Internet traffic, employee usage patterns can affect cross-communication between the production systems. Physical separation should probably be put in place, preferably with a private (or controllably shared) network between the two systems. Deferring large network loads until off-hours will also ensure the network's performance is up to par when it should be. Tweaks such as these that consider human factors and general policy levels can have more impact on your system's performance than any minor kernel tweak. Always assume that the problem exists at the highest levels before digging deep into the kernel networking code to solve a bandwidth issue.

Tuning and Performance Mechanics

IN THIS PART

8 Job Control   155

9 The Linux Kernel   163

10 Disk Configurations for Performance   195

11 Linux and Memory Management   211

12 Disabling Unrequired Services and Ports   223

Job Control

Linux (like Unix) has a small set of traditional job control facilities at the disposal of system administrators and, for the most part, users as well. These are as follows:

- "Plain" background mode
- The at facilities
- cron
- nice and renice

Job control gives both the user and the sysadmin the capability to manage workload by altering the way a job is performed, changing the priority of a job, or killing a job. These capabilities were one of the first things that set Unix apart. The first Unix systems were capable of multitasking in ways that most systems could not. Linux continues to carry on this capability quite well.

Background Mode

Putting a job in the background is not necessarily a separate facility—actually, it is more of a shell function (depending on the shell, of course). To put a job in the background, simply enter the task and follow it with whatever character the shell uses for specifying background jobs (most often &). For example, consider this rather large deletion run by root (so that you know there is no permissions problem):

```
# rm -rf /big_dir &
```

Monitoring jobs is relatively easy as well with most shells. Different shells report back differently—in some cases, they hardly tell the user anything.

For example, vmstat is started in bash on a Linux system. Here's what it looks like when you type the jobs command:

```
[jfink@kerry jfink]$ vmstat 5 5 >vmstat.out &
[1] 1273
```

The immediate output shown when a job is put into the background is the job number (starting at 1) and the PID of the job.

```
 [jfink@kerry jfink]$ jobs
[1]+  Running                 vmstat 5 5
```

The jobs command is more of a facility because it is built into the shell. Different shells have different ways of handling job control. The most common shell on Linux is bash, so we will look at some of the ways bash handles job control. As mentioned previously, simply typing jobs displays all currently running jobs. A job that is not in the background can be manipulated via the job control facility using certain keyboard strokes. On most Linux systems, if the keyboards have not been remapped, the Ctrl+Z combination will suspend a job in the foreground, and Ctrl+Y will stop a job. Additionally, bash can tell a job in the foreground to move into the background with the command `fg %<jobnumber>`. For example, to bring the `vmstat` job to the foreground, you would type this:

```
$ fg %1
```

Similarly, you would type this to send a job to the background:

```
$bg %1
```

> **NOTE**
>
> On most Linux distributions, bash, tcsh, and pdksh all display the same information.

Using background mode doesn't help a whole lot in performance monitoring (unless, for example, you are sending the output of a tool into a file), but it fits within the framework of job control and hence deserves mentioning.

The at Facilities

On Linux, the at facilities encompass a range of tools used to schedule jobs on the fly (unlike `cron` jobs, which recur periodically), list jobs in the queue, and delete jobs.

Using at

The `at` utility executes a command once at a specified time. It will accept either direct input or a file to be executed using `/bin/sh`. The syntax is as follows:

```
at  [-q queue] [-f file]TIME
```

The following is an example using the file mycommands:

```
$ at - -f mycommands 2200
```

The options used specify that the file mycommands (specified via the `-f` option) run at 2200 (or 10PM).

To see a listing of jobs running, the `atq` command is used:

```
[jfink@tesla ~]$ atq
10      2001-05-22 22:00 a
```

This lists the job number as 10, gives the date and time that the job will be executed, and shows the queue. The higher the character is, the higher the queue is. Queues from A to Z are treated as batch jobs.

To remove a job from the queue, use the `atrm` command:

```
[jfink@tesla ~]$ atrm 10
```

This removes job 10 from the queue.

Using `batch`

In the old days (you know, the 1970s and part of the 1980s), many systems ran almost all user-land programs in `batch` mode. This was because processor time was expensive (in terms of both the processor and money). The difference between `at` and `batch` is that a batched job will execute only when the processor is available (which, by default, is when the system average is below 0.8).

The syntax of `batch` is similar to the syntax of `at`:

```
batch  [-q queue] [-f file] [TIME]
```

The following is an example similar to `at`:

```
$ batch -f mycommands 2200
```

In addition to just scheduling an `at` or a `batch` job, the queue into which a job goes can be modified with the -q option.

Batch processing (and the prudent use of at) can help reduce the load of the system because the program will run only when the CPU is below the watermark. This is helpful, for example, if you want to run a compile job of some new software you are trying out, but you want to run the job at off-hours for minimal impact on the system.

Using `cron`

The `cron` facility is related to performance tuning in several ways. First, it allows for the periodic execution of commands, scripts, or programs, which lends itself to periodic performance data collection. Second, it allows for the periodic scheduling of tasks when the system is known not to be in use. In addition to scheduling periodic tasks appropriately, `cron` is flexible enough that jobs can be modified so that they do not interfere with the system, if that is a requirement.

Access to `cron` can be restricted via /etc/cron.allow or /etc/cron.deny; simply enter the username. The default on most Linux systems is to not have either of these files, thus allowing global access. If a username is listed in both, cron.allow takes priority.

To use `cron`, you can write and submit a crontab file to `cron`, like this:

```
$ crontab mycron
```

Or, you can simply edit the `crontab` implicitly, like this:

```
$ crontab -e
```

In either case, the format is exactly the same.

To view all current cronjobs, simply type this:

```
$ crontab -l
```

To delete all current jobs, type this:

```
$ crontab -r
```

> **NOTE**
>
> There is no warning for `crontab -r` on systems with a lot of users who use cron, so a wrapper should be created to prompt them first.

The cron Format

8

The following is a sample list of cron entries:

```
03 02 * * * /usr/local/bin/lbackup 2>&1
00 03 1 * * /usr/local/bin/monthly 2>&1
...
```

The fields, from the left, are as follows:

```
* minutes from 0 to 59
* hour from 0 to 23
* day of the month from 1 to 31
* month from 1 to 12
* day of the week from 0 to 7 where 0 and 7 are both sunday.
* command or script etc.
```

The format is pretty simple and easy to understand. As an example, to run `get_mem` at 3:00 every morning, the entry would look like this:

```
00 3 * * * /usr/local/get_mem 2>&1
```

The * indicates a wildcard. In addition to using single numerical values, ranges can be specified in fields, as in this example:

```
00 03 1-2 * *
```

This indicates that a job runs at 3 A.M. on Monday and Tuesday. A comma-delimited time list also can be used:

```
0,15,30,45 * * * *
```

This indicates that the job will run at the beginning of the hour and every 15 minutes. A simpler version of this can be specified with an interval in the form of `*/N`:

```
*/15 * * * *
```

This also states that the job will run every 15 minutes.

Command-line options are fully supported. Actually, regular syntax is supported as well within cron:

```
*/15 * * * * cd /var; ls -1R ftproot > ftproot/ls-1R; gzip ftproot/ls-1R
```

In this example, the FTP server provides a full listing of its contents every 15 minutes.

nice and renice

The nice value of a process indicates how "nice" a process is to other processes. The nicer (or higher) the nice priority is, the slower the process will be to use system resources and the nicer it will be to other processes. Likewise, a lower nice priority of a process means that the process will be "less nice" and will use more system resources. This can be somewhat difficult to understand, but, in a nutshell, a lower nice value translates into a higher priority (not nice priority—just priority) for the process, from the kernel's perspective. Most people like to simply think of it in reverse order.

The nice and renice commands are used to modify the nice priority of a program. The nice command is used to modify a program at the time of invocation before it has an associated process. The renice command is used to modify a program after it already is running and is attached to a process.

The default nice priority actually does vary from distribution, but the most common one is 0. Additionally, the standard range is 20 to –20.

The nice Command

The nice command syntax is as follows:

```
nice  [OPTION]… [COMMAND [ARG]…]
```

For example, to set a compile job to run at a nice priority of 5, the command string is this:

```
$ nice -n 5 cc mybigprog.c -o mybigprog
```

This assigns a nice priority of 5 (7 less than the standard 12) for the compiler.

The `renice` Command

Sometimes a process's `nice` priority must be changed. Most often this comes in the form of jobs that simply must get done faster or that should be slowed down after they have started because they are using a lot of the system's resources. When such a situation arises, the `renice` command can be employed to alter a running process's `nice` priority.

In the simplest form, the process ID's `nice` priority is changed like this:

```
$ renice 10 1029
1029; old priority 0, new priority 10
```

Here, 10 is the new priority and the PID is 1029.

Only the owner of a process can assign a higher `nice` priority, and only root can assign a lower priority with `renice`.

How `nice` Comes into Play

Renicing the right command can sometimes help pull a system out of a bad situation without having to kill it altogether. As an example, a Linux system once had an `rm -rf` job that was interfering with production. However, it happened to be a job that was making room so that production could continue. This case is a classic catch 22; the wrong decision could have cost a great deal of money in production time. The ultimate decision was to raise the `rm -rf`'s attached PID and lower a few of the production processes' attached PIDs, to even out the load.

Summary

Linux provides the user, programmer, administrator, and engineer with many tools to aid in improving performance and make prudent use of every session. Helpful tools include `cron`, the at facility, and `nice`. Use them wisely, and spread the good word.

The Linux Kernel

The Linux kernel is the core of the Linux system. Technically, Linux *is* the kernel, and the rest of the system that rides on top of the kernel is simply a collection of utilities and applications that have nothing to do with the kernel itself. Some people argue that a Linux system should be named GNU/Linux because, as a whole, the kernel is only a piece of the entire system—overall, it is actually a small part of the code base of a fully outfitted system. This easily can open into an almost religious debate among those in the open source and free software movements, but for the purposes of this chapter, consider Linux to be the kernel, not a specific instance of a certain vendor's collection of utilities.

A little bit of background is needed for those new to the idea of modifying a core part of the operating system. Many people who come to Linux from other operating systems such as Windows 2000 find the concept of replacing a component such as the kernel jarring. They end up thinking that to upgrade the core, you need to upgrade the whole system. The kernel provides an interface to hardware and manages processes running on the machine. It can perform other operations, but this is the core of the kernel's responsibilities.

The graphical interface is handled through X Windows, or a frame-buffer system, but, for the most part, the kernel could care less about graphical interaction. Likewise, support for nearly all server-oriented services is provided by normal applications, and the kernel handles only the operations of getting data from hardware to the userspace software. `tar` couldn't care less about the kernel, and the kernel couldn't care less about `tar`. Because its role is so clearly defined and involves only providing an interface to hardware, replacing your kernel generally has little impact on user-level applications. Even jumping from the 2.2 series to the 2.4 kernel requires very little to be modified throughout the system.

This does not mean that you can run around swapping kernels left and right on production machines, especially between large revisions. Depending on what the machine is doing, some modifications might need to occur on the user side of the kernel wall. For example, as mentioned before, support for large files is now included, but to fully utilize this capability, you need to have both a 2.4 kernel and a version of the C libraries that knows how to take advantage of the 64-bit file handling calls. Refer to your vendor's documentation for instructions on how to put this into effect, if this information isn't there already. Another example is that, during the jump from 2.0 to 2.2, the kernel interface for PPP interaction changed. This required an update to the PPP daemon to handle the new semantics.

Generally, these changes are fairly simple and not very far-reaching, but you should check for known issues when making large kernel revision jumps. Before a development series becomes the new default stable series, a list of nonkernel changes must occur before making the jump. It is usually a good idea to make a note of this list and see if any of the specified changes have an impact on your system.

Why Alter the Kernel?

Before you go in and start replacing your kernel, make sure you know the reasons for doing so, and determine whether it makes sense in your situation. Here are a few possible reasons:

- New capabilities or scalability is present in a new kernel.

- A security flaw was found in the version that you have and is fixed in a newer revision. (Yes, security holes in the kernel do occur, but they are rare.)

- Support for a new driver has been integrated into the kernel. Sometimes this can be added to your existing kernel with a patch, as described later.

- External software requires a new kernel. This is rare, but some software does need this. For example, the VPN software FreeS/WAN integrates IPSec support into your kernel via a patch and requires you to update your kernel so that the patch can apply correctly.

- By removing unneeded components from the kernel, you can reduce the memory footprint and ensure that you're not running anything you don't absolutely need. This will increase your speed.

- Your vendor's default kernel might not be configured for what you need the machine to do. You might need to configure a small kernel with support for a strange device that isn't supported by default, and the vendor's version might not be configured to handle it. Generally, most vendors ship kernels with support for many types of devices and a large number of different patches. This might not be what you need, but because you have the source, you can do anything you want to it.

Modular and Monolithic Kernels

Linux provides an easy mechanism for loading and unloading different parts of the kernel. The core architecture of the kernel itself is monolithic, meaning that, in general, a large portion of the kernel is irreplaceable. The presence of the module loader, however, allows things such as drivers, protocols, and other components to be swapped in and out with relative ease.

If you have a driver for a piece of hardware that might not always be present, you can let the system run without the driver most of the time and load the driver only when needed. This saves the trouble of dealing with a system that starts reporting all kinds of errors when a driver fails because the hardware isn't present. A real example would be support for a Zip drive. With a modular driver, you can load the driver into the kernel when you need to use the drive, and then you can remove it when you are done. This way, you aren't using kernel memory for a device that isn't always present. Here's an example of a system with a couple modules loaded:

```
#lsmod
Module              Size   Used by
vfat                8752   0
fat                 29600  0 [vfat]
emu10k1             39968  0
```

9

THE LINUX
KERNEL

This machine shows modular support for the `vfat` filesystem (and `fat`, which `vfat` uses) and a module for the SoundBlaster Live! Value card, represented by the emu10k1 module. The `lsmod` command shows all loaded modules and their dependencies. Here is the same machine after loading the modules needed to support a second audio card that is onboard:

```
#modprobe via82cxxx_audio
#lsmod
Module                 Size  Used by
via82cxxx_audio       17008   0  (unused)
ac97_codec             8592   0  [via82cxxx_audio]
vfat                   8752   0
fat                   29600   0  [vfat]
emu10k1               39968   0
```

As you can see, now there are two more lines—one for the ac97 codec support and one for the via chipset driver that actually drives the onboard sound. Note that, again, the dependency that via82cxxx_audio has on the ac97 codec is shown by the `ac97_codec` line. Now let's say that you want to use only the one audio feed present on you emu10k1/Sound Blaster Live! Value card. All you need to do is remove the module drivers for the via chipset, as in this example:

```
#rmmod -r via82cxx_audio
#lsmod
Module                 Size  Used by
vfat                   8752   0
fat                   29600   0  [vfat]
emu10k1               39968   0
```

Using the `-r` switch on rmmod will remove any modules on which the requested module depends, if it can. If any particular module is still in use, rmmod will fail on that removal. This way, if two applications are triggering usage of the same module in the kernel, the commonly used module won't be removed. If two modules were using the `ac97_codec` module and you remove the `via82cxxx_audio` module with `-r`, removal of the `ac97_codec` module would have failed because it is still in use. If all applications that are using the device behind that driver are finished, the module should unload cleanly. If it doesn't unload cleanly, it's probably a sign of broken driver code or something wrong with the device itself.

A couple other points about modules must be specified here. In addition to the presented examples, the commands `depmod` and `insmod` are generally useful. The `depmod` command handles dependency checking similar to what `modprobe` does, and `insmod` performs individual module loading. This can be handy if you are installing a hierarchy of problematic module dependencies because you can watch kernel messages after each module is loaded. For safety's sake, it is generally a good idea to have a root login running `tail -f /var/log/messages` during all module interactions, just to be sure that everything is going as planned. There also are switches to the module commands to log to syslog, which makes it easier to track down what happened down the road if something goes awry.

You can configure a whole slew of configuration directives to automate the loading and unloading of drivers and their dependency trees. Some drivers, especially if you are loading multiple instances of hardware, might require you to specify options during the module load. (Performance can be greatly affected by what parameters are handed to the driver, so check your vendor's documentation for what options are available.) Here's an example of loading the NE2000 network driver with a parameter to specify IRQ 5:

```
#modprobe ne irq=5
```

You probably don't want to specify these parameters every time you use the driver, though. By specifying driver parameters and aliases in /etc/modules.conf, you can automate this process and even have the driver load on access to the hardware. In addition, you can specify actions to take before and after the module load. By aliasing devices to driver names, you can greatly simplify interaction with the driver. Here is a sample /etc/modules.conf file that should reflect basic capabilities:

```
alias net-pf-4 ipx
pre-install pcmcia_core /etc/rc.d/init.d/pcmcia start
alias usb-interface usb-uhci
alias parport_lowlevel parport_pc
pre-install plip modprobe parport_pc ; echo 7 > /proc/parport/0/irq
alias eth0 8139too
```

As you can see, this makes use of several options. If you have a pcmcia setup, such as a laptop might have, you'll be making use of the pcmcia core. The configuration makes sure to run the pcmcia script in /etc/rc.d/init.d before doing any module configuration. Likewise, for parallel port drivers, the plip command is run, followed by a kernel setting being pushed to the /proc interface. Aliasing driver names to devices also is handy. In this case, eth0, the first Ethernet device, is aliased to be driven by the 8139too driver. You might also get a second network card that relies on a different driver. Adding eth1 and the name of the module for the second card instructs the system to automatically use the other driver for eth1. If you were using the ne driver here, as demonstrated earlier with modprobe, and you wanted to specify that IRQ 5 should be used, you would insert a line such as options ne irq=5.

What happens if you get source code for your hardware, but you don't know how to integrate it with the kernel? If the vendor supplies a raw module file, you might need to have a specific instance of a specific vendor's kernel installed. If you've rolled your own, this might not work, and you'll need to contact the vendor. This tends to happen with vendors who say that they support specific instances of individual distributions. In reality, the code can be modified to work with any distribution and any kernel, but it might not work perfectly out of the box. More vendors are providing source, though, so you might end up with a set of files and a Makefile.

Follow the vendor's instructions for building the source. In most cases, you will end up with an object file (a file ending in `.o`) in the directory of the source. Depending on the driver, there might be several object files. Check their instructions, but, in most cases, you can run `insmod` or `modprobe` on the local module file. This should load the driver into the kernel without really installing it anywhere on the system. `modprobe` and the like know to check your current local directory and the default location for module files, which is under `/lib/modules/kernel-name`. If you are running kernel 2.4.3, the root path to the modules is `/lib/modules/2.4.3`. From there, these are separated into subdirectories based on their type. For testing purposes, though, it is beneficial to maintain separate instances of the driver. If you are testing hardware capabilities with each, loading one, testing, unloading, loading a second, and testing can be helpful in tracing the right fit for your needs or determining which one has a bug in the code.

In some rare cases, you could end up with the source for the driver only, with no utilities to build the module. This generally doesn't happen, but here is an example of how to handle simple drivers. This won't handle everything, but it will give you some idea of what is involved in creating a binary module from source:

```
#ls
driver.c
#gcc -DMODULE -D__KERNEL__ -O2 -c vendor.c
#insmod vendor.o
```

This will compile a simple driver, build a local object file, and load it into the kernel. Check your `/var/log/messages` file to see if the driver dumped any useful information about its status. To install this driver, simply do the following:

```
#install -m 644 vendor.o /lib/modules/`uname -r`/appropriatesubdirectory
```

Replace `appropriatesubdirectory` with the correct location, depending on the driver—for example, use `net` for a network driver. Also make sure that you use backticks for the `uname -r` call. This replaces the subdirectory in the path with the name of the currently running kernel, making sure that the object file is installed with the right kernel version. You might need to repeat this install command for other kernel versions with which you are working. Keep in mind that this situation doesn't often occur, and this solution won't apply all the time—this is only an illustration.

In the end, you could have just as easily compiled support for the hardware in question directly into the kernel. It all depends on your needs and whether you can afford an outage long enough to install a new kernel. With multiple instances of hardware, such as multiple network cards, it is usually easier to run drivers in a modular fashion. If the machine will be fairly static, though, it could be simpler to build support directly into the kernel for the device. In today's frantic server environments, though, it is helpful to be able to swap drivers in and out dynamically, and modules might be needed in order to pass specific performance-related parameters to the kernel.

Tuning via the /proc Interface

As explained earlier, the /proc filesystem is an in-memory filesystem that provides hooks to the kernel. By echoing values to certain files in the filesystem, an administrator can modify the behavior of the kernel without interrupting general usage. With a root login, simply echoing specific data to a file under /proc/sys will modify kernel behavior. It should be noted, though, that this is not to be handled lightly. For nearly all applications, the kernel is well balanced to handle expected loads. Only if you know that there are specific updates to be made should you start tweaking the kernel—and even then, make sure that you know what is being changed on the other side of the kernel wall.

More information, including the source for all of these controls, can be found under /usr/src/linux/Documentation. Presented here is an overview of what is contained under /proc, along with a few examples of how to interact with it. If you really want specific details on how these values are manipulated within the kernel, the source code is the best place to get solid details. However, this generally requires more of a time commitment than the average administrator wants to invest.

Note that to be able to use the sysctl/proc interface, you must have support for it in your kernel. This always should be the case because vendors ship kernels with the interface enabled, and the kernel configuration (when rolled by hand) defaults to on for /proc and sysctl. It is important to make this distinction, though: /proc is a view of the kernel, but sysctl provides the means to actually push new behavior data into the kernel. The only time that sysctl is generally turned off is in very small systems, such as embedded architectures or boot disks that need to conserve every bit of available memory. So far, we have generally discussed /proc as an interface to the kernel, and although this is true, it is important to understand that sysctl is the component within /proc (/proc/sys) that allows the administrator to actually modify the behavior of the system, rather than just read it, as the rest of the /proc interface provides.

Top-Level Information

At the top of the /proc interface, many files provide easy access to the kernel's view. Most can be viewed easily with just cat, as shown here:

```
#cat /proc/version
Linux version 2.4.2-ac24 (root@host) (gcc version 2.95.3 19991030
➥ (prerelease)) #10 Fri Apr 6 13:54:00 EDT 2001
```

As you can see, this retrieves the kernel version, information on what compiler was used to build it, and some other useful data. Retrieving data from the kernel this way is so simple that some system administration utilities use data directly from /proc to get their usage statistics.

Rather than covering every single entry in /proc, here are the most important entries:

- **cpuinfo**—This gives information on every CPU present in the system. It shows what precise instruction sets the CPU supports, and it also reports any flaws that the kernel knows about.

- **devices**—Depending on your configuration, you might have a normal /dev filesystem or devfs, which allows dynamic alterations of the device filesystem. devices lists the types of devices that it knows about. It also lists block device types that it understands, such as IDE or loop devices.

- **filesystems**—From this, you can see what filesystems are currently supported by the kernel. This can fluctuate over time depending on what filesystem driver modules are loaded into the kernel. Possible types are smbfs, ext2, reiserfs, and vfat, among others.

- **interrupts**—This is a simple dump of what interrupts are being used by what devices.

- **iomem and ioports**—These two show the current mappings in place for various hardware devices. Having to use these in practice for troubleshooting is rare.

- **kcore**—This gives a view of your memory. Unless you know what you are doing, this won't give you much useful information. However, it can be useful in debugging a live kernel. By configuring your kernel to use /proc/kcore in Executable and Linking Format (ELF) format and compiling with the -g option, you can use gdb to debug a live kernel through this interface.

- **kmsg**—Use this to trap kernel oops data. Oops data will be discussed in further detail later in the chapter, under the "Tracking Kernel Oopses" section.

- **ksyms**—Kernel symbol locations are presented here. This will be described in more detail later on in the section on troubleshooting kernel panics, in "Tracking Kernel Oopses."

- **loadavg**—This is the system load average data in 1-, 5-, and 15-minute intervals, as described in Chapter 2, "Aspects of Performance Tuning."

- **meminfo**—From this, you can get granular data on memory used, similar to using a command like free or vmstat, but without having the utilities prepare all the data for you.

- **modules**—This is a list of the currently loaded kernel modules, similar to running lsmod. In fact, the data presented here should be identical, without the column headers that lsmod provides.

- **mounts**—Similar to running mount or df, this gives information on all filesystems currently mounted, along with their type and other relevant options. The output is similar to what should be contained in your /etc/fstab file.

- **mtrr**—The mtrr is short for Memory Type Range Register, which allows write combining over the PCI or AGP bus. With this enabled, writes can be combined before bursting over the bus, which can greatly speed operations for applications such as X that make heavy use of the bus. This gives the information on the base addresses and memory configurations for your system.

- **partitions**—This is a simple list of the physical drive partitions present on your system.

- **pci**—Similar to the interrupts entry, this gives information on the PCI bus: what devices are present by name, what interrupts they are using, revision codes, and other data, depending on the type of device. lspci also can retrieve this data for you in a more succinct format, and lspci -v gives nearly the same data, although arranged in a simpler format.

- **slabinfo**—The slab information is a reflection on current memory allocation across the system. For the most part, this won't be useful to you unless you see instances of memory allocations going awry and the kernel dropping allocation messages to the ring buffer. (dmesg dumps the contents of the kernel ring buffer, and messages that go there also should be visible in the system log files.)

- **swaps**—This shows the current swap files and partitions in use, their priorities, and current usage.

- **uptime**—This is raw uptime data. You are better off running the command uptime to get the data in human-readable form.

That covers most of the relevant entries, but you might be thinking that this is a lot of possible places to look for data relevant to your issue. Not so. For the most part, you should have an inkling of what is going on, and you should be able to narrow your search for data to a couple files on average. If your swap usage isn't right, checking swaps should be the obvious choice. Also, a nice utility called procinfo pulls most of the commonly requested data from the /proc interface for you and presents it in a consolidated form. Rather than poking around, try it first—in most situations, it will have the data you need.

Per-Process Data

All the numeric directories at the top level of /proc correspond to running processes. This won't give you much of an opportunity to tune the machine, but it does give insight into what each process is doing and provides enough interesting data to allow troubleshooting in some cases. Some of these are normal user-level processes; others might be the init process or kernel daemons.

Let's assume that you have process number 22927 running vi. You should go into /proc/22927 and look at what the kernel is tracking about the process. In there, you'll see items such as cmdline, which is the command that started the process. cwd provides a quick symbolic link to the current working directory of the process, and `environ` gives a dump of the environment that the process is using. This can be extremely helpful in making sure that your process is running with the right settings. If your Apache configuration is misbehaving, check the environment as specified by the http child processes—it might be a simple matter of having the wrong environment configured. Other useful bits are a symbolic link to the running executable, status about the process's usage in memory, and a directory containing its file descriptors.

Data-Presentation Areas

Several directories provide information about the system, but they won't help you much in tuning, except maybe to point you in the direction of where some of the load is coming from. The `bus`, `fs`, and SysV IPC directories all fall into this category: They give you information about various subsystems, but they are not geared toward tuning. The `bus` directory, for example, gives you information about each type of `bus` your system has, devices present, and so on. The `fs` directory might give you NFS export data if you have that enabled, and SysV IPC can give you stats on current SysV usage on your system. The kernel's implementation of SysV does have some tunable parameters, which are described in the next section on kernel parameters. These values are used mostly with applications like Oracle. Also, the net hierarchy can get you some interesting data about the network subsystem.

Modifiable Parameters

Most of the interesting parameters relate to live tuning under the `/proc/sys` directory because this is where the `sysctl` interface of the kernel is active. Different areas that can be tuned include file limits, general system attributes, network parameters, and `vm` balancing data. If you don't see the values presented here, chances are good that your kernel doesn't have `sysctl` control turned on in the build. Refer to the section on "Recompiling the Kernel" for more information on turning on this capability.

Filesystem Limits

Under `/proc/sys/fs`, several parameters affect limits that the kernel places on file operations. Here is an overview of what some of the relevant ones do. More information on a per-field basis can be found in the kernel documentation.

- **dentry-state**—Dentries are name-to-`inode` translation structures that are cached aggressively. This entry can be used to modify the number of dentries being used for caching.

- **dquote-max/dquot-nr**—These two apply to the number of cached disk quota entries, both the maximum and the current number in use. This should hold up in normal circumstances but might need to be raised in the presence of a large number of users with quotas.

- **file-max/file-nr**—From these two, you can see the current number of file handles in use by the system. Actually, the number presented by file-max is the same as the third number presented by file-nr. The first two entries of file-nr are the current number of allocated file handles and the current number of file handles in use. The kernel allocates handles up to the maximum but does not release the handles; it instead keeps them and reallocates to processes that need them later. To raise the maximum number of file handles across the system, echo a new value to the file-max file, as shown here:

```
# echo 16384 > /proc/sys/fs/file-max
```

- **inode-nr/inode-state**—These are similar to file-max and file-nr, except that they apply to the inodes handlers behind the file. A good rule is to make sure that the maximum number of inode handlers is at least three times larger than the number of file handles.

- **overflowuid/overflowgid**—If you are writing to a filesystem that assumes a 16-bit UID and GID rather than the 32-bit range that Linux uses, you can use these two values to force UIDs and GIDs to be mapped down to whatever value is specified when writing to such a filesystem.

- **super-max/super-nr**—Although these are rarely used, they might need alteration in a large environment. These values track the current and maximum number of superblocks that the system uses. Because superblocks correspond to mount points, this is effectively the number of mount points you can have. The default is 256, but in a large, heavily networked environment, this value might need to be raised.

Kernel Parameters

/proc/sys/kernel provides several ways to interact with the kernel's handling of some parameters. Most will never come into play in a tuning situation, but some can be handy.

- **Ctrl+Alt+Del**—When 0, this causes the kernel to trap ctrl-alt-del key combinations and causes a clean shutdown. When this is set to 1, it forces an immediate and messy shutdown.

- **panic**—This is the number of seconds that the system waits before a reboot when a panic occurs.

- **printk**—These are the debug logging levels for the kernel, as specified in the syslog pages. If you are tracing what looks like a kernel problem, raising these levels to generate more debug data might point you in the direction of a solution.

- **threads-max**—This is the maximum number of POSIX threads that the system can handle. The default value should be adequate for most configurations.

- **msg* and shm***—These deserve special attention. Many books, especially those on configuring Oracle, have said that to raise the SHMMAX value to a reasonable level for your database, you need to modify the value hard-coded in the source, recompile the kernel, and reboot. This is absolutely false, and it applies only to commercial Unixes such as Solaris that need modification of a boot file to configure maximum values for SysV work. Under Linux, most of these values are modifiable directly through the /proc interface. For example, the SHMMAX for your system should be as large as your SGA plus other pools under Oracle. This way, Oracle can maintain its data within a single shared segment and doesn't have to spend time splicing datasets across multiple shared segments. To raise the value for the SHMMAX, just echo the value that you need in bytes to the file in /proc, and the kernel instantly allows segments up to that size. Under extremely high load, a couple values might need to be raised in the source, but for all but the largest databases, the source values are fine and any dynamic parameters can be changed through /proc.

Network Manipulation

The realm of network tuning is outside the scope of this chapter. But, if you know what modification you want to make to the kernel's network stack behavior, chances are good that you can make the change through the /proc interface. Depending on the physical network hardware you are using and the transport protocols, there might be different entries under /proc/sys/net, but most users will at least see an entry for IPv4. To give an idea of what can be done with the network here, some examples with IP are shown. However, it would take at least a whole chapter or book to cover all the possible repercussions of changing network parameters.

Depending on load, you might need to raise the keepalive time for incoming sockets. If there is a processing delay, connected sockets might timeout waiting for completion. Echoing a larger value to tcp_keepalive_time could help resolve the issue. Likewise, you might want to alter the parameters dealing with IP fragmentation. For nearly all tasks, though, the kernel's behavior is more than sufficient for handling the load. If you are convinced that you need to make IP stack modifications, make sure that you completely understand the underlying technology and implications; otherwise, you're probably chasing a false lead on a problem.

It also is worth noting that there are other parameters here that, although not directly relevant to tuning, might help in other configuration issues. IP forwarding is present here, along with settings for the maximum number of SYN backlogs, which could come into play if your machine is suffering performance loss because of a network attack.

Virtual Memory

The virtual memory (VM) subsystem is a very important part of the kernel. It has implications throughout the kernel because it controls memory usage. Historically, the VM subsystem has been very good at tuning itself—the 2.0 series was known for being nearly perfect. In the early 2.2 series, it could become unbalanced under heavier load, but this was sorted out later in the 2.2 series. New metrics are in place for the 2.4 kernel and generally keep it from needing human help. Nevertheless, there are a few entries present if you need to override the default settings.

bdflush is the file that tends to have the most impact on the system. In Chapter 2's example of irresponsible tuning, we showed an example of updating the bdflush parameters and a set of values that have been shown to generally increase performance. Here's some additional information about what each parameter means so that you can make more of an educated decision about how to tune the parameters for your machine.

The first value, as described earlier, is the percentage of the buffers that need to be dirty before a flush to disk occurs. This should default to 30 or so; although it is tempting to raise it directly to 100 to make sure that the buffer is always used rather than disk, keep in mind your expected load average. If the system waits until all buffers are dirty to trigger a flush, a large amount of slow I/O will occur during the flush, adversely affecting performance. If the system is prone to large influxes of activity, a lower number is recommended so that I/O flushes are spread out in a more gentle manner.

The second parameter is the number of buffers that bdflush can push through during a single flush operation. This number should be kept at the default value for nearly all situations. Lowering it will only cause flushing on more wake cycles because there will most likely be dirty buffers left after each flush, and the dirty count can more easily stay near the flushing threshold. Raising the value will cause more to be flushed per cycle, at the expense of more time being locked up with disk interaction. Depending on your memory requirements, you might want to allow more buffers to be flushed to disk per call.

The third parameter is the number of buffers that get added to the free list during a call to refill_freelist() within the kernel. This number should not be set much higher than the default value: It will result in fewer calls to refill_freelist(), but it will waste memory in the process.

Next is the threshold of dirty buffers to trigger bdflush when trying to refill buffers. Basically, when the system is trying to create new buffers to use, if this threshold of dirty buffers is passed, bdflush will be triggered to clean up some of the old buffers, making room for new buffers.

The fifth value is a dummy value, so it doesn't matter what you enter.

The sixth and seventh parameters are the age_buffer and age_super fields. These specify, in jiffies, the maximum age for data buffers and filesystem metadata blocks before updates must take place. A jiffie is a unit of time as measured by the kernel based on the clock present for the architecture. On most architectures, this hardware interrupt happens 100 times a second. A jiffie corresponds to this interrupt rate. When setting this value, make sure to use hundredths of a second as your basic unit.

As you can see, the bdflush parameters are fairly complex, and they can affect system performance in many ways. The example given earlier in the book is a decent example of finding a good set of numbers for a machine that is performing file-serving operations. Depending on your needs, you could come up with a different set, if you need to modify the parameters at all.

The next file, buffermem, enables you to specify the minimum percentage of system memory to be used for buffer memory. The default is 2% with most configurations, and rarely should you need to change this. Because Linux caches so aggressively, it will generally use a lot of the system memory for buffering, but it is rare that a configuration should be so tight on memory that it needs to steal the remaining fraction of buffer memory from the cache.

Next is the freepages file, with three values: the minimum number of free pages allowable, the low point to tell the kernel to start swapping heavily, and a high value to allow the kernel to gently swap. Depending on the architecture, the kernel maps memory in to 4KB pages internally. Based on your total system memory, it will decide on sane values for these variables. For the minimum number, the kernel watches that it never allows applications to claim enough pages to drop below this point. If this is reached, the remaining pages can be allocated only by the kernel itself so that it can continue to perform house-cleaning operations and keep the system going. If the system free page list hits this low number, swapping becomes a priority for the kernel. Until that point, it swaps as little as possible to keep performance up. The kernel uses the high value as a metric to start swapping data out, but not aggressively. Thus, free page counts anywhere from the high to low range are considered swapping ranges, to various degrees. If the system ventures into the high range only at peak load, then you have a memory shortage. However, the system will not grind to a halt immediately.

kswapd controls the activity of the kernel paging daemon. As the system becomes loaded, memory demands rise as allocations become fragmented. Kswapd runs as a kernel thread. If memory allocation problems occur, it makes sure that swapping is performed as needed to help matters.

There are three values here, two of which might come in handy if you are fighting to tune against bad swapping behavior. The first value is the tries_base. This controls the maximum number of pages that the swapping daemon will attempt to free in one round. Second is tries_min, which makes sure that some pages are freed even when kswapd is running at low priority. Otherwise, if it is running at low priority but doesn't work enough to free any pages, any time that it spent is wasted. Third is the `swap_cluster` variable, which is the maximum number of pages that `kswapd` will write in a single pass. Because this directly interacts with the disk, you should find a good balance between clustering requests to save disk spins while not blocking the VM system long enough to cause a large backlog of requests.

`max_map_count` is a simple setting that you shouldn't have to modify, except in rare situations. It is the maximum number of memory map areas that a process can have. Most processes will never hit this value, although heavy debuggers might need it to be raised.

`Overcommit_memory` is another simple one, at least on the surface. If it reads as 0, the kernel will error correctly when a memory allocation errors because there is no memory left. When this is nonzero, the kernel always pretends that there is enough memory.

Sounds pretty simple, right? But why would you want the system to let you allocate memory that it knows it doesn't have to give? In reality, policy on overcommitting memory has caused many arguments in kernel development. As explained earlier, the kernel uses a "copy-on-write" mechanism to conserve memory. When a process forks itself, generally the child doesn't really need all the internal data structures copied over. Realizing this, the kernel saves the memory that would be needed for this and allows the child to go on without duplication. If the child requests this data, the original structures from the parent are copied over so that it can behave as normal.

Herein lies the problem. Many applications out there, such as emacs, fork themselves but never request the child data. As these forks grow in number, a rising disparity grows between the memory actually allocated on the system and the amount that the kernel has promised to allocate through all those forks. If all those children cash in on those promised allocations, the memory might not really be there to support it.

The alternative to this system is to just duplicate all that data so that the child can use it, if needed. But this wastes large amounts of memory. So, the idea of overcommitting seems to have taken hold. Within the kernel, there is an out-of-memory killer that can wake up if all these allocations occur—the box would really be out of memory. The killer can wake up, select a likely culprit, and kill it off, bringing the machine back from the dead. Fortunately, the killer can use several metrics to determine the right thing to kill. Killing the largest process in memory is generally a bad idea because it can result in the death of X. Some good metrics to determine safe processes are ones that are not running as root, that have been running for a short period of time, and that are not doing privileged I/O operations. Although this approach sounds extreme, it prevents a system lockup and, in the end, might indicate that the system really does need more memory to effectively handle its expectations.

`page-cluster` and `pagecache` are fairly straightforward: They apply to paging of the disk. `page-cluster` controls the number of pages read ahead from the disk during a read because the next request is likely to continue reading data from the end of the last. `pagecache` acts the same way as `buffermem`, described previously, except that it is applying the behavior rules to the page cache to cache reads from the disk.

`pagetable_cache` maintains page tables on a per-processor basis. If you have a small system with less than 16MB of RAM or a single-processor system, you can set these values to 0 to conserve memory. On larger SMP systems, it could be beneficial to raise the values. The kernel will be sure to keep the page cache size between the low and high values. The benefit is that if each CPU in an SMP system can interact with the page cache rather than the VM system, it can save the overhead of obtaining kernel locks.

Well, that's a simple overview of what is contained in the /proc filesystem as it pertains to tuning and general control of the system. It might seem like a lot to digest, but most situations will not require you to do much more than what the kernel has already figured out for you. As with anything else in the kernel, changes are always being made. If what you have present in your system varies widely from what is described here, make sure that you get up-to-date information on what the new interfaces mean and how to work with them.

Recompiling the Kernel

You've determined that you want to make some changes to your kernel configuration. This chapter assumes that you are getting a new kernel and installing it fresh. This is often not the case, of course: You might just want to modify an existing kernel configuration, or you might only want to bring your kernel up to the latest revision. In the latter case, it is better for the kernel servers to just patch the latest source into your tree. Examples of this will be handled later in the chapter in "Patching Your Kernel." For now, assume that you are getting a brand-new copy of the latest kernel.

Getting the Sources

First, you need to get the latest kernel from the mirror system. Check out `http://www.kernel.org` to make sure you know what the current release is. There is a script that checks revisions present and gives a listing of both the current stable release and the current prerelease version that will eventually become the next full release.

Check out the mirror list for locations near you. Generally, you want to put your country code into the URL to get your local server, as in `http://www.us.kernel.org/`. From there, the path down, if not specified by the server, is `pub/linux/kernel`, which gets you to the directory of all the major release trees. Select the current one from that set, which currently is version 2.4. Download the latest revision as checked previously, preferably in bzipped form, which gives better compression rates and is faster to download. Nearly all modern distributions ship with the bzip utilities installed by default. If you don't have them, install them or get the gzipped version of the kernel.

Now that you have the source downloaded (hopefully as a normal user), copy the file to /usr/src. Depending on your installation, you might already have kernel sources present, probably in a directory called linux. If they are already there, you can either remove the entire directory with rm -rf linux, which will trash any existing source, or move the directory over to something more informational, such as the name of the kernel you are running. uname -r will give you the revision of the currently running kernel and will provide a good way to make distinctions between which source tree you are working with.

When this is out of the way, run tar xvzpf linux-x.y.z.tar.gz. Or, if you downloaded a bzipped version, run bz2cat linux-x.y.z.tar.bz2 | tar xvf - to unpack the source into a directory named linux. You can also just as easily unpack all sources to anywhere, such as your home directory, but many people like to keep the sources together in /usr/src if they have room. Keep in mind that if you got the bzip2 version, better compression is offered but this version is more CPU-intensive to work with.

There should now be a directory called linux with the current sources. If you know that you will be working with different versions—say, for testing purposes—you might want to rename the linux directory to whatever version you just downloaded and then symlink the linux name to it, as shown here (simplified to contain only kernel-relevant entries):

```
# ls -l
drwxr-xr-x   14 root      root            691 Apr 19 11:22 linux/
drwxr-xr-x   14 root      root            463 Mar 25 13:45 linux-2.2.19/
-rw-r--r--    1 root      root       19343412 Apr 19 11:24 linux-2.2.19.tar.gz
-rw-r--r--    1 root      root       20499361 Mar 18 19:12 linux-2.4.2.tar.bz2
# mv linux linux-2.4.2
# ln -s linux-2.4.2 linux
# ls -l
lrwxrwxrwx    1 root      root             11 Apr 19 11:29 linux -> linux-2.4.2/
drwxr-xr-x   14 root      root            463 Mar 25 13:45 linux-2.2.19/
-rw-r--r--    1 root      root       19343412 Apr 19 11:24 linux-2.2.19.tar.gz
drwxr-xr-x   14 root      root            691 Apr 19 11:22 linux-2.4.2/
-rw-r--r--    1 root      root       20499361 Mar 18 19:12 linux-2.4.2.tar.bz2
```

This way, you can move the symlink back to the 2.2.19 tree if you want to make some changes to the old stable tree and try it out for a while.

Before you move on to the configuration stage, make sure that you are running a supported compiler. Portions of the kernel rely on the writer knowing exactly what assembly will be generated during the build, so the kernel authors generally directly support only specific versions of compilers. Check the README file for the currently recommended compiler. For example, gcc-2.91-66 or gcc-2.95.2 are directly supported at this time, although many people also are using 2.95.3 without trouble. Using a supported compiler is recommended; otherwise, a bad compiler could generate bad code that would result in an unstable kernel.

Configuring the Kernel

Now that you've got the sources ready, you need to build a configuration. As with anything else in Linux, there are several ways to get this done. `make config`, `make menuconfig`, and `make xconfig` all will let you walk through the decision tree. If you are running X, you can run `xconfig` to get a graphical interface to configuration options. `menuconfig` will present a curses-based interface, which, although still console-based, is very nice to work with. The standard `make config` will run you through the questions in series on the console and can seem to take longer to work through. For most users, `menuconfig` or `xconfig` is the best route. Keep in mind that after you make a pass through the configuration once, your options are saved and are usable the next time around. After you get a base configuration working, the basic `make config` becomes easier to work with because you can simply select all the preselected options, which are now the default answer for each question. This makes later tweaks to the configuration easier to control.

Explanations of all kernel configuration options are beyond the scope of this book, but here is an overview for what you probably want to select during the configuration process. Always remember that you can get help about an option by hitting the ? key during a console configuration or by selecting help in either `menuconfig` or `xconfig`. Although these directions aren't exhaustive, they should give you a basic idea of what the option does and whether you should select it by default if you are in doubt.

- **Code maturity-level options**—This contains the option to allow questions about kernel options that might still be considered experimental. This is generally fine to turn on because, by the time most options are worked into the default kernel tree, they are fairly well tested. Some hardware drivers, although heavily used in the field, might still be tagged as experimental and won't show up as an option unless this flag is set.

- **Loadable module support**—This switch enables hooks to allow kernel modules to be loaded and unloaded at runtime. It is a good idea to have this on, even if you currently don't have any loadable modules. Enabling the kernel module loader also is a good idea: With it on, the kernel can decide when it needs to load modules into memory. For example, if you access a hardware device and the driver isn't loaded in memory, the kernel will load the dependency tree for you.

- **Processor type and features**—Flags under this tree deal with processor-specific settings, allowing the kernel to take advantage of whatever specific CPU you have. Depending on your CPU, it also can enable extensions for large amounts of memory and MTRR support, which can make better utilization of other hardware components. SMP support is triggered here as well. It is safe to leave it on, even if you don't have a second CPU, and this will save you the trouble of fixing the kernel to add support if you do add another processor.

- **General setup**—This one should be pretty obvious. General system settings live under here. You can control what busses the system supports, what kind of binaries it understands, and power management options. Also make sure that you enable SysV support, along with `sysctl`. Make sure that your kernel supports ELF format binaries and a.out, if you have any legacy binaries that use this format. For the most part, this is not needed anymore. The kernel does allow you to arbitrarily set up handlers for different types of binaries, which makes Java class files appear to be transparently handled as true binaries. This is left as an exercise for you, though.

- **Block device support**—Use this section to allow kernel drivers for different types of block devices, such as ramdisks, network block support, and some RAID drivers. Block devices are useful in situations such as when you need to layer a filesystem on top of a device that normally wouldn't appear to be one. Ramdisks are a good example of this because you can take a chunk of memory and drop a filesystem on top of it, making it appear to be something that it is not. Network block devices enable you to mount remote servers as a local block device and use it for file I/O or even as a swap device.

- **Networking options**—This is an extensive tree of configuration options that control what protocols the kernel will work with, along with how it will work with them. For example, you can enable network quality-of-service capabilities from this section, along with network packet filtering. Generally, this turns certain sets of possible behavior on in the kernel, and userspace tools are used to control exactly how the kernel should behave. In the example of packet filtering, you would use the iptables user-space tools to control the kernel's tables of rules for what to do with different packet traffic. If you need a specific protocol enabled, it is handled here—anything from DECnet support to IPv6 and ATM.

- **ATA/IDE/MFM/RLL and SCSI support**—This enables support for the various subsystems, such as IDE and SCSI, and it presents drivers for each. A good rule, especially in a server environment, is to at least have SCSI enabled as a module. This way, even though the box might be serving Web data off an IDE drive, when load demands a SCSI drive, you can add the hardware but have the machine down only long enough to physically add the card. When it is back up, you can dynamically add the SCSI driver to the kernel without requiring another set of reboots to make sure that the driver is correctly built into the kernel.

- **Network device support**—Network cards of various types are enabled here. Everything from ARCnet to FDDI is supported, and many drivers are integrated into the kernel tree for the myriad of normal Ethernet devices on the market. Note that many similar cards are grouped under the same driver, as is the case with 3COM hardware. A single driver works with all types of cards listed.

9

THE LINUX
KERNEL

- **Character devices**—This might be a misnomer to newcomers. Various types of devices fall under the character device umbrella. Anything from different mouse types to real-time clocks to direct video rendering support can be enabled from here.

- **Mutltimedia devices**—The only component present under this is Video 4 Linux, or V4L. This enables applications using the V4L set of system calls to work with video and audio capture hardware. Cards such as TV tuners and radio cards are present here, but other types that might be qualified as multimedia have fallen in other configuration areas.

- **File systems**—As you might guess, you enable Linux's support for various filesystem types under this tree, along with partition types. Linux has support for many types of filesystem formats, although normal users won't need support for most of them. Ext2 is the default filesystem format, although ReiserFS is rapidly becoming a favorite because it doesn't need to run extensive filesystem checks if the system crashes. Network filesystems also are in this area, which means that you can enable support for either NFS client or server support, along with SMB filesystem support so that you can mount drives that are remote Windows shares. You can even enable support to read your NTFS drives on your system. For most of the options here, they can be compiled as a module and inserted on the fly without rebooting, so don't worry about making sure that you directly support everything that you might need in the kernel.

- **Sound**—Again, as you might guess, this is the support for various sound cards. Many drivers are integrated into the kernel, but the ALSA project (`http://www.alsa-project.org`) also maintains a separate set of drivers that could work better for your hardware. If your hardware is only marginally supported in the kernel, either because it is poorly documented or because it is new on the market, you might want to look at the ALSA baseline.

- **USB**—If you have USB devices, this will enable the USB subsystem. As with the SCSI subsystem mentioned previously, it might be a good idea to enable this, to save the trouble of enabling USB down the road if you don't have a device using it now.

This covers the general sections of configuration—for the normal user, the best preset configurations should be chosen for you already, with a few possible exceptions. If you aren't the normal user (and you know who you are), you might need to make many changes to get things just the way you want them. If you are looking to reduce the memory footprint of the kernel, building your own kernel is a good way to trim any unneeded `fat` from the running system. This won't save you as much as correctly configuring all applications present and disabling unused services, but running a slim kernel can save some space and remove ambiguities about what might or might not be present in a running system.

make dep, make bzImage, and Similar Commands

After building a configuration, you will generally need to run a make dep, which runs down through the kernel tree and applies your configuration rules to the build. Depending on what you have chosen, different dependencies arise in the code, and make dep will resolve these for you.

After running the dependency checking, it's time to build the kernel. A simple make bzImage at this point will do the job. Multiple types of images can be built, but bzImage is the default for nearly any user. If you need a different type of image built, you know exactly what you need and how to do it. (The reasons for doing so are outside the scope of this chapter.) After issuing the make bzImage, give the machine some time to work through the source code. The kernel is large, and, depending on what options you have selected, the build could take some time. With modern hardware, though, the build time should take only a few minutes. At the end of the build, you should see something like this:

```
# make bzImage
gcc -D__KERNEL__ -I/usr/src/linux-2.4.2/include -Wall -Wstrict-prototypes
➡ -O2 -fomit-frame-pointer -fno-strict-aliasing -pipe
➡-mpreferred-stack-boundary=2 -march=i686 -malign-functions=4
➡-c -o init/main.o init/main.c
...
tools/build -b bbootsect bsetup compressed/bvmlinux.out CURRENT > bzImage
Root device is (3, 1)
Boot sector 512 bytes.
Setup is 4500 bytes.
System is 794 kB
make[1]: Leaving directory `/usr/src/linux-2.4.2/arch/i386/boot'
```

This means that the kernel is built and resides in a file named bzImage under /usr/src/linux-2.4.2/arch/i386/boot. It has also built a file named System.map that lives in /usr/src/linux, which can be used to map kernel symbol locations, if needed.

Here is another step that needs to take place before you install the new kernel: If you enabled anything as a module, you need to install the modules for that kernel version. This can be done with a simple make modules; make modules_install command, which will build any needed modules and install them in the right location, under /lib/modules/kernel-version.

If you are making small modifications to an already configured system, this build process can be simplified with something like the following command, after the configuration has been updated:

```
# make dep bzImage modules modules_install
```

In this case, make will work through all the requested builds in order and will quit if it sees an error along the way. This is a simpler solution in most cases because you can walk away and do something else while it is building.

Installing the New Kernel

Installation is a relatively straightforward process after the kernel is built. The end result is that you need your drive to be prepared to be capable of booting the new kernel image. On some systems, a make bzlilo command will install the newly built kernel for you, but in most cases, it's worth the trouble to make the modifications yourself.

Most distributions use the lilo boot loader. Some give the option of using the GRand Unified Bootloader (GRUB), which is the GNU offering, but both of them perform the same function: They provide a clean way of booting multiple kernels and multiple operating systems. First, let's look at how to configure lilo to use the new kernel, along with all the old ones.

Your new kernel, as shown previously, is sitting in /usr/src/kernel-name/arch/i386/boot, with the possible exception of the i386 portion if you are building on another platform. The best thing to do is to copy that file over to /boot and give it a relevant name. Most distributions default to an image name, such as vmlinuz, but if you are looking to use multiple kernels or are just testing, it's a good idea to name it something like 2.4.2, with an optional trailing name specifying what set of capabilities it has enabled. If you are testing the RAID options, for example, naming it 2.4.2-RAID might be a good idea. The idea goes back to the premise that you should never change multiple components at the same time when working on a system.

Now that the file is in /boot, you need to add an entry to your /etc/lilo.conf to reflect this. Looking at your default file, it should appear to be something close to the following:

```
# cat /etc/lilo.conf
boot=/dev/hda
map=/boot/map
install=/boot/boot.b
vga=normal
default=linux
keytable=/boot/us.klt
lba32
prompt
timeout=50
message=/boot/message
menu-scheme=wb:bw:wb:bw
image=/boot/vmlinuz
    label=linux
    root=/dev/hda1
    initrd=/boot/initrd.img
    read-only
```

```
image=/boot/vmlinuz
    label=failsafe
    root=/dev/hda1
    initrd=/boot/initrd.img
    append=" failsafe"
    read-only
other=/dev/fd0
    label=floppy
    unsafe
```

As you can see, lilo understands several options, down to details such as color scheme for the boot menu. By pointing the boot line to different disks, you can update the boot sector for each, although you generally will point it only at your boot drive. You shouldn't have to modify most of the options present if lilo is already in use. The default line might be worth looking at if you want to change the image used as the default. (The default line corresponds to the label name for each image.)

Each one of the images listed is a kernel that can be booted or a pointer, as with the other line that points to the floppy drive for a kernel. To add your new kernel to the list, add a new set of image lines, as shown here:

```
...
menu-scheme=wb:bw:wb:bw
image=/boot/2.4.2
    label=2.4.2
    root=/dev/hda1
image=/boot/vmlinuz
...
```

As you can see, you don't necessarily need all the options enabled for your kernel. After lilo.conf is saved, return to the console and run /sbin/lilo: You should see a line of output for each kernel entry in the list, with a * next to it. With this example setup, you should see something like this:

```
#/sbin/lilo
Added 2.4.2
Added linux *
Added failsafe
Added floppy
```

This means that 2.4.2 has been added, but because the default line still pointed to the default linux label, it will still be the default if no options are selected before the timeout passes. The timeout is in tenths of a second, so, in this case, there is a 5-second delay before the default kernel is selected.

The next time you boot, enter or select the new kernel from the list and then test the system with it accordingly. If you don't have a graphical list of options, hit tab at the LILO prompt for the list of available kernels to choose from and also to disable the pending timeout. If there are problems, you might want to try booting in single-user mode, which is a good way to test the system before all services are started. This is an invaluable means of performing tests and doing administrative work that shouldn't be done when the system is running in multiuser mode. A surprising number of administrators never know how to enter a kernel in single-user mode under Linux, but all it takes is typing the word `single` after the name of the kernel that you want to boot.

So far, we haven't said anything about GRUB. In theory, it performs the same operation and gives you the same list of kernels or other operating systems to choose from at boot time. The major difference with GRUB, from a normal user's point of view, is that you don't have to initialize the boot sector of your drive with it every time you add a new kernel. After GRUB is installed, you have to modify only a single file to enter the new kernel option. This file is typically `/boot/grub/menu.1st`. After you enter your new kernel into the list and reboot, the option will be present in the list without running a utility such as lilo.

GRUB also provides some nice capabilities that might make it a better choice, depending on your environment. Besides being compliant with all relevant standards, it enables you to download images over a network, making centralized management of kernels simpler. It also supports diskless systems. Although the GNU developers have not declared it to be complete yet and have not made public announcements about its status, distributions are beginning to offer it as an optional bootloader, with some even making it the system default (Caldera and Mandrake, for example). At this point, most users are still more familiar with lilo, although that could change.

One more operation should be done, although it is not critical to the operation of your new kernel. The kernel build left a `System.map` file in the `/usr/src/linux` directory, which can be used to get symbol locations. It is generally good practice to copy this file over to `/boot` and name it something like `System.map-kernelname`, where "kernelname" is whatever you named your kernel. Then remove the existing `System.map` in `/boot` (or rename it to something meaningful) and symbolically link `System.map` to the new file, as shown here:

```
# cp /usr/src/linux/System.map /boot/System.map-2.4.2
# cd /boot
# mv System.map System.map.original
# ln -s System.map-2.4.2 System.map
```

This enables you to change symbol tables easily when trying to debug different kernel versions, but it is not an absolutely necessary step in the process. The system can run without having the map, although some distributions will dump errors about the wrong map being in place.

Now you should have a good idea of how to manipulate your set of kernels. The capability to keep multiple versions around is very useful in practice. For example, if you are testing a new series of kernels on your hardware, you can easily add the kernel source, configure, boot the new kernel, and still have the old one around just in case. If something goes wrong, such as a driver not being up to par yet, the old kernel is only a reboot away, and the system will be back as it was before the upgrade.

Leaving the old kernel as the boot default might be a good idea until you are comfortable with the new one in all situations. This way, if something goes wrong with the box and it forces a reboot, the old safe kernel will be the default when the system comes back up. One thing to keep in mind is that both kernels should have similar capabilities. If you add a drive with a ReiserFS filesystem using the new kernel's support for ReiserFS, but the old kernel doesn't understand the filesystem, reverting back to the old kernel is no longer a safe option. If you are changing the kernel only and not the underlying system, as you should, this problem shouldn't occur.

Choosing the Right Drivers

How do you know which drivers to use? A good rule of thumb is that, for your given hardware, it is usually a good idea to go with the version of the driver that is integrated into the kernel. To get into the kernel, drivers are reviewed by more people and get wider testing because more people have direct access to it. But there are exceptions to this rule. Sometimes the kernel driver is stable, but the developers have pushed the driver much further ahead and can now take advantage of advanced portions of the hardware—they just haven't submitted a new version to the kernel list. Sometimes you need to be able to use that extra capability and need to use the external version. (A good example of this is the bttv driver, which provides a driver for TV tuning cards. The kernel version tends to lag well behind the current external stable version. In this case, it exists with the kernel, as an external set of drivers, or as a patch to the kernel to bring the kernel driver up to speed.) Sometimes the only source of a driver is the hardware vendor, and that is your only choice.

Whatever the cause is, there can be justifiable reasons to look outside the kernel for drivers. Regardless of whether the driver was in the kernel or was external, though, the system should be thoroughly tested to ensure that it is up to handling the expected need. It should never be assumed that if the driver is in the kernel source, the system should be deployed with it immediately.

In reality, having multiple versions of a driver can be a good thing. Depending on your needs, you might end up with a choice, such as between a more stable but less hardware-capable kernel version and a newer version with less testing but one that lets you take better advantage of the hardware. If you need stability over the absolute latest hardware tweak, the obvious choice

9

THE LINUX
KERNEL

is to use the kernel version. Having this option can be a lifesaver in a dynamic environment in which needs might shift. If the driver is installed as a module, swapping out the versions can be as simple as using a series of commands that load and unload the appropriate drivers.

Changing Driver Configuration

Actually changing driver configuration requires knowledge of exactly what your hardware can do and what specific options are needed to reconfigure the driver. For the most part, the driver pokes at the available hardware and chooses the right configuration to use. In the case of the 3COM drivers, support for nearly all the available cards is provided by a single driver module. As the driver is loaded, it probes to see what specific type of card is present. In some driver cases, it also needs to take into account what revision of the hardware is present. Based on what it finds, options are set.

Sometimes these options need to be overridden, though. For example, sometimes network drivers don't put the hardware in full-duplex mode, resulting in a performance loss. Using options specific to the driver, you can override the defaults and force it to use the hardware in a specific manner. Refer to your driver documentation or vendor for specifics on what options the driver can handle. After the correct setup is found, it can be configured in the module configuration files to use the same options whenever the hardware is used.

Patching Your Kernel

In some situations you need to add an external source file to your kernel. This is conventionally done via `diff` and patch, which output differences between files and apply those differences to a file, respectively. Here are a few reasons you might need to patch your kernel:

- A vendor gives you drivers in the form of a patchfile that is to be run against various source versions of the kernel. This is a rarer instance than the vendor providing source to be built outside the kernel, but sometimes small modifications need to be made to the kernel internally to allow the driver to work correctly.

- You need to test different approaches to a solution. If you are testing different people's approaches to, say, a VM subsystem fix, the fixes will most likely exist in the form of a `diff` from the original source. By applying the patches one at a time and then reverting them back out, you can objectively test different solutions to the problem.

- You need to integrate fixes that haven't been worked into the standard source tree yet. For example, 2.4.3 has been out for a while, and the developers are taking patches for fixes against it that will eventually become 2.4.4—but 2.4.4 isn't out yet. You are in the unfortunate position of being one of the people experiencing problems that have been found and fixed, but you can't wait until a final 2.4.4 is wrapped up and released. In this case, every few days a patch release is done that is meant to be run against the current base of 2.4.3. If your fix was rolled into patch level 5 against 2.4.3, you can roll the fix into your base kernel without waiting for the final version. (You still need to be careful about what else comes with this patch, of course. It might make sense to get the individual patch for the specific problem from the original author rather than getting the intermediate patch for the whole kernel.)

Regardless of how you get here, sometimes you're left with a problem and a patchfile that you know needs to be applied to your kernel source. (Of course, the solutions described here can occur with any piece of source code you have, whether it is in your own project, in another local application that you are building from source, or somewhere else. It in no way has to be the kernel.) If you are working with your vendor, it might provide fixes through another route, possibly by releasing precompiled binaries of the patched kernels. For the sake of vendor neutrality, though, we assume that you are working on your own personal instance of the kernel source. Let's look at the tools involved to get a better perspective on how this works.

diff is a utility that generates patch files to reflect the differences between two versions of a file. When it's run on a source file, it provides nearly human-readable files that specify the exact steps needed to go from one version of a file to the other. Let's look at simple example: Assume that you have a simple C file with these contents:

```
#include <stdio.h>
int main (int argc, char **argv) {
    printf("diff tsting\n");
}
```

This file is saved in a file named dtest.c. As people use this wonderful little program, someone notices that there is a spelling error. They need to fix it and get the patch to you. So, the bug-fixer creates a copy of the file named dtestupdate.c and makes the change so that the program now reads as follows:

```
#include <stdio.h>
int main (int argc, char **argv) {
    printf("diff testing\n");
}
```

Now, to get the patch back to you so that you can apply it to your local copy, diff is run in the following fashion:

```
# diff -u dtest.c dtestupdate.c > dtestpatch
```

By default, diff writes the output to stdout, so it needs to be redirected into the patchfile. The contents of this dtestpatch look like this:

```
--- dtest.c Thu Apr 19 15:59:52 2001
+++ dtestupdate.c   Thu Apr 19 16:02:39 2001
```

```
@@ -1,4 +1,4 @@
 #include <stdio.h>
 int main (int argc, char **argv) {
-    printf("diff tsting\n");
+    printf("diff testing\n");
 }
```

In this simple case, the patch file is larger than the program in question, but you should get the general idea. The first file sent to diff is the original file, and the second is the destination. The patch can be seen as reflecting the path that you would need to take to get the first file to the state of the second one. As you can see, the output in unified format (provided by the -u switch) isn't really too cryptic. It is obviously saying that you need to remove the line with the misspelling and replace it with a line without the problem.

As a patch recipient, though, you should rarely have to deal with the diff end of the process. For the most part, you will be applying patches that are the result of someone else's work, and the diff will likely be over more than one file. Usually kernel patches are meant to be applied to the root of the kernel source tree because they typically touch many files throughout the code base.

Upon receiving a patchfile, such as the one just generated, the patch utility can be used to apply the differences and bring the original dtest.c up to par. The process is fairly simple, especially in this case. Assuming that the patchfile was saved locally as dtestpatch, it would be applied to the local copy of dtest.c with the following command (assuming that both files are in the same directory):

```
# patch -p0 < dtestpatch
patching file dtest.c
# cat dtest.c
#include <stdio.h>
int main (int argc, char **argv) {
    printf("diff testing\n");
}
```

As you can see, the change specified in the patch file has been applied to the local file. When dealing with kernel patches, the same ideas apply, although on a larger scale.

You might be wondering exactly how a patch works. As you can see, it reads its patch data from stdin, which means that it can apply patches that reside anywhere on the system; the patch doesn't have to reside directly inside your source tree. (In general, that would be a bad idea anyway.) The -p0 specified is a parameter that needs to be present, and it determines the number of leading / characters that should be removed from the paths specified in the files embedded in the diff file. Most of the time, in a kernel patch, you use cd to navigate to the /usr/src/linux directory or whichever kernel tree you want to apply the patch to. In the previous example, you used -p0 to specify that no leading slashes were to be removed (because there weren't any.) This same value applies in most cases. If you get a patch that contains the full path to the files in the embedded `diff` paths, such as `/usr/src/linux/mm/vmscan.c`, you still use the patch. Go to the root of the tree from where you would like to apply the patch, and run patch with the `-p4` switch. Because you are running it from the root of the tree, you need to make sure that everything up through the / after linux is taken out of the path.

Patching is a fairly straightforward operation, but trouble arises when it's not done correctly. For starters, applying patches to the wrong kernel version can result in a corrupted source. Generally, the patch being applied comes with a notice of some kind specifying what version it should be run against—and don't expect a patch against 2.4.4 to run cleanly against 2.0.36. A good rule to follow is to do a dry run with the `--dry-run` switch to patch. This enables you to see the output of what would happen if you did run the patch so that you can keep it from clobbering your source tree. Sometimes, if there are large implications of the patch from which you might not cleanly recover, you should use `tar` and `gzip` to create a copy of your base tree to make recovery simple.

Another factor to keep in mind is that patches might step on each other. If the patch exists outside the general kernel tree, it might want to make a change to the kernel base. The possibility exists that another patch you need to add might step on the same piece of code. In this situation, notify the maintainers if you don't feel comfortable merging the source changes yourself. For the most part, these differences can be resolved. In addition, it's rare that conflicting patches last for too long because there is usually crossover between developers when they are working on the same area of kernel code. If you still want to try applying the conflicting patch, patch will go ahead and try; it will save the unmatched fragments in files ending in .rej for review. Based on the contents of those files, you can deduce the problem with the patch and determine a merge point.

As mentioned previously, you can use patch to apply different solutions to the same problem onto the same kernel source. With the `-R` or `--reverse` switch to patch, you can easily revert a patch back out of your tree. This works through the modifications in reverse, leaving you with the original version of the file. So, if you have two patches you want to test, the following series will allow you to test each one:

```
# cd /usr/src/linux
# patch -p0 < /usr/src/patch1
(build kernel, install, test)
# patch -p0 -R < /usr/src/patch1
# patch -p0 < /usr/src/patch2
(build kernel, install, test)
# patch -p0 -R < /usr/src/patch2
```

After all these tests are finished, you have objectively tested each approach and your source tree is just as clean as it was when you started.

9

THE LINUX
KERNEL

Where do all these patches come from? That's a very good question. As always, it depends on what you are trying to do. If an application is trying to patch the kernel, the patch most likely comes with the software. If you are applying a patch to solve a kernel issue, it could have come from anywhere. For most kernel problems, the patch becomes available through whoever wrote it and posted it to the kernel mailing list. If the patch is small, it might be contained in the message, or it might be on a Web site, referenced on the list. Sometimes a vendor might supply the source patch through whatever channels are appropriate for that vendor.

Generally, if you are patching a kernel, you most likely will be using one of the default patch sets against the current baseline. Two trees typically are in active use: the one controlled by Linus Torvalds and another by Alan Cox (although there more could spring up until the works get rolled into the main kernel). Linus runs the development tree, whereas Alan runs the stable tree. The older trees continue to be in use, but development on them typically drops off, to the point of only significant bugs being fixed. Depending on time, Alan also maintains a patch set against current trees (development or stable) that incorporates different fixes considered too radical to be rolled into the default line without more testing. For example, the current stable tree is 2.4; because it's in a stable testing pattern, Linus keeps a patch set of fixes against it. Likewise, Alan keeps a patch set. Linus is focused only on letting high-importance patches in—and only when they don't involve major repercussions. Alan, on the other hand, is more accepting in his tree and accepts some riskier bits and pieces for testing. When they have been proven, these bits generally get sent to Linus, who keeps them in his patch set to be rolled into the next version release. (Refer to the kernel mailing list summaries at `http://kt.zork.net` for more information and insight into Linus' and Alan's current work.)

During normal development cycles—say, when 2.5 development begins in full swing—Linus will change his focus to that tree, leaving Alan to continue work on the 2.4 series, integrate drivers as needed, and merge fixes as needed. Eventually the leadership will change hands to someone else when Alan needs to focus on the 2.6 stable tree. Currently, he is still maintaining the 2.2 tree. The 2.0 leadership has been handed over to David Weinehall.

Now you know more than you ever wanted to about the kernel development process. The names might shift over time, but the overall model holds up and will likely continue for the foreseeable future. But how do you know when a fix is out in a patch for your problem? The best way is to watch the Linux kernel development list, but that's not feasible for most people because of the volume of mail involved and the fact that not everyone wants to spend their life watching kernel development. News services such as *Linux Weekly News* (`http://www.lwn.net/daily`), which gives up-to-the-minute announcements or Kernel Traffic (`kt.zork.net`), which gives weekly summaries of kernel development, can help keep you up-to-date when Alan or Linus release patch updates. In both cases, a changes document is attached to the release, specifying what exactly is updated. If you see something that pertains to your problem, it might be worth patching.

The patches usually reside on the same kernel servers as the rest of the source, except that they reside in the directory of the person who made the patch. Several people have directories here; depending on their focus, they might have patches in which you are interested. In general, though, the location of the patch that you need should be specified in the changes file.

When you get the patch, you need to apply it. It is assumed that you are applying the patch to a clean copy of the previous version of the kernel. For example, if you are running 2.4.4 and need to apply the 2.4.5 prepatch 2, which will eventually be 2.4.5, it is assumed that your kernel source is a clean version of 2.4.4. Likewise, if you are running 2.4.3 and want to patch up to the full release of 2.4.4, it is assumed that you have a clean copy of 2.4.3 to patch against.

In reality, you might have applied patches to 2.4.3—it is just a matter of whether the changes in 2.4.4 conflict with the patches you have applied. If so, you'll probably need to revert the patches, apply the patch to 2.4.4, and get the new copies of your other patches that have been done against 2.4.4. Also remember that if you want to make a larger jump—say, from 2.4.0 to 2.4.3—you need to apply the patches in sequence: In this case, you'll need to apply the patch for 2.4.1 to bring up the base so that it's the same as the real 2.4.1. Then you'll need to apply the 2.4.2 patch, to bring the 2.4.1 base up to 2.4.2, and so on. Depending on the age of the source, it could be simpler to just get the complete new version—going from the old stable series of 2.2.0 to 2.2.19 requires a lot of downloading and patching.

To wrap up this idea before leaving this section, let's walk through an example. Assume that you are running kernel 2.4.3 and are experiencing problems with your qlogic card. Looking at the latest news, Linus is up to version 2.4.4pre4, which means that four patches have been released since 2.4.3 came out. Looking at the release for patch level 4, you see that there were fixes for the qlogic driver integrated into pre3. Because these patches are cumulative against 2.4.3, you can get the 2.4.4pre4 patch, patch it against your system, and test to see if it solved the problem. While you're at it, it might make sense to look at the source difference in the qlogic code, to see whether it really could fix your problem or whether it's completely unrelated.

Tracking these patches sounds like a daunting task, but with the help of news sources, distribution vendors supplying fixes, and a quick release schedule, getting the latest code really isn't that difficult. It ends up being fairly rare that a specific patch set is needed for very long before it is resolved within the kernel or whatever source base that it touches.

Trapping Kernel Oopses

In the process of testing all these patches, you might crash the kernel. How do you take the kernel oops message and reconstruct meaningful data to fix the problem? Fully understanding the methods involved in tracing internal data can takes years of practice, so this section just points you in the right direction of getting the data to someone who can trace the meaning of it.

In most cases, the kernel log daemon can trap data as it does all other kernel messages. If it has a valid System.map file, it can translate the memory values involved to their human-readable symbolic values. This is why moving and replacing the current System.map file is recommended when configuring your kernel. From this data, you can reconstruct clues to what happened and find a solution.

In the case of dynamically loaded modules, the kernel symbols were not present in the kernel image and thus cannot be translated if a module causes an oops. There are ways to get relevant data in this situation, but it might be better to build the driver into the kernel so that tracing is easier. If the problem goes away when the driver is statically built into the kernel, the problem is probably not the driver's general operation, but rather how it deals with the kernel when loaded as a module.

If you end up with a hard crash, in which the interrupt handler was killed before the data was written to disk, you might have to write the oops data for yourself and type it at the next boot. In this case especially, but also when symbol translations were not done, you need to install ksymoops from the ftp.kernel.org mirror system. ksymoops can reconstruct the relevant symbols needed to generate useful debug information. The internals of ksymoops cannot be described here in full detail; check with the ksymoops documentation for a full description of how to use it.

After you have the data, check the MAINTAINERS file in the Linux sources for someone who would likely be able to trace the problem. Or, if you started having this problem as a direct result of applying someone's patch, mail the information to that person. If you cannot find anyone who seems capable of solving the problem, post your problem to the Linux kernel mailing list, at linux-kernel@vger.kernel.org.

Summary

This seems like a lot to handle all in one chapter, and it is. The Linux kernel is by no means a simple beast. In reality, it does a lot of work for you, and it shouldn't require much in the way of tuning. For more specific needs, the information presented here can be a nice springboard into making changes in your environment. Always keep in mind that Linux is always under development; although this information provides a good base from which to start, you should continually check for any improvements or changes made during the development cycle, as well as information from someone who has already solved your problem.

Disk Configurations for Performance

Managing Disk Space

To effectively manage your network, the most important factors are consistency and scalability. Historically, machines have been managed on an individual basis, resulting in complex network deployments that require much more management and general attention than they warrant. Using the following technologies, management of your network storage should become much simpler, while at the same time allowing for more capabilities as your system grows.

GFS/SAN

SAN architectures are offered through many vendors and can conveniently keep all your storage in the same area. This simplifies backups and failure management, among other things. Check with your hardware vendor to see whether a SAN would fit in your environment. Within your *Storage Area Network (SAN)*, you can segment your storage so that different attached machines can see different portions of the disk set. With something like the *Global File System (GFS)*, all machines involved can share the same drive area concurrently, and all normal disk operations are coordinated through the file system. GFS and SAN technologies seem as if they overlap, and in a way they do. GFS allows multiple machines to share the same physical storage at the same time, whereas a SAN tends to be focused on the physical centralization of your network storage. So in a way they are the same, but not completely. A GFS system could be used within a SAN, but it doesn't have to be this way—the GFS cluster could just be a small group of machines coordinating around a shared drive array, whereas the SAN exists for the rest of the data on the network.

Normally, a *namespace* (a consistent naming system, generally having an enforced hierarchy and rules against duplication) is created on a per-machine basis between the filesystem and the underlying disk. In the case of networked filesystems such as NFS exports and SMB shares, extra handling is injected to make sure that file manipulation is coordinated among users. In the case of GFS, this coordination can be handled by machines that are sharing access to the same physical drive set. Although this case assumes a SAN architecture, this could just as easily be a normal shared SCSI drive array or a network block device to which all machines are sharing access. The advantage is that the machines involved don't have to bottleneck at the network like the rest of the system, and they can have direct hooks into the storage array. This allows for faster access to the data that the machines need and also reduces the load of file traffic on your network.

GFS works by coordinating file locking through a *Device Memory Export Protocol (DMEP)* server, which can be implemented in either software or hardware. DMEP is a protocol providing a global locking space for all nodes involved in a clustered filesystem. When machines are running their own local filesystem or connecting to a share, they are free to do all the locking on files themselves, or relying on the network share server to deal with the locking mechanisms. But with multiple machines sharing the same physical storage, there needs to be some coordination in place to determine who has what access to individual pieces of data. DMEP provides the mechanism to support this. Because it is a relatively new standard, DMEP in hardware is not common yet, but it has been operational in software for a while through a memexpd daemon, which is a software daemon implementation of DMEP. Machines that have access to the drive array coordinate all the interaction with the files in the GFS pool through this server, so it is helpful to have this implemented in hardware for safety and speed. If it is deployed in software, it is highly recommended that a failover server be in place to take over in an emergency. The software implementation requires persistent storage for the locking data. Therefore, the failover machine needs to have direct access to this data so it can carry on the duties of managing the cluster. Because the locking data can be a bottleneck, it is important to make sure that this storage is fast. A solid state drive might be appropriate for this situation.

Under the hood, a lot of coordination is going on to maintain consistency in the drive pool. With GFS, no single machine is the master of the storage space, with the possible exception of a software implementation of the locking daemon. Because of this, each machine needs to be capable of removing any other from the cluster if it fails to respond correctly. To allow this, all machines must constantly ping or perform a heartbeat-like check against the global lock and check each other's locks. If a machine stops talking to the lock and becomes unresponsive, that node must be taken out of the cluster to prevent corruption of the filesystem—the unresponsive machine might have held locks that are no longer valid. Taking the questionable machine out of the loop can be done in many ways, ranging from using hardware to physically cutting the machine's power supply, to disabling it with software methods.

GFS can be very useful in environments where storage is centralized and there is a pressing need for large amounts of file operations that do not place heavy loads on the network. GFS can simplify the management of the SAN because a large portion of the disk array can be handled as one segment rather than doling out small pieces to each individual server. Sharing the filesystem is as helpful as it normally is through conventional methods such as NFS or Samba, although it allows direct physical access to the hardware and saves the overhead usually placed on a file server. The hardware side of the implementation is still catching up, but GFS can make working with centralized filesystems much easier than it has been in the past. As it stands now, a GFS implementation exists for Linux at `http://www.sistina.com/gfs`. It will work; however, management of a GFS cluster will become simpler and faster when the DMEP protocol becomes more prevalent in the underlying hardware, reducing the dependency on a software implementation as with memexpd. As far as SAN support goes, vendors are constantly moving their SAN solutions forward, and you should refer to your vendor for the latest information on Linux support for their SAN products.

LVM

Although the concept of SANs and GFS clusters is usually recommended for most medium and large networks, using GFS or a full-fledged SAN might not be suitable for your needs. Let's look at another way to manage your centralized storage, known as the LVM. The *LVM* is a component that allows for transparent resizing of existing partitions, along with addition, deletion, and other resource allocation of physical storage within the context of a running system. For now, assume that physical management of the disks is taken care of in a centralized manner, whether that is a true SAN or just a central external drive array. Centralizing storage in capable housings is the first step in the process of proper storage management because it usually results in the capability to add and remove storage to the overall system without physically rebooting machines involved, disassembling production hardware, and causing costly downtime. Usually, when storage is dispensed on a per-machine basis, the result is that each machine needs to be physically rebooted to add the new drives as its storage requirements change. With a SAN or a simple drive array, this is generally not the case, so drive capacity can be added and removed at any time. Combined with the LVM's capability to restructure your partitions on the fly, the amount of downtime needed for storage upgrades becomes much less.

Now you have all your storage in front of you. Whether it is physically close or over a Fibre Channel link, it should be viewable as a hardware storage device. The question becomes how to manage it when it comes to allocating partitions, predicting usage, and adding new storage to existing partitions as usage grows. First you'll look at the traditional means of doing so, and then you'll focus on how to use the Logical Volume Manager in the 2.4 kernel to simplify growth.

First, assume that the system in question is running the old 2.2 series of kernels and cannot take advantage of the LVM. In this case, you need to allocate your partitioning scheme carefully; it becomes difficult to move large amounts of data around a production system without scheduling an outage. Assume the following partition scheme:

```
/boot     /dev/sda1     50 megs
swap      /dev/sda2     1 gigabyte
/home     /dev/sda4     12 gigabytes
/         /dev/sda3     26 gigabytes
```

Remember that this is not a recommended layout, by any means—it is simply here as an example. Assume that this takes up all available space on the drive. Over time, the drive fills up, resulting in a full /home partition. At this point, there are a few options: The administrator can add drives or start stealing drive space from the other drives through a set of messy symbolic links so that portions of /home actually live on the root partition. This results in a mess on a per-machine basis. The administrator must keep this setup in mind at all times so that as data is added to some parts of the /home partition, it doesn't endanger the free space that might be needed on the root partition. In a hectic environment with multiple people managing a box, this can spin out of control quickly.

The LVM is the preferred method for handling dynamically growing usage patterns. The LVM creates logical volumes that sit between a regular filesystem and block device, or a set of block devices.

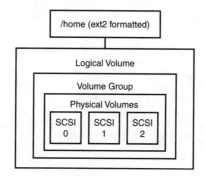

FIGURE 10.1
The structure of a partition using the LVM.

There can be a single drive in the set or multiple ones, depending on need. A volume group might be created at the start with one physical device, and other physical devices might be added as needed. Let's look at the same layout as before, but now assume that the whole drive is managed with the LVM:

```
/boot      /dev/vg00/boot     50 megs
swap           /dev/vg00/swap    1 gigabytes
/home      /dev/vg00/home    12 gigabytes
/          /dev/vg00/root    26 gigabytes
```

Now, as /home grows, the root volume can be shrunk by stealing space from the root partition, without introducing messy spillover. But this is only a minor advantage of the LVM. On a production server, you most likely will be splitting all this over multiple disks. In this case, it might make sense to have /home as its own volume group, while other, more static partitions on the machine share another volume group. This would allow volume management on the machine's local drive set, but /home, which might reside within a separate drive array, can be managed completely independently. These partitions can reside on normal disks, RAID devices, or anything else that the kernel can view as physical storage.

You might be wondering which terms mean what. The LVM contains a lot of names, all of which seem to mean the same thing. Here is a list of the common terms and what they mean, from the highest level in the system to the lowest:

- **Volume group**—This is the highest level in the LVM hierarchy. Logical and physical volumes live inside this group.

- **Logical volume**—It is helpful to compare this to a disk partition on a drive, where the drive is the volume group and the logical volume is the partition. This is what is exposed to the system as a block device for a filesystem. In the previous example, /dev/vg00/boot is a logical volume.

- **Logical extent**—The logical volume is broken into extents, which are used as meters of size and growth of the volume. This is vaguely similar to the blocks present on a disk.

- **Physical volume**—This is normally a hard drive, although it can be anything that the system can mount as a normal storage disk.

- **Physical extent**—This is the physical equivalent of the logical extent described previously.

This might seem confusing, but it's really not that bad. A volume group is made up of logical volumes, just like partitions on a disk. Underneath the logical volume might be a set of physical volumes, which correspond to disks (or anything disk-like). Both the logical and physical volumes have extents, which determine what size chunks will be used to grow the volumes in the future.

Now let's step through a couple of tasks to help ground all this. First, you need to initialize your disk to have the right partition type to be included in an LVM set. Using fdisk, cfdisk, or whatever is handy, set the partition type to be 0x8e. On that partition, you need to run pvcreate as follows:

```
# pvcreate /dev/sdb1
# pvcreate /dev/sdc1
```

See? That wasn't too hard. pvcreate just created the low level physical volumes on the partitions involved, the first partitions on the second and third SCSI drives on the system. Now the drive has a physical volume descriptor at the front of that partition. Now run vgcreate, which creates a volume group over the two disks that have been configured as physical volumes:

```
# vgcreate test_vg /dev/sdb1 /dev/sdc1
```

Here we've created a volume group named "test" with two physical volumes inside of it—the two created with the pvcreate commands previously. The vgextend and vgreduce commands can be used later to add or remove devices related to this group, respectively. At this point, there is a volume group comprised of a couple of physical devices. In the future, though, there might be a need for more devices to be added to the set. vgextend would be used to add this new partition to the set. If there is a need to get drive space over to a full partition, and a device is currently a member of a partition where it's not being used heavily, vgreduce would be used to remove it from the set. You can run vgdisplay to view the contents of the set at this point. The next step is to allocate a logical volume, or partition, on top of the volume group, or drive. The lvcreate command handles this job:

```
# lvcreate -L2000 -ntest_lv test_vg
```

The syntax looks a little strange, but it is creating a logical volume named test_lv of 2GB on top of the volume group we created previously. There should be a file named /dev/test_vg/test_lv now, which is the logical volume that can be formatted and mounted as a filesystem. Some other tools are involved for removing and extending logical volumes, among other things, but this should be enough to demonstrate the concept of building a logical volume.

Now, you might be thinking, what exactly does this get me? The result is still a device that can be formatted, mounted, and so on just like a regular filesystem. You can inject more drive space into the set at any point by adding a drive to the volume set. If you are using a resizable filesystem (like ReiserFS), you can dynamically grow your partition space without even notifying users, let alone trying to schedule an outage to reboot the system or perform tape backups to convert between the old filesystem and the new. Because you can extend logical sets, you can also configure a large set of disks, allocating only a base amount to each filesystem and then growing each partition as needed. This helps ensure that storage usage is more easily watched and that, in an emergency, extra storage can be injected anywhere you need it.

When you create volume sets, they also can be striped, which means that data will alternately be written to different drives in the set. This can yield performance improvements, although it might be better utilized in hardware. A host of other little side benefits also exist, but that covers the large ones. The end result is a much more manageable system, with a much simpler growth-management strategy.

Depending on the age of your distribution, the LVM might not be included by default. If it was based on the 2.2 kernel and you added your own installation of the 2.4 kernel, you will likely need to get the userspace tools by hand or as a package from your vendor.

When it comes to a high-availability machine requiring high amounts of data throughput, the underlying bus system should be considered carefully. With SCSI-2, it might have been worth putting multiple busses on the same machine. With the data rates that SCSI-3 or the next standard brings to the table, however, the card might swamp the PCI subsystem in some situations, although the data rate coming off individual drives isn't enough to do this. Usually, multiple cards are needed only if there is a need for a lot of physical devices.

But as mentioned before, localizing the storage in this manner is not recommended. Running a link to a centralized storage facility is highly preferred because you can centralize your storage, backup, and management. This also centralizes the need for failover systems such as the various RAID levels.

Aside from volume management and location, there are other ways to manage your storage effectively, although most rely on policy rather than the operating system. As with the network, high bandwidth requests should be deferred to off-hours. In addition, it is generally a good idea to watch the drive usage closely because most filesystems experience performance drop-offs as the partition on which they are residing fills up. This depends on your filesystem, but 75% usage is generally a good number to watch for. This can prevent overusage slowdown and can alert you to storage shortages before the situation gets out of control. As you saw with the LVM, recovering from a mostly filled partition is very simple.

Disk I/O Utilization

For most server configurations, SCSI and Fibre Channel are preferred methods of interacting with your storage system. Even when using Fibre Channel, it is usually just a transport method to an array constructed of SCSI drives. In general, SCSI is known for having confusing parameters, depending on what card is used, what speed devices are present on the bus, and so on. In general, there isn't much you can do to the kernel to speed it beyond what you configure in the driver section when setting up the driver. If you have a prebuilt system, specific options might be enabled for speed reasons. If you are rolling your own kernel, be sure to find out what these options are and then apply them to your set of changes. By default, there is little in the kernel build that will help performance, except for making sure that queue debugging is off; this will inject consistency checking code into the SCSI subsystem. Nearly all performance gains will be found by tweaking the module settings for the specific driver in question.

If you need to test the throughput of your card and drives, the standard dd tests apply as described elsewhere in the text. Other tests include these:

- **dt**—This is similar to dd, but it can do a lot more than just copy data. It will test all kinds of SCSI devices for you.

- **lmdd**—This is part of the lmbench suite, which is also recommended in testing your drive systems. lmbench is a suite of benchmarks for various components of your system.

- **sg_dd**—This is part of the SCSI generic suite, which can be used to test various types of SCSI devices. sg_dd is a component of the sg_utils suite, and is similar to the dt program noted previously.

- **sard**—This gives I/O statistics on mounted partitions and other devices. It collects data through a kernel patch that adds more informative statistics to the /proc interface, and it can provide more insight about your system than the normal higher-level tools.

- **bonnie**—This pressures your drive subsystem with various types of tests. It generates statistics on overall results, comparing your hardware with that of other systems.

In some cases, you might need to tune some IDE/UDMA drives. Although the bus isn't as capable as SCSI, these standards have enabled transfer speeds of 33, 66, and 100MBps. However, if any question arises about the capabilities present in the hardware, Linux defaults to the safest setting for the drives it finds. As with nearly anything else in Linux, this can be overridden if you know that the drive is physically capable and that it is safe for the settings to be enabled. You can do this through the hdparm utility. For full details on how to use this utility, check the hdparm man page. Here are a few useful parameters that are generally turned on by users:

- **-d #**—Enables (1) or disables (0) the using_dma flag for the drive. This can greatly improve performance on drives that use UDMA.

- **-a #**—This sets or gets the number of sectors used for read ahead operations. The default is 8, yielding 4KB read aheads, which is good for most operations. Usage tendencies that result in random seeks won't see much of a performance gain from this.

- **-k/-K**—Gets or sets the keep_settings_over_reset and keep_features_over_reset flags for the drive, respectively. Not all drives support this, and they should only be used when you are sure that the settings in place are the right ones for your environment. Another option is to place the configuration of hdparm in an initialization script, if the drive doesn't support these options.

- **-W**—Gets or sets the drive's write-caching setting. This is off by default. If used, keep in mind that it introduces an ambiguity in whether data sent to the disk has been written.

- **-m #**—Sets the sector count for number of sectors that can be transferred during a single interrupt. The default is one sector, but 8 is a common value.

- **-c #**—Enables (1) or disables (0) 32-bit I/O support. A special value of 3 is present to allow special sync sequences, but this is not as common an option as 1, and it might not be safe on your hardware.

- **-u #**—Enables (1) or disables (0) interrupt mask flag for the drive. This allows other interrupts to be unmasked while the drive is handling its interrupt, and it can greatly help responsiveness in general. This should be used with care.

- **-r #**—Enables (1) or disables (0) the read-only flag for the device.

- **-t/-T**—Enables testing of current settings. The -t/-T options should be used around all configuration changes, in order to get a better feel for whether you are on the right track in tuning your disk. You could see improvements in your application during tuning, but the use of these options will make sure that the speed increases are really coming from the disk and not another subsystem.

Remember that when working with these settings, these options are enabling capabilities that might not be properly handled in your hardware. This could result in data loss or loss of drive integrity, which works out to the same problem in the end. That said, here is a commonly used set of options that gives good performance rates without placing your drive at risk. (Again, make sure that your hardware can handle the following options before attempting them.)

```
# hdparm -d 1 -m 8 -u 1 -c1 /dev/hda1
```

You also should make sure that your drive subsystems can handle impairment: If you are running everything off a RAID drive, multiple tests must be run to make sure you can handle any load. Run an I/O test while the drive array is fully operational, and run another while it is missing a drive from the set or is rebuilding. Performance will be degraded, but you still need to be sure that the performance during these times is enough to carry the load. If not, RAID itself won't stop you from having system failure—it will only keep you from doing a restore from tape. Although this represents an improvement over offline backups, it is decidedly not optimal.

Swap Strategies

Although swap space gets a lower priority than the rest of the system, it still requires some planning. If you end up using your swap space aggressively, this is usually indicative of a more general problem of memory starvation. However, the swap space does need to be present to handle unexpectedly high loads.

In some situations, it might be beneficial to have swap on multiple drives, although whether each one is used in a balanced fashion is up in the air. Under heavy load when you are sure to be using large amounts of your swap, you might get a slight bit of performance back.

In general, though, it could be a better idea to add swap on a drive that doesn't get as many system requests. Placing swap on the same drive as your central file-serving directories won't help matters; in fact, it'll probably hurt performance because of the extra drive work. Instead, add the swap to a drive that might house only semi-used data, and on a I/O channel that isn't being heavily used, such as a storage partition that isn't used in general. This way, the extra drive spinning likely won't effect the rest of the system as much.

Using RAID

In most situations, a redundant array of independent (or inexpensive) disks (RAID) will help with both performance and data reliability. Your needs might vary, but, from this selection, you should find a type of RAID that will help you speed your subsystem. This list is noninclusive because some types of RAID never made it to market, but it does cover most of the common types of RAID systems.

- **RAID 0**—Although it's not technically RAID because it is not redundant, RAID 0 stripes data across multiple drives present in a set. By distributing the write (and read) load, drives can provide data to the bus faster because each one is acting independently. If you need speed but not redundancy, this is the path to take. Also make sure to use stripe sizes that are larger than average requested records so that queries can be completed in one request against the set.

- **RAID 1**—This is a simple mirror set. For each drive, there exists one counterpart that has its data constantly updated with the master. In some situations, there can be more than one mirroring drive. Throughput is not as fast, but redundancy is maintained.

- **RAID 5**—This is the most common balance of redundancy and distributed data. In this case, a parity drive exists for the sole purpose of maintaining parity status for the data on other drives in the set. The other two drives have data distributed between them. Although writes can be slower than striping, RAID 5 offers fast reads and can survive the death of a drive in the set. However, this will impact performance. Performance during the rebuild is also degraded, although the rebuild can be done online. Make sure that this degradation of performance is permissible in your environment. If it's handled correctly by either hardware or software, a RAID 5 failure should never cause an interruption in service or a loss of data.

- **RAID 10**—This is a hybrid of RAID 0 and 1; it performs striping across sets of mirrored drives. In this system, sets of drives are set up to be mirrors of each other, and then a stripe set is built across them. This requires more drives to be present because each drive needs to be duplicated. Data availability is very high, and overall interaction, such as reads, writes, and rebuilds, is very good. If RAID 5 doesn't offer quite the right performance during a rebuild and you have the drives to spare, RAID 10 is probably the right choice.

Other types of RAID not mentioned here are RAID 2, 3, 4, 6, 30, and 50, and JBOD (Just a Bunch Of Disks) configurations. These aren't very common, though, and they generally don't offer much more in performance aspects. If none of the options listed fits your needs, however, you might want to check out the other levels. For most uses, if storage is available, RAID 5 and RAID 10 are the most recommended because they provide both good performance and redundancy.

Software RAID

RAID is assumed to be handled by hardware. By abstracting the operations out to hardware, you lift a large load from the system and get less reliance on the operating system. In general, most hardware RAIDs are even resilient to power fluctuations because they can battery-back their operations. Local caches can be controlled on the RAID card, treating the subsystem separate from the rest of the box. In nearly all situations, hardware RAID is preferred.

10

DISK CONFIGURATIONS FOR PERFORMANCE

Occasionally, though, whether due to budget restrictions or a simple lack of options, it might be worthwhile it to implement RAID in software. Linux offers kernel support for RAID levels 0, 1, 4, and 5. Because hardware devices usually abstract many of the details from the user, we will do a short walkthrough of a RAID device configuration, as presented in the RAID HOWTO. Refer to the original document at www.linuxdoc.org for more details on setting up other types of RAID.

Although the RAID code supports sets on either IDE or SCSI, assume here that SCSI is in use. Not only does IDE place limits on bus usage, but it also doesn't handle hot swapping at all. If you need to use IDE for your RAID set, it is just as simple as the SCSI build—but don't expect to be able to hot-swap drives in the case of a drive failure. If you are more interested in data integrity than hot swapping and speed, IDE might serve your purposes well, without raising the cost of the system by more than the inexpensive cost of the IDE drives.

First, you need at least a 2.2 kernel with the RAID patches (a 2.4 kernel is preferred). Decide which type of RAID you want to configure, and build your /etc/raidtab similar to the following configuration for RAID 5:

```
raiddev /dev/md0
    raid-level       5
    nr-raid-disks    7
    nr-spare-disks   0
    persistent-superblock 1
    parity-algorithm         left-symmetric
    chunk-size       32
    device           /dev/sda3
    raid-disk        0
    device           /dev/sdb1
    raid-disk        1
    device           /dev/sdc1
    raid-disk        2
    device           /dev/sdd1
    raid-disk        3
    device           /dev/sde1
    raid-disk        4
    device           /dev/sdf1
    raid-disk        5
    device           /dev/sdg1
    raid-disk        6
```

If you have more than one RAID device on the system, add more raiddev configurations. When you have this configured and the kernel and the userspace tools are ready, run this command:

```
# mkraid /dev/md0
```

This creates the RAID device, as specified in the /etc/raidtab file. Repeat as necessary for any other devices. The drives should be working away at building the set; you can retrieve information about what is going on from /proc/mdstat. Here is the output of a functioning RAID 5 array:

```
# cat /proc/mdstat
Personalities : [raid5]
read_ahead 1024 sectors
md0 : active raid5 sdb1[1] sda1[0] 35760384 blocks level 5, 32k chunk,
➥ algorithm 2 [3/2] [UU_]
unused devices: <none>
```

The mkraid command might take a long time to complete, but, while it is working, the set is functional—it's just not fail-safe. Feel free to start putting a filesystem on it, if you're impatient. Depending on the filesystem used, it might be beneficial to use special format commands to make sure that filesystem data is distributed intelligently across the set. This depends on the chunk size you chose and the filesystem you want to put on top of it. Refer to the HOWTO for more information on this, and feel free to experiment with different values yourself. When things are running smoothly, you can take the set online and offline with the raidstart and raidstop commands. Autodetection is probably also worth configuring; the HOWTO has full details on how to implement this. Essentially, the kernel needs to have autodetection enabled, and the partitions involved in the RAID set need to be set to type 0xFD.

The RAID capability in the kernel previously existed as a set of patches, but it has been integrated into the main kernel tree as of the 2.4 kernel. Depending on the distribution used, you might need to get the userspace tools as specified in the HOWTO. Because the RAID code is now part of the kernel by default, more vendors will most likely start shipping versions of the userspace tools along with the default distribution. The RAID code has been well tested and has been used extensively in the field. Surprisingly, even with a hardware failure while working on the drive set, the software RAID is amazingly resilient. Even so, it is probably worth working through some failure tests. To test integrity in the face of a missing drive, unplug a drive from the set while the power is off. This will give the desired test result but will not endanger your disk. (Depending on the drive housing, dropping a disk on the fly might have no electrical repercussions, either for the drive or for the bus. This we leave up to you.)

Understanding the Limitations of the Bus

Sometimes, no matter what you try to tune, your disk subsystem will remain the bottleneck. This is probably because of the limitations of the SCSI or the IDE bus, and also the physical construction of the drive. It is a well-known fact that drive speeds lag well behind speeds of the rest of the system. Although there have been advances, most likely this will still slow you down if you are unlucky enough to have a disk I/O-bound architecture. Even with numerous advances, IDE still doesn't scale well, it has significant problems handling negotiations on the bus, and it utilizes the host CPU. Although SCSI is much better, it still offers a speed that will cause other parts of the system to block work while waiting for the drives. Firewire is built to handle this kind of problem—it offers 400Mb/sec rates, and was designed to handle the bandwidth requirements of video and other high-demand operations. Although Linux has support for Firewire devices, this bus has never achieved the universal acceptance its creators hoped for; however, it might be worth investigating for your use.

This is not meant to discourage you. It is meant only to point out that, in most situations, the disk system will be the bottleneck. The best you can do is attempt to mitigate that fact.

Alternative Solutions

In some situations, disk optimizations just don't cover the problem, and it's not enough to just sit back and accept the fact that the disk is the bottleneck. Presented here are some different steps you can take in sidestepping the problem of a slow disk.

First, consider looking at a solid-state disk for high-speed work. Solid-state drives are much faster, offering seek times much faster than conventional mechanical drives. With solid state drives, there are no moving parts, so there is no rotational latency, allowing the disk to get data to the bus at speeds much higher than those of normal disks. Although the cost is much higher than that of normal drives and the capacities are usually much lower, moving high-activity data to a solid-state disk can yield large performance gains on operations when the CPU is waiting for large amounts of data from the disk. It is not uncommon for overall system speed to increase by four times when reliance on rotational drives is lessened.

Shifting work directly to a ramdisk also might offer gains. Linux buffers your data in RAM when it can, but, even in this case, it eventually needs to interact with the disk. If you are dealing with volatile data that isn't needed for more than a short period of time, or if you simply want to make sure that a portion of your work never goes to disk, a ramdisk is probably what you need. Remember that the data is volatile, though—after the machine is rebooted, any data that was sitting in that ramdisk is gone for good. Don't store data there that you need over time, unless you set up a job that periodically backs it up to a more permanent storage solution.

Configuring a ramdisk is relatively easy. As of the more recent kernels, ramdisks can grow as needed by stealing pages from the buffer cache and flagging them as being protected. Make sure that your kernel has built-in support for ramdisks, or compile and use insmod to load the ramdisk support as a module (rd.o). First, use dd to move an appropriate amount of data into the ramdisk device; 4M is the starting default size. Then layer a filesystem on top of the device, and mount it. From that point, you can use the mount as a normal filesystem. When you are done, simply unmount it. Remember that the process needs to be done on a per-boot basis. Here's an example:

```
# insmod rd
# dd if=/dev/zero of=/dev/ramdisk bs=1k count=4096
# mkfs -t ext2 /dev/ramdisk
# mount /dev/ramdisk /mnt/ramstories
```

As you can see, this is a very simple process. If your system of managing data can make use of ramdisks, this method is highly recommended. This can be the perfect place to drop data that needs to be manipulated with a set of scripts or pipes because it gives you all the file I/O operations without any of the slowdown.

In general, drive tuning will have the most impact on the overall speed of your system. The downside is that you might not be able to speed operations, short of the alternatives presented in this last section. Tuning your individual SCSI driver or enabling capabilities on your IDE drives can buy you a little more speed, but the physical construction of the average disk will still provide a bottleneck that is difficult to sidestep.

Summary

For the most part, there are two types of bottlenecks. Problems tend to be processor bound or I/O bound. Depending on the problem, it could be feasible to apply more processors or a Beowulf cluster to the problem, where each node handles a small piece of the problem. I/O problems tend to be the hardest to work around, and can cause the most headaches in the process. For some situations, the problem can be alleviated by throwing more hardware at it or tuning. In general, it can be a simple matter of being limited by the technology of the physical drive.

As mentioned, tuning can be effective by making sure that the kernel driver makes good use of the underlying hardware, and the correct options are on to make sure that the kernel is allowing the right commands to be sent to the hardware. If these tuning operations don't quite cut it, other approaches such as ramdisks or solid state drives could be the optimal route. In addition, upgrading your hardware to a more capable bus could be the answer. There is still a possibility that there will be a slowdown to the physical construction of a rotational drive. But, these problems can be mitigated by making sure that all other factors are taken out of the picture, and then making sure that tests run on the drive result in numbers that push the raw throughput of the media.

Linux and Memory Management

It is the systems administrator's job to decide what hardware, if any, a system needs. One aspect of that decision process is memory requirements. Within the realm of performance, the proper application and use of memory is by far one of the most (if not *the* most) important process.

Random Access Memory (RAM) is where system operations, processes, and tasks are stored until called upon by the CPU. The kernel also uses swap space (discussed later in this chapter) as virtual memory in case there is not enough physical memory or for use on a convenience basis.

The first part of this chapter looks at deciding how much RAM is needed for a new system. The second part examines buying additional RAM and also discusses swap space.

Determining Physical RAM Requirements

You can determine how much RAM a system needs in many ways. The Unix industry as a whole has certain places where standard usage information is kept, as do many vendors of both software and hardware products related to Linux. The best way to determine how much RAM is needed is to figure out what type of role the new system will be playing. Most often there are very clear methods of determining the amount of RAM that a system will need, based on its role. This role really revolves around two factors: How many users will be accessing it, and what software will be up and in use? That question then puts the topic into two vague categories:

1. Single-user systems (workstations)
2. Multiuser systems (servers)

Looking at these separately makes things a great deal simpler.

Single-User Systems

Obviously all Linux systems are multiuser systems, but "single-user" in this context means that one physical person is using the system. Now it is quite easy to start figuring out the memory requirements for a single-user system; there is a general step-by-step approach for doing this:

- If the system will be run in console mode and will not be running any services except typical single-user ones, then 16MB to 32MB should be fine.
- If the system requires X Window and the user is comfortable with fvwm or blackbox, then 32MB to 48MB should be enough.
- If the user requires a larger X environment or will be doing graphics manipulation or large-scale programming, a high-end graphics adapter and 64MB to 128MB is recommended.

Linux and Memory Management

CHAPTER 11

213

11

LINUX AND
MEMORY
MANAGEMENT

- If the user requires a test database, test Web servers and other heavy developmental tools and X Window, 128MB+ should be adequate.

These are all just estimations, really. Often the situation might be more complex and would not fit well within this framework. This comes into play more with high-end workstations that might be required to run graphics tools (such as the GIMP). A classic example is that some of the Oracle management clients use Java. A system might be better off with a faster processor rather than tossing memory at it to help render the Java client faster.

The RAM amount usually revolves around central usage; for example, a Linux server running an Oracle database would need enough RAM to contain Oracle's common running processes, while a small workstation that is primarily used for remote management via Telnet or secure shell would require a minimal amount of RAM.

Multiuser Systems

The larger multiuser server environment is a completely different animal. Some Unix power-house systems go well into the range of terabytes of RAM. In any case, the best bet is to always err on the high side. Heavily loaded file-sharing systems that use NFS and SMB services require extra memory for additional overhead, but not as much as you might think. For example, a 100GB file server that services a norm of 20 concurrent users mainly transferring documents would need only about 128MB of RAM or so, but if you pile on print services, the entire formula changes. In this case, with same number of concurrent users doing printing and using a database, it might be wise to move the RAM all the way up to 1GB.

On the flip side, static Web pages on a Web server surprisingly use very little RAM at all. It is quite possible to use 128MB of RAM for static pages that take in, say, 2000 hits per hour. However, if a dynamic engine that generates Web pages on the fly is connected to a database either on the Web server or elsewhere, a rather large hike in RAM will be required, again bouncing into the gigabytes ranges. Of course, the experienced database administrator knows that even 1GB on some systems is trivial compared to the sheer volume of large companies, where terabyte ranges are the norm.

With the ever-growing acceptance and use of Linux in the mainstream computing world, a whole new monster has reared its head: the high-end database server (actually, the high-end anything). Until about 1997 or 1998, Linux was mainly used for low-end systems, the smaller home hobbyist system, or, of course, the nefarious "server in a closet." It is worth noting, how-ever, that when intensely high ranges become the norm, the topic begins to move more into the realm of overall networking and load balancing than pure Linux administration.

RAM Requirements

So how does it all add up? Simple. As an example, a system with the following requirements must be designed:

- NFS server for 10 clients
- SAMBA server for 200 clients
- mSQL
- Apache Web Server
- PHP4

The first step is to think about file server. Earlier in the chapter, you learned that roughly 64MB should be good for up to 20 continuous connections. Following that logic, it is safe to say that around 1GB should service the 210 file-sharing connections just fine, knowing that they will not all be reading and writing concurrently. Next, consider the database server and Web server. With both on the same system and an already pretty high amount of RAM, moving up to 1.5 or 2GB should be fine. Actually, this measurement is pretty accurate for that system (I have one that is almost identical).

Of course, RAM is not a one-size-fits-all item. Plenty of users fall well outside the normal ranges, such as power users, administrators, and home hobbyists, who all seem to have incredibly unique needs. The sysadmin needs to be subjective about designing systems and (whenever possible) pad for emergencies.

Getting Additional RAM

Getting additional RAM is far easier than deciding on RAM for an entirely new system. In most cases, more RAM is being purchased to address a specific need or to enhance something that is already in place (the latter of which is always the best possible scenario). When getting additional RAM, it is easy to know how much is needed—for example, on a system that is "thrashing" or just locking up occasionally, it is probably a good bet that twice the amount of RAM would help. Likewise, if the system is slowing down occasionally and all other appropriate tuning actions have already taken place, then a last resort might be to throw a small increment of RAM at the problem.

After you have ascertained the amount of RAM needed, the next step is to address swap space.

Swap Space

RAM is not the only consideration when you're setting up the memory on a Linux system. Swap space and how it is configured can be immensely important—or not very relevant, depending on the case. Many Unix pundits have used the following "formula" to figure out the amount of swap space needed:

$2 \times RAM$ = swap space

With today's enhanced technology, this can be done with more precision. The idea behind this is that all Unix systems should use $2 \times RAM$. However, Linux systems—as well as many other Unix-like and Unix systems—have advanced to the point at which much less than $2 \times RAM$ can be used for swap space.

Calculating Swap Space

The following is a method for calculating swap space that is popular among Linux systems administrators:

1. Estimate your total memory needs. Consider the largest amount of space that you will need at any given time. Consider what programs will be running at the same time. The easiest way to do this is to set up bogus swap space and load all the programs that will be used at once. Then see how much memory is being used.

2. Add a couple of megabytes in as buffer space for anything that might have been missed.

3. Subtract the amount of physical memory from this total. The amount left over will be the minimum swap requirement.

4. If the total of Step 3 is three times the amount of physical RAM, there will be problems. Consider getting more RAM. This is because most systems run well when the kernel requires up to about twice the amount of RAM for swap space. However, if up to three times of RAM is needed under a normal load, the system is not operating as efficiently as it could.

Obviously, this method scales per user as well. If it shows a system that has no need for swap, make some anyway because the system will use virtual memory on a convenience basis. Most of the time, creating swap areas as big as physical memory or a little lower is sufficient.

Of course, like so many issues, swap space becomes immensely more complex when more software systems are added to the core system. When dealing with extraordinarily large systems, it is better to throw a disproportionate curve than to go strictly by a given formula. As an example, if the previous formula proved that one user uses 6MB every time he is logged in and doing as much as he can at once, that does not mean that 10 users necessarily will equal 64MB. In a case like that, it is always better to sandbag the result up to, say, 72MB.

Assigning Swap Space

After you have decided on the amount of swap space, the next logical step is to create it. Most Linux distributions have the administrator initially assign swap during the installation. The assignment of swap space has three steps:

1. Decide where.

2. Decide how much.

3. Decide whether any priorities should be changed.

On systems that use hardware RAID (RAID5+) or striping, determining where to put swap space is pretty much a moot point. This is because the kernel sees all disks as one. Many first-time users simply set up a swap partition on the first hard drive that the system recognizes. Although this is acceptable, it might not always be the most efficient way to set up swap. As an example, consider a system with three hard drives, all IDE type:

/dev/hda 2GB hard drive

/dev/hdb 8GB hard drive

/dev/hdd 12GB hard drive

On this system, three disks can be utilized for swap. One common approach might be to add a safety net for swap space. So, on /dev/hda1, the expected amount of swap could be set up, and then some additional swap space could be set up on /dev/hdb, /dev/hdd, or both.

If the model of /dev/hda is older than the other two, it might make more sense to put the swap space on a higher-performance disk. You should be trying to evaluate how you should split the load across the disks.

Managing Swap Space

Now that you know the different approaches to setting up swap space, it is time to look at the actual mechanics of swap space. This chapter mentioned earlier that on most Linux distributions, swap space is assigned during the installation. However, if additional RAM has been purchased for a system or the administrator assigned a minimal amount of swap space to suffice until the installation is finished, then some knowledge of how to assign and configure additional swap space is required.

Configuring Swap Space

The swapon and swapoff commands are used to specify devices on which paging and swapping will take place or be disabled, respectively. During bootup, swapon is called from startup scripts to specify the system swap areas. The syntax for swapon is as follows:

```
mkswap -c [ [ device_name ] [ blocksize ] ]
```

The mkswap command comes with several useful options. In the examples shown in this chapter, -c is used to check for bad blocks; it will also print any if it finds some. See the man page on mkswap(8) for more options.

Linux and Memory Management

CHAPTER 11

217

11

LINUX AND
MEMORY
MANAGEMENT

Before a raw device can be used for swap, it must be marked with a utility such as disk druid, fdisk, or the more "primitive" method of using mkswap.

As an example, the device /dev/hda2 with a size of 64MB will be used. To determine the block size of a partition, the fdisk utility can be used with the -1 option. For example, here is the output of fdisk -1 on a system:

```
[root@kerry /root]# fdisk -l


Disk /dev/sda: 255 heads, 63 sectors, 3276 cylinders
Units = cylinders of 16065 * 512 bytes

   Device Boot    Start      End     Blocks   Id  System
/dev/sda1    *        1       64     514048+  83  Linux
/dev/sda2            65     3276   25800390    5  Extended
/dev/sda5            65     2104   16386268+  83  Linux
/dev/sda6          2105     2487    3076416   83  Linux
/dev/sda7          2488     2742    2048256   83  Linux
/dev/sda8          2743     2934    1542208+  83  Linux
/dev/sda9          2935     3062    1028128+  82  Linux swap
```

First use mkswap to create the swap area on /dev/hda2:

```
# mkswap -c /dev/hda2 1024
```

Here, 1024 is the block size. Next, use the swapon command to activate it:

```
swapon [ device_name ]
```

For this example, the command would be as follows:

```
# swapon /dev/hda2
```

To use a swap file, the operation is a little different; it uses the previous example, but with a swap file instead of an entire partition.

Use the dd command to initialize the file. Basically, dd sends an input file to an output file. The bs parameter is the block size, and count is the number of blocks copied:

```
# dd if=/dev/zero of=swapfile bs=1024 count=65536
```

Using /dev/zero, you can effectively "zero out" a file that can be used for swapping. This has the effect of making the file look like a raw partition.

Then use swapon to activate the swap file:

```
# swapon swapfile
```

The swapoff command will deactivate a specified swap device, or all devices, if the -a option is given. Take a look at this example:

```
swapoff /dev/hda2
```

Swap Priorities

To set or alter swap priorities, the swapon command is used with the -p option. Swap priorities are in ascending order—in other words, a higher swap priority number has a higher priority. As an example, three partitions already are set up for swap that need to be activated here:

```
Physical memory: 64MB


    /dev/hda2  64MB REALLY_FAST_HARD_DISK
    /dev/hdb1  32MB A_SLOWER_HARD_DISK
    /dev/hdd1  32MB A_SLOWER_HARD_DISK
```

In this case, the desired result is to give /dev/hda2 the highest swap priority and then give /dev/hdb1 and /dev/hdd1 lower priorities:

```
# mkswap /dev/hda2 1024
# mkswap /dev/hdb1 1024
# mkswap /dev/hdd1 1024
# swapon -p 2 /dev/hda2
# swapon -p 1 /dev/hdb1
# swapon /dev/hdd1
```

Notice that no priority was assigned to /dev/hdd1 because the default priority is 0. In this setup, /dev/hda2 has the highest priority, followed by /dev/hdb1 and finally /dev/hdd1.

The premise for such a configuration is that when the higher-performance disk is exhausted (rather close to exhaustion) the system calls upon the next swap area.

The last step for activating new swap is to make an entry in the file system table, /etc/fstab. Using the previous examples, the entries for the swap partitions look like this:

```
/dev/hda2 none swap 0 0
/dev/hdb1 none swap 0 0
/dev/hdd1 none swap 0 0
```

A swap file would look like this:

```
/path_to_swapfile none swap 0 0
```

Swap Partitions Versus Swap Files

The Linux kernel and distributions are advanced Unix-like systems. One of the more powerful features offered is incredible flexibility. Swap files and partitions are one of these flexible features. Aside from reassigning, reprioritizing, and handling other management aspects of swap partitions is the judicious use of swap files.

Linux and Memory Management

CHAPTER 11

219

11

LINUX AND
MEMORY
MANAGEMENT

There are definite pros and cons to swap files. For example, if a swap file is used on partition that is also used heavily by userland processes, it can obviously interfere with the userland processes.

Swap Files

To simplify the discussion, it is better to look at the pros and cons of each individually. A swap file is more useful on a lower-end system where I/O contention is not of great concern. It is also a good idea (although not necessary) to put a few swap files on different partitions. Swap files do not have a predefined limit unto themselves, so they can easily use up an entire partition. It is important to note (and, yes, this has been known to happen) that creating a partition, mounting it, and then putting one swap file on it and using it for nothing else really defeats the purpose of swap files unless there is a special need (such as a quick test, as mentioned earlier, to figure out how much memory is needed). Otherwise, it makes more sense to simply create a partition for swap.

Another case for the swap file is the "flat install" of a Linux system. Sometimes the person installing a Linux distribution installs everything to one drive and uses a swap file. This practice is discouraged unless it absolutely will not fill up the entire partition. This is because a swap file is actually the swap space, and processes are put into it when needed. It is quite possible to fill up a partition with it.

There is no doubt about what the best use for swap files is: When a system's swap partitions are thrashing, a quick method for stemming the tide of swap usage is to assign a swap file and then attack the real culprit, whatever that might be. Other uses include trying to determine the needs of RAM requirements on a temporary test system.

Swap Partitions

Using swap partitions brings two cons, although they are of little consequence to the seasoned system administrator. First, a swap partition is a little more difficult to set up and manage after installation. Second, a swap partition is finite in regard to the size of the partition it is on: It will not take up additional space, and it is easier measure. However, as noted in the previous section, you can easily play with swap files to help stem swap usage from a swap partition until the problem is solved.

The primary advantage of swap partitions is performance. Because swap partitions are on their own partition and do not have to contend with a filesystem layer and buffers, they tend to work better than swap files. They are directly managed by the memory and virtual memory subsystems of the Linux kernel.

Advanced Topics

This chapter's earlier coverage of the initial estimation of memory was vague (at best) because there is no concrete method for precisely figuring out how much RAM a large system will need. This section readdresses that topic in the context of what a system is doing and where an administrator can get help for figuring out memory requirements.

Industry Guidelines

The first tool at the administrator's disposal is industry and organizational guidelines. Many mid- to high-end application systems such as databases have published documents that an administrator can use to determine how much memory the system will need. Most often these are extreme cases, so they should be properly weighted.

As an example, a database product might have the guidelines shown in Table 11.1 for a Linux system.

TABLE 11.1 Sample Guidelines

Number of Processors	RAM	Swap	CPU	Disk
1	1GB	2GB	1GHz	100GB
2	3GB	7GB	1GHz	100GB

It is quite clear that there is an upward curve, but one thing that is not taken into account with this particular table is the number of concurrent connections. For example, this could be an internal database for a company that has 50 employees, only 20 of whom would ever use this particular database. This also could be the only application on this system. In such a case, it would be safe to say that these estimates are a wee bit on the high side. The exact location of such guidelines are scattered across the Web in user group sites, vendor pages, and application-centric Web sites.

By far the easiest way to figure out the real requirements is to take a set of baseline requirements when the system is under a minimal load and then steadily load it down again using the methods described for memory estimation. A completely different situation arises when a system is already in production. In this case, the best way to estimate possible future needs is to take measurements throughout the day to establish user patterns and then take the appropriate steps. You might find that having certain processes run at certain times stems possible expenses.

Application Effects and Memory Operations

11

Another useful tool for the administrator is to understand how an application uses and manipulates memory. Some applications load a large amount of data into memory all at once. Others are written to use as little memory space as possible. A good example of this is that a particular X Window manager is designed to still be fully functional, but it uses the class capabilities of C++ for software reuse. Thus, it uses memory a bit more efficiently than one of its cousins. Finding nitty-gritty details like this can sometimes be as simple as reading information about the software or as difficult as probing newsgroups and mailing lists. The most common ways to profile how applications use memory are to either watch them, write a script to watch them, or use some of the more advanced monitoring tools mentioned in this book to keep track of the amount of resources they are demanding.

Sometimes application effects on systems are quite apparent. For example, many databases load the management area of the database directly into memory. Obviously, it helps if the host system can actually hold the entire image it needs. Again, normally some sort of documentation can be found with or about the product, to explain how this works in detail. In any case, after the database instance is started, it is pretty easy to tell how much memory it needs just to be able to run, let alone operate, efficiently.

The Crash Test Dummy

In today's new world of commodity hardware, having a test system is no longer such a difficult feat for a system administrator. Any benchmark, no matter how vague, is better than nothing. Being able to acquire and use an older system to size how applications will affect its operation is an important and highly recommended practice. This does not mean that the administrator necessarily has to duplicate the environment on a one-to-one basis; instead, simple proportionate math can do the job for him.

As an example, a new system that will be installed must have optimum flexibility for users when it comes to screen-based editors. This means installing a lot of free editors such as emacs, elvis, vim, nvi, and so on. In this case, there will be 20 developers using the system. The memory requirements then must be capable of running the largest editor with, say, 80 concurrent sessions. Four concurrent emacs sessions per user is probably a good maximum estimate. Then add padding, if possible, just in case!

For simplicity, each emacs session takes up roughly 1MB of RAM. This means that 80MB is a good estimate for memory needs, plus 10MB or so for padding.

Summary

Memory is tricky, but, with patience and some thought, a good administrator can make the best possible use of memory through smart swap assignment and thorough testing. In today's commodity and high-end environments, understanding memory sizing is crucial for systems at every level of the scale.

Linux System Services

A "Typical" `inetd.conf` File

The Linux system runs constant services. These are processes or, in some cases, facilities that are always available and working. As an example, the sendmail service might run in the background in daemon mode to facilitate the movement of mail messages. In some cases, services are facilitated through another process. For example, inetd (the Internet Server) can facilitate a great deal of services such as FTP, Telnet, secure shell, and so on.

A Linux system does not always have to be running a great deal of services. One way to enhance the performance of a Linux system is to shut down services that it does not need. Regardless of the amount of disk space, size of memory, or processor speed that a Linux system has, it will perform better if it is running only the services that are absolutely necessary.

Services are managed and started one of three ways:

1. As an initialization script
2. Via the command line
3. As run levels

An initialization script can be added to /etc/rc.d/rc.local (which is discussed later) and can be called directly. To start a service form the command line (for testing before installing an init script of some sort), the user simple invokes it. For example, this command would be used to test sendmail as the mail user and group:

```
$ sendmail -bd -q30m
```

Finally, an init script is linked to a run-level directory that is called during bootup.

In this chapter, two main aspects of services will be discussed:

1. The Internet Server (inetd)
2. The system rc scripts

It is important to mention at this point that invariably some services will never need to be disabled. Perhaps the most prominent one that comes to mind is syslogd, the logging daemon. The administrator should take extra care when deciding which services to leave running and which ones to disable. If possible, the administrator should test changes or at least warn affected users of possible problems that might arise.

The Internet Server inetd

The Internet Server (also referred to as the Internet "super-server") runs as a daemon and listens for connections to certain ports. The ports are dependent upon the local configuration. When a connection is received, inetd invokes a program to service the connection. In a nutshell, inetd multiplexes all the daemons for which it is configured into a single daemon. This helps ease management and reduce the overall system load. Not all services use inetd; in these cases, the service might be a frequently used service such as a Web server process.

The file that dictates which services will be used and which options for those services exist is /etc/inetd.conf. It has several fields in it. The following is an example of an /etc/inetd.conf file:

```
#
# inetd.conf     This file describes the services that will be available
#          through the INETD TCP/IP super server.  To re-configure
#          the running INETD process, edit this file and then send the
#          INETD process a SIGHUP signal.
#
# Version:     @(#)/etc/inetd.conf    3.10     05/27/93
#
# Authors:     Original taken from BSD UNIX 4.3/TAHOE.
#          Fred N. van Kempen, <waltje@uwalt.nl.mugnet.org>
#
# Modified for Debian Linux by Ian A. Murdock <imurdock@shell.portal.com>
#
# Modified for RHS Linux by Marc Ewing <marc@redhat.com>
#
# <service_name> <sock_type> <proto> <flags> <user> <server_path> <args>
#
# Echo, discard, daytime, and chargen are used primarily for testing.
#
# To re-read this file after changes, just do a 'killall -HUP inetd'
#
#echo    stream   tcp   nowait   root    internal
#echo    dgram    udp   wait     root    internal
#discard    stream   tcp   nowait   root    internal
#discard    dgram    udp   wait     root    internal
#daytime    stream   tcp   nowait   root    internal
#daytime    dgram    udp   wait     root    internal
#chargen    stream   tcp   nowait   root    internal
#chargen    dgram    udp   wait     root    internal
#time    stream   tcp   nowait   root    internal
#time    dgram    udp   wait     root    internal
#
# These are standard services.
#
ftp     stream   tcp   nowait   root    /usr/sbin/tcpd     in.ftpd -l -a
telnet    stream   tcp   nowait   root    /usr/sbin/tcpd     in.telnetd
#
# Shell, login, exec, comsat and talk are BSD protocols.
#
```

```
shell    stream    tcp    nowait    root    /usr/sbin/tcpd    in.rshd
login    stream    tcp    nowait    root    /usr/sbin/tcpd    in.rlogind
#exec    stream    tcp    nowait    root    /usr/sbin/tcpd    in.rexecd
#comsat  dgram     udp    wait      root    /usr/sbin/tcpd    in.comsat
talk     dgram     udp    wait    nobody.tty    /usr/sbin/tcpd    in.talkd
ntalk    dgram     udp    wait    nobody.tty    /usr/sbin/tcpd    in.ntalkd
#dtalk   stream    tcp    wait    nobody.tty    /usr/sbin/tcpd    in.dtalkd
#
# Pop and imap mail services et al
#
#pop-2   stream tcp    nowait root    /usr/sbin/tcpd    ipop2d
#pop-3   stream tcp    nowait root    /usr/sbin/tcpd    ipop3d
#imap    stream tcp    nowait root    /usr/sbin/tcpd    imapd
#
# The Internet UUCP service.
#
#uucp    stream    tcp    nowait    uucp    /usr/sbin/tcpd
/usr/lib/uucp/uucico    -l
#
# Tftp service is provided primarily for booting.  Most sites
# run this only on machines acting as "boot servers." Do not uncomment
# this unless you *need* it.
#
#tftp    dgram    udp    wait    root    /usr/sbin/tcpd    in.tftpd
#bootps  dgram    udp    wait    root    /usr/sbin/tcpd    bootpd
#
# Finger, systat and netstat give out user information that might be
# valuable to potential "system crackers."  Many sites choose to disable
# some or all of these services to improve security.
#
finger    stream    tcp    nowait    nobody    /usr/sbin/tcpd    in.fingerd
#cfinger stream    tcp    nowait    root    /usr/sbin/tcpd    in.cfingerd
#systat    stream    tcp    nowait    guest    /usr/sbin/tcpd    /bin/ps    -
➥auwwx
#netstat    stream    tcp    nowait    guest    /usr/sbin/tcpd    /bin/netstat
➥-f inet
#
# Authentication
#
# identd is run standalone now
#
#auth    stream    tcp    wait    root    /usr/sbin/in.identd in.identd -e -o
#
# End of inetd.conf

linuxconf stream tcp wait root /bin/linuxconf linuxconf --http
#swat       stream    tcp    nowait.400    root /usr/sbin/swat swat
```

Each line is read by the shell, so those with a # in front of them are not in use. To activate a service, simply remove the # from the line.

The following list describes the /etc/inetd.conf file's layout, starting from the left side:

- **Name**—This is the name of the service, as listed in the /etc/services file. The /etc/services file contains mappings of human-readable service names to their numbered ports.
- **Type**—This field contains the socket type information, usually either stram for byte delivery or dgram for packet delivery.
- **Protocol**—This is the name of the protocol used, as listed in /etc/protocols. The /etc/protocols file translates protocol names into numbers.
- **Wait-status**—This field is normally either wait or nowait. Basically, stream types of deliveries are nowait, and packet-based (dgram) ones are usually wait. For wait services, inetd waits for a program to launch before releasing the port; for nowait services, it continues to listen for further connections.
- **User**—This field contains the username under which the process will run.
- **Daemon**—This field is the absolute path pointing to where the server runs.
- **Arguments**—This field holds any arguments that might need to be passed to the service.

TCP Wrappers

The inetd server is a great way to manage Internet services, but it is not very secure. The best way to add security to inetd is to use TCP wrappers or tcpd, written by Wietse Venema. Most Linux distributions already have TCP wrappers installed and set up. Basically, tcpd adds logging and access control to inetd. The logging usually goes into /var/log/secure and logs all connections in a format like this:

```
[service_name[pid]]: connect from [client]
```

Access control is done using two files, /etc/hosts.allow and /etc/hosts.deny, to decide whether to allow a connection from a particular client. It does this using basic pattern-matching rules:

1. If an entry is in /etc/hosts.allow for a client, then allow the connection.
2. If an entry is in /etc/hosts.deny for a client, then do not allow a connection.
3. Otherwise, allow the connection.

The /etc/hosts.allow and /etc/hosts.deny files have the same format and follow general shell script rules (# for comments, \ for multilines, and so on), and they also allow for very complex rule sets. Each access rule has a format like this:

```
[daemons] : [clients] [ option [ : option ... ]]
```

The hostname matching can use a string (as long as it will resolve) and IP address, and can also have the netmask. A netgroup might be used for NIS netgroups.

Finally, the allowable daemon and client fields are as follows:

- **ALL**—This always matches.
- **LOCAL**—This matches any host whose name does not contain a dot.
- **UNKNOWN**—This matches any user whose name is unknown or any host whose host-name or address is not known.
- **KNOWN**—This matches any username that is known or any host for which both the address and hostname are known.
- **PARANOID**—This matches any host whose address and hostname do not match, and it could be indicative of a spoof.

The following is an example:

```
ALL : ALL: ALLOW
```

This will let everyone in. Additionally, the use of DENY and ALLOW at the end of rules can let the sysadmin use only /etc/hosts/allow. The following is an example:

```
ALL : .evil.domain : DENY
ALL : ALL : ALLOW
```

With /etc/inetd.conf configured appropriately for the server's use, it is time to look at rc scripts.

The rc.d Scripts

In addition to services activated within the inet daemon, additional services usually are enabled via rc scripts. On most Linux distributions, these are contained in /etc/rc.d.

The scripts in /etc/rc.d are symbolic links to scripts in /etc/rc.d.init.d. Each service or application is linked from its main script file in /etc/rc.d/init.d to the appropriate run-level directory (for example, /etc/rc0.d/linuxconf). The scripts in /etc/rc.d/init.d can stop, kill, start, or restart a given process. In the run-level subdirectories, each link starts with a *K* or *S*, to kill or start a process, respectively. The following is a set of partial listings from the output of tree -n on a Red Hat Linux system:

```
rc.d
|-- init.d
|    |-- amd
|    |-- anacron
|    |-- apmd
|    |-- arpwatch
```

```
|   |-- atd
|   |-- autofs
|   |-- bootparamd
|   |-- crond
|   |-- dhcpd
|   |-- functions
|   |-- gated
|   |-- gpm
|   |-- halt
|   |-- httpd
.   .   .
|-- rc
|-- rc.local
|-- rc.news
|-- rc.sysinit
|-- rc0.d
|   |-- K00linuxconf -> ../init.d/linuxconf
|   |-- K05innd -> ../init.d/innd
|   |-- K05keytable -> ../init.d/keytable
|   |-- K10pulse -> ../init.d/pulse
|   |-- K10xfs -> ../init.d/xfs
|   |-- K10xntpd -> ../init.d/xntpd
|   |-- K15gpm -> ../init.d/gpm
|   |-- K15httpd -> ../init.d/httpd
|   |-- K15pvmd -> ../init.d/pvmd
|   |-- K20bootparamd -> ../init.d/bootparamd
|   |-- K20isdn -> ../init.d/isdn
|   |-- K20nfs -> ../init.d/nfs
.   .   .
|-- rc1.d
|   |-- K00linuxconf -> ../init.d/linuxconf
|   |-- K05innd -> ../init.d/innd
|   |-- K05keytable -> ../init.d/keytable
|   |-- K10pulse -> ../init.d/pulse
|   |-- K10xfs -> ../init.d/xfs
|   |-- K10xntpd -> ../init.d/xntpd
|   |-- K15gpm -> ../init.d/gpm
.   .   .
|   |-- S00single -> ../init.d/single
|   `-- S20random -> ../init.d/random
.   .   .
.   .   .
```

12

LINUX SYSTEM SERVICES

This is initially confusing, but there is a great deal of logic behind it. Each rc directory with a number in it represents a run level. A run level refers to what stage the system is in—for example, run level 0 is halted and run level 1 is single-user mode. On most Linux distributions, there are 10 defined run levels, two of which are reserved for shutting down the system. The lowest run level for system interaction is run level 1 (also referred to as single-user mode). Run level 2 allows access to multiple users and might have networking services; however, it might not have optional networking services, such as a news server. The default run level for systems not running X Window is 3, and the run level with X Window is 5. To switch run levels, the init command followed by the appropriate run level can be used. For example, to go into single-user mode, you would use this command:

```
# init 1
```

In addition to the rc numbering scheme, each script has a number following either K or S. This number is used to define the order of start and kill processes. For example, S00single will start up before S20random. The reasoning for this is simple: One particular process might have a dependency that must be started first.

It is now easier to see how the run-level directories relate to the state of the system.

Two ways exist to permanently change the state of an init script. One is to simply remove its capability to execute in /etc/rc.d/init.d. The other is to use a front end to manage services. The Linuxconf utility and tksysv, a Control Panel program, can be used as an easy front end to services.

The Role of Other Files in /etc/rc.d

So far, the /etc/rc.d run-level directories and /etc/rc.d/init.d scripts have been covered. There are other files in /etc/rc.d that play a significant role as well, and these vary among distributions.

/etc/rc.d/rc File

This file's job is to start or stop services when a run level has changed. It also can do very rudimentary setup functions that are not in their own rc scripts, such as setting the hostname.

/etc/rc.d/rc.local

This script is executed after all other init scripts. It can be used if the sysadmin does not want to install a full Sys V–style init script.

/etc/rc.d/rc.sysinit

This script is run once at boot time. It performs several critical checks and configuration actions, such as setting the system path and ensuring that the filesystem is all right by running bcheckrc and related tasks.

Starting, Stopping, and Restarting

The system administrator might not know for sure whether a particular process or service is actually required (hopefully this is all ironed out before the system is in production). An easy way to stop, start, or restart a service is to simply invoke the script in /etc/rc.d/init.d directly. The following is an example of stopping and starting dhcpd:

```
# /etc/rc.d/init.d/dhcpd stop
# /etc/rc.d/init.d.dhcpd start
```

A service also might be restarted for changes to take effect. It is important to know how to restart a service because, in most cases, this is the only way to reread the configuration or settings of a service without rebooting. A good example of this might be to alter inetd.conf to allow a service to run:

```
# /etc/rc.d/init.d/inetd restart
```

Summary

One of the easiest ways to enhance performance on a Linux system is to run only the services that are absolutely necessary for the system to accomplish the task that will be (or is being) performed. When this is done, this task is finished.

12

LINUX SYSTEM
SERVICES

Capacity Planning

PART

V

IN THIS PART

13 Thinking About Capacity Planning   235

14 Methods for Capacity Planning   261

Thinking About Capacity Planning

What Is Capacity Planning?

Before diving into the topic of capacity planning, it might be helpful to know exactly what capacity planning is. It is the process of determining a plan of your system's needs, both for the present and for the future. Whether you are building a Web farm, a database cluster, a normal file server, or a transaction system, the capacity of the system in question is nearly as important as whether it works at all. If the system is designed to handle the exact requirements as laid out at the time of construction, be prepared for the system to crash and burn in the real world. If you don't allow for growth in your system, any slight fluctuation in usage could bring the whole thing to a standstill.

Capacity planning means stepping back and looking at all your needs—past, present, and future. Valuable data can be gleaned from growth patterns and previous bottlenecks that the system has faced (not to mention information held in a log book over the previous maintenance periods). If you have a history of ending up with processor bottlenecks, this should give you some clue to what needs must be addressed in detail when planning for the future. If you presently have a running system, it can provide a perfect testbed for usage statistics that can drive your next planning session. Assuming a similar system or an extension of the existing infrastructure, the current layout can show you what works well and what doesn't, along with what components are overworked and which ones are ready for explosive growth. Looking to the future with a view of what requirements are coming and in what areas you would like to grow, you should be able to determine growth rates for various system aspects and plan accordingly.

If you are planning a system from scratch, it is helpful to have domain experts involved in the process. Otherwise, the system's specifications can go horribly awry, resulting in structural problems down the road. In general, this can result in a complete reconstruction of the system, which can be more costly in both development time and cost than simply having that expertise on hand from the start.

When you have past, present, and future data, it might be as simple as plotting some of these values to see exactly what kind of growth pattern you should expect. If it comes down to plotting average memory usage per customer based on database load, it should be a straightforward process of taking a past ratio, a current one, and anticipated future rates and then plotting a growth track. Depending on other changes brought into the system by new products and new technology, the future data points might need to be weighted differently, but at least a target should be decided upon and followed.

In the end, don't assume that capacity planning will solve all your issues. Capacity management is just as important as capacity planning, as time moves on. No matter how much domain expertise you have or how precise your requirements look, shifts will occur. Some of these will be caused by last-minute requirement changes that cannot be avoided. This usually raises the bar of expectations rather than lowering it. To balance this, technology is always shifting; by the time the system is deployed, there might be a new drive standard that enables you to double your workload. Other times there might just be a simple industry shift that wasn't anticipated. For example, planning around a proprietary or custom protocol was the norm years ago, but now many transfers that once required custom transfer mechanisms have started to use open protocols, such as HTTP, extensively. Not all these pitfalls can be seen—some might help, and others hinder. Planning for the future doesn't involve looking into a crystal ball and finding out specifically what should be done in all cases, although that would make many system architects' lives much easier.

Never a Quick Fix

Capacity planning should never be thought of as a Band-Aid solution. If it's done correctly, the need for quick fixes should never enter the equation. Assuming that the system has been artfully specified and that extremely detailed requirements have been defined, there should be no kind of capacity problem or throughput bottleneck in the system, right?

Wrong. Because of forces beyond anyone's control, there will always be some factor that comes into play when the system comes together. Sometimes the network wasn't specified correctly and there is now a slowdown over a certain link. Or, maybe the network was built correctly, but someone has determined that a subcomponent, such as a database replication server, needs to work over the same link, even though that was not planned in the specifications. So now data is traversing that link during times when it should be reserved for other services. The possibility exists that as users start utilizing the system, a feature request is putting increased strain on one of the application servers.

Some of these issues might be simple policy problems that need to be worked out. But in any system, growth will happen. Although some of it can be planned for, some tangential growth spurt will occur in an area that wasn't anticipated. Because these spurts aren't accounted for in the global view of the system's data flow, they can have large repercussions on system operation. Consider the database replication problem mentioned earlier. If users on two physically disparate systems need data replication, a DBA might schedule replication between the sites at certain times of the day. As the userbase grows and needs to see the other end's data with more real-time updates, the frequency of the replication scripts might have to change. If there was data growth over the lifetime of the system, the data being replicated might have grown. Combine larger amounts of data with more frequent replication over what might be a slow link, and you've just introduced a problem that breaks the preferred methods of data flow that the system was built upon.

The point of all this is that when you're responding to these kinds of problems, dropping a quick fix into the mix isn't the solution. In the replication example, to fix the problem, the quick solution might be to upgrade the link between the sites. As a short-term solution, this might be valid. But rather than just double the speed of the leased line, it could be more beneficial to take a step back and ask some questions about what has changed.

First of all, compare how the system works now to how it was specified in the original documents. If the system was to be equally balanced at both sites in the original planning specifications but now business practice has moved most of the activity to one end of the line, it probably makes sense to change the architecture to reflect this. In this case, stopping the replication completely might be the solution. You might need to have the users at the other end of the leased line query a single server at the main office. The repercussions of this could reach different areas and even require some user retraining. However, you'll end up with a more centralized database-management platform and better utilization of the leased line—and this probably will make your users happy.

Making the effort to realign your architecture might take time, but your system is probably better off in terms of growth potential. Without replication happening over the leased line, you don't have nearly the same bandwidth restrictions, and the centralized database has much more potential to grow as a result of this. But you can't expect to be able to make these judgments overnight and deploy the changes the next day. There needs to be a process of stepping back, looking at the problem as a whole, and determining how it can be solved while avoiding any other capacity problems hidden in some of the other solutions. Depending on the problem, there could be a large number of solutions—some of these could be discarded right away, while others might need to be analyzed and possibly prototyped to determine their effectiveness. You could face severe pressure to roll out something quickly, but time needs to be spent making sure that you're taking the right path. When your solution saves three man-months of network management down the line, or saves several million dollars in operating overhead over the system's lifespan because of correct resource planning, you will be comfortable with the knowledge that you didn't just make a bad snap decision.

Having a Global View of Requirements

As you might have guessed, having a full view of your requirements is absolutely necessary. Without requirements of how it will work within the larger whole, all of your work most likely will be fruitless. In the case of a processing cluster, you might have specified enough hardware, configured your software, and found that it suited your needs. As it gets worked in as a component of a larger system, however, your capabilities likely will be woefully inadequate. Knowing what you must build at a local and global level, you can get more detail and the system can be constructed more intelligently, saving trouble down the road. Otherwise, as time goes on and you learn more of the global view, holes will begin to appear in the system's capacity. You can avoid this by knowing all scopes up-front.

A good rule to follow is to always build your components—whether hardware, software, a product, or any combination thereof—in terms of how it will be implemented in the next-largest scope. This relates perfectly to the point of knowing your global scope. Although this generally applies more to software design, it can be just as applicable in this case. If you don't know how the system will be used outside the current scope, there is no reason to believe that it will work at all. If you have details of how it will interact with other systems, you can draw a more concise picture of what exactly the system in question will have to do in terms of internal usage and what interfaces, protocols, and other items it needs to present to everyone involved.

Generally, this applies to code interfaces, but in the system sense, it might mean planning based on a common knowledge of working outside of your group. Consider the case in which you anticipate having database replication requirements in the future, through different groups within the enterprise. If the rest of the enterprise is using Oracle, it might make sense to work that in as a requirement, so as the system moves forward, integration with the rest of the system becomes much easier.

By looking at the global plan, you also can avoid functionality overlap. If all the component systems are architected and developed by individuals who don't understand the bigger picture, application, expertise, hardware, and data redundancy likely will occur across the units. By seeing these overlaps ahead of time from the global perspective, many of these redundancies can be easily avoided. This results in cooperation and consolidation of domain expertise rather than replicated work throughout the components, as well as centralization of hardware and management operations, and cleaner requirements for each component system. Of course, the greatest benefit will most likely come from the large time and money savings from avoiding duplicated work. This redundant work should be avoided at the functional level only—planned redundancy within the system definitely is not to be stripped out if it can be helped. Planned database replication is an example of redundancy that is good—it provides load balancing, failover, and other bonuses. But having two customer databases within the enterprise that operate independently is an example of the type of redundancy that should be eliminated.

A Twofold Approach

Don't assume that doing everything from the 10,000-foot level, or the perspective of the highest levels of management will solve all your problems, though. Again, stealing terms from software development, you need two views of planning: top-down and bottom-up. As in software development, *top-down* refers to the concept of knowing exactly what you want the system to do, from the global perspective. Based on this set of high-level requirements, you can drill down and specify subcomponents that will perform the work you need to do. But also involved in the process is a *bottom-up* approach, in which you take fine details about the lowest-level components of the systems involved and build up subcomponents that will satisfy intermediate requirements. The two approaches converge in the middle.

Although this might sound strange, it works out fairly well, if you consider the repercussions of selecting only one methodology. If you start with a fully top-down approach and specify components only from that angle, you might ignore viable paths that lead you to the appropriate lowest-level components.

Likewise, if you start with only a bottom-up philosophy, you might end up building subcomponents that piece together a high-level architecture that might not have the top-level goals you had in mind. By joining the two, the design should meet somewhere in the middle, between where high-level directives are made and where the rubber hits the road in the server room. Another possibly more important angle of this is that it can yield interesting results that were never anticipated from either end. For example, from the top-down approach, a designer might not consider certain technologies while trying to fulfill his requirements. But someone working with low-level details might come up with some application of new technology that fits into a new midlevel component. This can allow for a new high-level capability that wasn't considered previously.

This might be as simple as joining some new networking technology in an interesting way that forms a bridge between two previously disparate systems. When joined, this offers interesting capabilities for the business as a whole. Doing all the planning for capacity and requirements at the highest level might never have uncovered this angle, and it never would have been seen from the lowest level. By involving both ends of the spectrum, synergies such as these can be found in all sorts of interesting places. A simple example would be in planning a quote alert system. At the highest level, management knows that it wants to hit the existing markets solidly. But, in talking to the low-level tech people, management learns about a new wireless technology that is coming in a year or two, and thus roll those factors into the planned system so that everyone will be ready as the technology arrives. On the other hand, some low-level software people might have been looking at new ways of disseminating some business intelligence level using some new distribution protocol. On hearing about this plan, they learn about a new market that the company is working to capture. As a result, they can plan code to accommodate the upcoming needs.

Grounding Planning Reliability in the Real World

Global planning might not always be perfect, though. As mentioned before, there are always unknowns. Even if you develop as much as you can to fit the global view and still allow for different capacity fluctuations, some factors beyond your control might change. Consider the case in which your business acquires some companies, and all of these new companies' systems are rolled into yours to prevent duplication of effort. Although you might have factored in normal business growth rates, chances are good that the system isn't ready to double or triple its throughput without some serious reorganization. That said, doing everything that you can from the global perspective with growth in mind will result in as resilient a system as you can reasonably expect.

Classic System Requirements

A myriad of different factors might exist in your system, but a few core requirements need to be addressed first. This might sound elementary, but it is a good way to focus your planning process without feeling swamped with all the possibilities. These areas include the processor, memory, drives, the network, and, to a lesser extent, bus subsystems. (They usually go hand in hand with the processor architecture you are using.) Sounds simple, right? It should.

After you have laid out the requirements for these core subsystems, the rest should fall into place more easily. Because so much relies on these parts, after this is solidified, narrowing down the specifics on the types of peripheral systems can become your focus, without being meshed in the cloud of the whole system. This is not to say that the process can be completely taken apart—obviously, if specific requirements call for a set of physical cards on a certain architecture, this must be taken into account when selecting the CPU, the architecture, and the level of expandability on the machine. In general, though, focusing on the core components can simplify the process.

Application-Specific Requirements

When doing capacity planning for a system, hardware is generally considered more important because it is harder to manage from within production. However, you should also consider application requirements very carefully. Whether it is an in-house application or a large application server, the requirements placed on hardware should determine what hardware ultimately is needed.

Aside from being able to list the items on the application's handy list of features, it is always good to know the software inside and out—especially when it comes to how it will behave under the load you are preparing for it. Short of being an expert on it, knowing its real system load as compared to what the vendor promises is advantageous.

Following the application's market is also a good idea. If you know (or can guess) where the application will be in a year or two. Based on trends in the industry, you might want to be able to handle its upcoming capabilities. Something being released down the line might fit in nicely with your application when it hits the street. However, this likely will incur some additional overhead for the system or require a specific type of hardware that you can get today. If you plan ahead for it, when it does come, you'll have the hardware in place. What's more, you will only need to perform a normal software upgrade to take advantage of the new features.

13

In the end, the software drives the need for hardware. Although you can judge hardware needs based on what kind of hardware you are using today, this might not give you the insight to handle the upcoming advances on the software side. You don't want to be blindsided six months after deployment with a software requirement for which you didn't account. The lesson here is that you should be prepared in all aspects of the deployed system.

Actual Versus Potential Needs

In the course of performing capacity planning, it is assumed that planning is done to specify the system while taking into account current plans and future growth potential. Without this process, it can hardly be called capacity planning. But another angle needs to be considered as well: Does the current capacity plan take into account potential needs in addition to what has been determined as actual growth rates?

This almost sounds like the same question, and it can be confusing at first. Let's step back and take a closer look at it to make sure that everything is perfectly clear. Assume that you are tasked with doing capacity planning for a certain system. As mentioned earlier, various factors must be taken into consideration, including previous usage statistics, current needs, and future growth needs. Based on the numbers, you might plan on a system that validly assumes a growth potential of, say, 10% per year in terms of network bandwidth usage, 23% growth in the SAN architecture, and some modest growth in management overhead to compensate for increased usage.

As specified, the system should sustain these growth rates over a period of five years, at which point the system components should be reassessed according to advances in various technology involved. At this point, new technology can be rolled into place to extend the system, most likely at a lower cost than it would take today to outfit everything for 10 years. New software can be injected into the process flow to allow better use of the system. This should be viewed as the process of finding the *actual* needs of the system, as determined by the capacity assessment. The final result takes into account what is perceived to be the actual planned growth of the system. This act of determining actual needs is one aspect of the capacity-planning process.

Now let's look at the other side of the assessment process. This is known as looking for the *potential* growth of the system. Although a 23% annual growth rate in storage might seem valid for actual growth, it could be beneficial to allow other factors involving potential growth to come into play. For most situations, this requires heavy interaction with the company's group of people responsible for business development. These minds most likely will be involved in looking for interesting ways to grow the business, so their input about where the business development is growing can be very important. If the current plan is to merge an existing product with your system or apply your system to a different market, separate capacity planning must be done to take these extra growth rates into account. Because they are not necessarily going to happen, the growth rates should be classified as *potential* rates.

Potentials also need to be figured in when developing a small testing system (both in capacity and possibly component types) that will have to scale by large amounts if it does well in the testing market. In this case, the system's actual growth rate is less of a factor than the potential rate because the system might not need to handle moderate growth well—instead, it should have the capacity to potentially grow by leaps and bounds. The actual growth rate likely will be moderate and easily predictable, whereas the potential growth rate will be large and will assume more architecture work up front.

Each metric's applicability might still be somewhat vague, so let's run through an example of how to apply the two in a situation. Assume that, as a system designer, you are working on a normal, run-of-the-mill Web site that hooks to a transaction server and a database on the back end. When designing the system for deployment, the normal annual growth rate of users is assumed to be 25% (a random number) annually, once word gets out and the initial customer base is in place. This rate is determined from a number of factors, based on other competing products and where the target market is heading over the next few years. To account for this rate, you construct a sufficiently powerful Web server, application server, and database server to handle the eventual load. In discussions with the heads over at business development, however, plans are uncovered to open this product to another group of users. An in-house prototyping project is going on that, if successful, is close to what your system does; this would be rolled into your capability set, which could raise your load significantly.

Suddenly, although your normal growth rate remains the same, your potential growth rate is phenomenally high. How do you prepare for this? You need to change your target on your initial architecture to reflect this new shift in potential. Where you had one Web server, you now might need a load balancer and a failover node to correspond with it. Your single Web server's requirements can now be lowered and distributed across several nodes in the load-balancing pool. Small modifications are needed to scale the transaction system; where you had one database, it now makes sense to install a parallel cluster, resulting in two machines where there previously was one.

Now, for the slight hike in pricing, your previous architecture can load-balance an arbitrary number of servers, and your database system is much more scalable. In the end, the cost might not be that different, but your capacity for *potential* growth has gone through the roof.

The lesson to be learned here is that both methods need to be applied, and risks between the two need to be assessed up front. If you absolutely must build for potential growth, take those factors into account. But if those risks are too high for your environment and the focus should instead be on actual growth, that path might be more important. Some combination of the two is probably beneficial, allowing for normal actual growth and maximizing your preparation for a large jump in potential. As applied to this example, a good intermediate solution might be to apply the database cluster, maximizing growth there because it would be most disruptive to deploy after the system has gone to production, compared to a load-balanced Web cluster. Find the right trade off for your environment, and apply what makes sense for your future needs.

Pay Attention to Requirements and Administrators

The technical details of specifying and building a system often are left up to systems administrators. They have the technical expertise needed to build everything with the right components and to choose what technology to fit where. The flaw in this process is that, for the most part, this process is not integrated with those who need the system in the end, and some of the requirements might not make it to the designers. In a perfect world, a requirements document would be constructed by people who are laying out the high-level system architecture. This then would be given to the system administrators to plan individual component usage and build. Unfortunately, this rarely works well in practice.

In the real world, extensive communication must occur between those doing the high-level planning and those implementing the details of the solution. Refer back to the sections "Having a Global View of Requirements" and "A Twofold Approach" for more information on how this applies. In addition to making sure that the right fit is found for all technologies involved, this process also ensures that requirements specifications are fully comprehended at all levels of the operation.

Otherwise, system administrators might get some requirements documentation and apply it without a global understanding of all the issues at hand. The people in the server room are just as important to the success of the business as those at the higher levels, and they need to be fully briefed on the needs of the system. The best system administrator in the world doing capacity planning without requirements knowledge might just as well be replaced with anyone off the street.

To make sure that this point is clear, let's go back to the example from the section on "Actual Versus Potential Needs" in relation to capability planning. Without interacting with the people in business development, the system administration team might have no idea what is in store for them down the road. The potential needs might not have been explicitly addressed in the requirements document. This results in what is basically a large communication gap within the business organization.

The important part of this process is that communication needs to take place among all involved parties—and even parties who might *possibly* be affected. As the communication takes place, needs will be assessed at all levels, yielding several benefits: All angles of expertise are applied to the problem in all affected areas of the business, the pending capacity needs are fleshed out, and the right technology is used for the job. This communication is the most effective means of ensuring success across the board.

Structured Approaches

An emerging product, such as a prototyping effort or a market possibility, always involves a certain number of unknowns. Good system capacity planning depends on having good knowledge of your domain and targets, so this can present a problem.

When possible, the unknowns involved in planning should be mitigated. In theory, any unknown can have disastrous consequences on what was considered to be a solid capacity plan. Adding several unknowns to the mix, with various interactions among them, can turn any system resource-planning process into a useless exercise. If an emerging system is being constructed, assumptions need to be placed on the process at some point.

Market unknowns might prompt a need to build this to handle 5,000 users a day according to the naysayers, or maybe 75,000, if the optimists are correct. In the end, some kind of agreement must be reached on where the right range is, and that number should be used as a baseline. Realistic estimates must be made across the board, and research must be performed to make sure that this range is as tight as possible.

This amount of research needs to go into normal system capacity planning, too, not just areas where there are definite unknowns. If the project is well known and domain expertise is present, a structured approach is much easier to take.

Depending on the scale of the system, different approaches might apply. If this is a prototyping effort, a looser set of restrictions can be placed on the design process because the primary focus is the concept. For most other projects that are considered in this text, though, a formal process needs to be put in place to make sure that everyone involved offers input on the system and also gets to review the contents of the capacity plan. Organizational systems within companies vary widely, but the process should follow the same steps for the most part, just acted on by different groups depending on the environment.

If possible, capacity planning should be approached as a normal system, from an organizational perspective. This implies specifications of the systems in question, the need for change, the approach recommended, and the rationale for the chosen path. Inside a normal business process flow, this should be reviewed by all parties involved, with comments being collected and discussed until the needs of every party are satisfied.

This might sound too formal for most uses, but why else would it be called a structured approach? In reality, it doesn't have to be performed in council-style round-table discussions, as long as everyone involved gets their voices heard and their needs addressed. By reviewing, modifying, and re-reviewing the proposals, more experts can take a look at the system. Flaws in assumptions about growth patterns and plans of attack can be addressed from all angles and fixed before the planning process goes down the wrong road. The industry shifts, and there needs to be some effort in keeping up with newer trends. For Linux trends, refer to the chapter on "Where to Go From Here," but for developments related to your specific environment, make sure to keep up-to-date with your vendors and the relevant areas of the industry. This structured approach ultimately will result in a well-thought-out plan for future growth, and the system involved will show it.

Thinking Outside the Box

As a side effect of the multifaceted review process proposed in the previous section, many of the parties involved will be forced to consider options outside their normal problem domain. Making sure that people don't get themselves in a closed set of choices is always a good idea. This is especially true in technology, when paradigms shift all the time and thinking the same way invariably leads to outdated, troubled solutions.

Cross-pollination is a good means of enforcing this kind of behavior, as described in the other sections. Having tech leads interact with business leads will help both sides understand the other's targets with greater detail, and this can open new opportunities. A technical person's explanation of a new piece of hardware to someone on the business side could spark an idea for a new business application. Likewise, a businessperson's explanation of where the current markets are heading can give the technical team a heads-up on what the next capability targets might be. External groups, such as consultancies, while not always appropriate, can provide a good source of different ideas. Regardless of the source, the exchange of ideas causes the other side to evaluate how things are done and forces them to think about things in a new light.

New technologies are appearing all the time, and keeping up-to-date with them can introduce new ways of getting work done in your system. Whether it is a new networking protocol or a new component architecture, it can have a profound impact on the operation of your system, if it is found to have an application. Even if the technologies aren't directly used, they can be helpful in maintaining a clear perspective of where the market is going, and they could inspire an idea for a related branch that might itself have an effect.

Any type of standard thought process must be questioned to make sure that all avenues are considered and sufficiently explored. If there is any aspect of the capability planning process that is taken for granted, it must be taken out, ripped apart, and replaced with a new perspective. In this arena where things move at an absurd rate, there is no time to allow in-grained assumptions to cloud the thought process involved in considering all options.

Let's look at an example. When building or expanding a system, it is easy to assume that a certain type of hardware is sufficient for a given task. Consider the case of building a medium-range database server that needs to handle, say, 50 simultaneous users with 100GB of data, using some fairly simple SQL queries and with a 10% annual growth rate. If you have built database servers before, you probably already have at least an inkling of something in mind to handle this load. Even without the numbers, if the system in question was something simple, such as a "medium-range database server," you still would have come to nearly the same conclusion, with some alterations made to the physical hardware. This is exactly what shouldn't be happening. Rather than just defaulting back to what has been done before, the planning process must question everything. (Note that this is not meant to write off previous experience as detrimental—it is some of the most valuable information you have at your disposal.)

In this case, though, you might want to jump up to more expensive hardware. As the potential growth rates and possibilities are analyzed, a more expensive hardware solution will be less expensive in the long haul. Over time, the higher-end hardware will most likely involve lower maintenance costs and will be capable of handling a higher load. Compare this to a lighter solution that is less expensive up front. As the system grows, major costs might be incurred while trying to scale it up. This is due to outages experienced during redundancy insertions, code that must be updated to utilize the new hardware, and so on. In addition is the valuable employee's time wasted while you spend months trying to update an existing system when you could have been pursuing new goals.

This is just one example of making sure that you see everything in a fresh light. Whether it is hardware choices, software technology, or development mentalities, everything affects the growth of the system. The lack of these fresh perspectives can lead to a capability plan that heads down the wrong path. By including these fresh perspectives, new capabilities will start to become apparent throughout the entire system.

The Interrelationship of Performance Tuning and Capacity Planning

Proper planning and tuning are definitely connected. Although it always makes sense to tune your applications carefully, the need for this might not occur if the system has enough extra capacity planned into the architecture. A balance between the two should be found, resulting in a healthy balance between solid usage of hardware and software. If enough detail is present, it is a good idea to build specific tuning points into the capacity plan. Over time, the plan will attempt to predict the points at which hardware will become overloaded and tuning should become a factor. By doing this and watching growth rates as system usage rises, you can keep cost analysis in mind when deciding when is a good time to tune and when it is a cheaper matter of making changes to the hardware.

Planning May Preempt the Need for Tuning

Given a large amount of extra capacity, there might not be an immediate need for application or operating system tuning. Assuming large growth potentials, it could be a long time before tuning enters the picture. In some ways, this is a necessary evil. This is not to say that you can build a system and assume that you don't have to touch it for the next two years. It simply means that tuning shouldn't be as much of a priority at the beginning as it should as time moves on. If tuning needs to be done from day one to make the system operate accordingly, this indicates a system that will not scale well over time. If the system was built to withstand normal growth rates for years, tuning should not enter the picture immediately unless there is a huge unexpected explosion in usage. This indicates that the system was improperly planned or that the general market changed directions faster than anticipated. (Although this is stressful, it isn't such a bad thing.)

Fortunately, hardware is inexpensive these days, and it is fairly easy to build a system that can safely scale to at least intermediate levels. Given standard low-cost Intel hardware, most systems can be built to handle relatively high loads, which can buy enough time to deploy a more capable infrastructure in the face of the suddenly rising demand.

In general, though, if things go along at about the rate planned, don't expect tuning to enter the picture significantly until at least the second half of the expected lifetime of the system's current incarnation. When this happens, a blend of tuning and hardware upgrades should be adopted—hardware might have advanced and general tuning has already been performed.

Because hardware is relatively inexpensive, it is usually preferred to heavy tuning. Upgrading a drive array or the memory in a server likely will be cheaper than paying several employees to spend weeks of company time looking for bottlenecks and chasing minor speed gains. Only at the tail end of the system's life should heavy tuning be adopted, when the cost of deploying new hardware in scale becomes more expensive than having employees or experts come in and tune operations.

In general, because continued growth is usually expected, the time bought can be used to begin preparations for deploying major upgrades to the infrastructure. If the system is reaching the end of its life span or there is no growth potential for it in the future, then software tuning is recommended. When the performance is brought back up to par, the system can be considered perpetually stable in most respects.

Predictive Analysis Versus Actual Results

If your system was carefully planned, it should have room to grow. As time goes on, though, constant checks on its health must be performed to see whether the plans put in place are valid and whether the growth rate is on track. When you're figuring the growth plan for the system, past data points should be taken into account. As time goes on, the new data points should always be merged into the various sets of data reflecting system usage over time. If this curve is moving ahead of schedule, hardware upgrades or tuning might need to be done sooner than planned.

Constantly plotting usage trends can save a lot of heartache. If the system's memory usage is rising ahead of schedule because of new user load, predicting the point where this turns into heavy swap usage allows you to take evasive action. This could be simple tuning, memory upgrades, or maybe the addition of a spare machine to the cluster.

It is very important to remember that capacity planning does not involve predicting usage, building a system, deploying it, and then waiting until the scheduled time when the system should need upgrades to start looking at usage patterns. It cannot be said often enough that although usage patterns can follow a predictable pattern, they also can spin out of control in a fairly short amount of time. By constantly monitoring all aspects of system use, you will be the first to know about new trends on the system instead of finding out through angry users.

Actual results of system monitoring, not the predictive results from a year ago are what drives the upgrade path. As much as you would like to deploy systems and forget about them, if you suddenly have an increase in usage by several thousand percent, you need to see that curve coming and deploy fixes before it finishes growing. Hopefully, scalability was built into the capacity plan, so simple upgrades will be all that is needed.

The Never-Ending Need for Data

You probably spend much of your time awash in a sea of data, trying to make sense of it all—and all that the systems seem to do is give you more to think about. But when your task is to determine the usage path of a system path over time and to plan its future extensibility, there is no such thing as too much data. Any bit of data that you can extract from the system to give insight on what should drive the capacity-planning process is invaluable.

Quality Versus Quantity

Generating massive amounts of data is easy to do. Set up your SNMP polling device to check the status of every machine's entire SNMP tree (which provides large amounts of system statistics), once every minute, around the clock. Or, set top to update processor status every tenth of a second. Chances are good, though, that most of this data is useless to you. To avoid drowning in your data, make sure that you collect exactly what you need. Tracking some peripheral data could be helpful, but to be truly effective, focus your needs on a central group of data points that most accurately describe the status of your machine.

But what exactly do you want to watch? There should be a few obvious things: Processor status, memory, swap, I/O status on the drive subsystems, and network statistics such as transmission and error rates should round out most of the biggest indicators. Beyond that, individual statistics that matter to your system might vary widely. Sometimes individual network card rates can indicate problems. If you have multiple cards in your system and one seems to be getting much heavier use when the two should be balanced, those numbers need to be tracked.

If your specific application supports external statistic polling, values present there should be tracked to make sure that it is behaving correctly under the load.

In the end, though, it all depends on finding the data that you need to watch and making sure that it is collected at a useful interval for your environment. This might vary over time, depending on shifts in load types, but as long as you keep a good handle on the basic set of statistics and the specific extra set in which you are interested, usage patterns on the system should rarely spin out of control.

Ways of Gathering Relevant Data

If you need to gather data, there are a number of methods to do so, ranging from standard means to hacks. By far the most common method is SNMP: It is flexible, and different vendors hook into it for application-specific data. If you are serious about getting true statistics from your systems, SNMP is probably what you are looking for.

You might not be interested in data directly from the systems, but instead have metadata about the overall architecture. In this case, methods range from pings around the network to port checkers and the like. Most of this information can also be retrieved through SNMP, by hooking to various data points or by judging outages by holes in your data gatherings.

For live data, the standard monitoring apps will probably do the trick. Refer to "Methods for Capacity Planning" for information on what applications are used to collect data. These can monitor most data you are looking for, or you can have a script poke at various components for you and report statistics back. This watches only transient data points, though, so it generally is not recommended. Also keep in mind that the process of tracking statistics imposes a skew in the system itself—due to the Heisenberg Principle—because by causing activity on the system to retrieve statistics, you are causing extra work for the system. In the case of SNMP, you are causing the kernel to handle the extra network interrupts and stack work to handle the request, and process overhead to handle the request in the SNMP daemon. In addition is the work involved in getting the statistics themselves. In general, this should be a light operation, but it is important to figure on the fact that you might be skewing the system slightly by monitoring it.

If you need to look at a particular application's status but you cannot get to it through SNMP or other standards, there are probably other methods of hooking into it for usage data. Most applications of significant size have their own monitoring applications to keep tabs on the process's health. The downside of this is that, depending on how the data is collected, it might not be integrated easily into a collection facility. This is why SNMP access is favored, but sometimes native data generated by the application is the only route available.

Sometimes you have to break down and do some work yourself to collect the data you need, through custom code or scripts. If you can't get memory usage data any other way, you could set up a cron job that collects the data from vmstat and saves it in a file. This is done by using a simple script that runs vmstat for a couple rounds and redirects the output to a file, along with the date of the capture. Another script could parse this data and inject it into a collection facility such as a database or a spreadsheet for analysis. Although this is a strange example—and definitely is not recommended—these situations do occur and sometimes call for inventive solutions.

Data Storage: When Enough Is Enough

You've been saving processor usage data at three-minute intervals since 1997 and recording swap usage rates since early 1998. How much is enough?

Usually, most of this can be discarded. Overall statistics for the period should be kept as is relevant, but after a time, granular data to this degree is simply overkill. When doing capacity planning, you need to be able to plot statistics of given types over time. Over larger time frames, however, most of these values can be rolled into averages, mins, maxes, standard deviations, and the like. From those data points, enough data can be determined to plug something into the graph for that time range.

If your architecture has completely changed, some of the data might not even be relevant anymore. Although this does not mean that you should immediately throw it out, it does mean that you can take it offline without worrying too much. If you are planning a new system based on a purely Fiber Channel storage interconnect, having usage statistics from a semi-equivalent system from several years ago that was running an old narrow SCSI drive set won't help you much—it will probably only confuse issues.

Likewise, if your system capabilities are completely different now than in the previous iteration, comparing throughput rates on the new and old could be like comparing apples and oranges. There's simply no value in it. In this case, too, the data can be taken offline.

Usage statistics should be kept online and figured into prediction models only when the data present in the statistics is from a system of similar capabilities for what you are planning—or at least one that shares some attributes. If you are working on planning a Web farm and you have some statistics around on the last iteration of Web usage and bandwidth rates on the company's other project, this data should be factored in. If there is crossover, keep it. Otherwise, get it out of the picture so that you can focus on the problem at hand. The timeframe for this is entirely subjective, but choose something reasonable for your needs. If your system has a lifecycle of 10 years with upgrades only every two years, it would make sense to clean up every couple of years. With a more dynamic system, where components are upgraded every six months, it would probably make more sense to take invalid data out more often.

Tuning the Data Collection Process

As collection goes on, you might find yourself adding more statistics to the mix, and more data might need to be polled from the servers involved. This can spin out of control if it's not watched carefully. By interacting with the system in the slightest bit, you are affecting its load. If you have too much data being polled from it over extremely short intervals, you could be affecting server performance by extracting performance data from it.

Care should be taken to make sure that relevant data is polled only as needed. Processor statistics might need to be checked fairly often, but having multiple administrators run instances of top with quick updates will cause unnecessary context swaps on a machine that might already be under heavy load. A better solution would be to have a remote machine poll every few minutes and then display the results externally to the server in question. (Admittedly, this might not be possible in all situations. If local, application generated data is the only way to get data, this obviously needs to be taken into account.) Also, for disk usage statistics, unless the system is very dynamic, these statistics can be polled over a much longer interval. This can vary from a few times a day to a couple of times a week—and still provide the data you need to keep your capacity plan in check. Having a remote process walk the entire SNMP tree as fast as it can will generate more data for you, but the results might not be reliable because of the load. The payoff for increased data granularity simply doesn't balance out for the cost of retrieving it.

Another factor to take into account is the network. In a large environment, the preferred method of management is SNMP. Pulling all the available SNMP data over the network for every machine present probably will induce undue strain on the network. Although SNMP is fairly light and it could be worse, if you are highly dependent on getting every bit out of your network, this could be a detriment to your overall system performance. One solution is to deploy a management network that can bypass the production systems. This is referred to as being out of band, as it exists beside your normal operating network. Think of it as a big brother network that lives alongside the normal network, and only exists for management operations. This network could be more easily used for a variety of tasks, from normal SNMP monitoring to custom in-house code, to commercial applications such as BMC's Patrol. Refer to Chapter 14, "Methods for Capacity Planning," for more applications. Another solution is to make sure that you are pulling only the data you need at the granularity you need. In the latter case, your impact on the network should be minimal, but it would be helpful to make sure that no systems are impacted by the overhead.

Aside from incurred overhead, you might need to tune your collection process down over time because you are collecting more data than you need. By simplifying the data that you have to wade through to get usage statistics, the picture of the system's health should become clear. Or, you might have found another piece of data that provides a good metric about a certain aspect of your application, and you need to add that to your dataset. Either way, it is always a good idea to keep tabs on your collection process to make sure that you are getting the most accurate image of your system possible.

How to Evaluate Your Need for Capacity Planning

Depending on your size, different approaches to planning exist. Some ideas are fairly simple to identify. If the company includes approximately 10 people and is looking to grow to 20, there's probably no need for a load-balanced system consisting of machines that all have at least eight CPUs for internal use. At the other end, with 10,000 employees, don't plan on centralizing the human resources systems on a single low-end Intel machine and hope to be in business long. Look at what you need, within reason, and look how at far you realistically expect to grow. Even if seeing far down the road at this point is difficult, some ranges should be visible based on the numbers you have.

Large Enterprise

If you are a member of a large enterprise, you need to put a great deal of thought into your capacity plan. This is not to say that you don't have to think about planning if you're in a small group, but, with a large deployed system, many more architectural issues need to be clearly thought out and implemented. It's true here that the larger they are, the harder they fall. When you're deploying a large system with a high cost, not thinking things through correctly up front can have a much larger impact than when deploying on a small scale.

Let's take a step back and consider the factors that need to be addressed within a large organization. Each one of these can have large ramifications for your deployed architecture, so they all need to be attended to in detail.

Scalability

Whether it is an internal system or a project that will be open to the world, it most likely needs to scale heavily, possibly over a short period of time. If it is an internal system, it probably needs to scale immediately to the size of the company at inception. You need to plan for the company's expected growth rate when looking at the capacity plan for the system over time. If it is for an external system for customers, you might be developing for an already large established user base.

Assume that your company has some large corporate partners and customers who tend to have a lot of crossover within your product line. If you are looking to deploy a new system, starting small and assuming normal growth rates is probably not a good idea because you might have a large influx of customers right from the start. This might load your system to its capacity within weeks rather than years. All architecture plans essentially need to scale well in capacity, but, in a large environment, that growth curve could be accelerated or could start from a higher value.

Group Crossover

It is very important within a large organization to use talent that you already have in-house. There is no reason to reinvent the wheel when another group has already done 90% of the research that you need to get the job done. By using this talent, you can plan your project more efficiently—and the end result is a system that is much less likely to have architecture problems down the road. Rather than bringing in outside expertise for an extra cost, who might not completely know your business, internal crossover can mitigate many risks while at the same time cross-pollinating ideas within the organization. This could lead to interesting possibilities down the road.

Another factor in group crossover is prevention of duplicated work. As described previously in the section "Having a Global View of Requirements," it is very important to avoid functionality overlap when possible. This is a waste of management resources within the organization, it wastes research and development time in building and planning the system, and it wastes large amounts of hardware resources. For an external project, it might even make life more difficult for the customer.

Consider the simple case of customer information replication. If you have multiple product lines but customers tend to be involved in multiple products, it would be a good idea to centralize your customer data into a single database. Although this component needs to keep in mind the various products using it, capacity planning for the customer data can be segmented off for the most part and can be managed individually. This saves the trouble of having customer-management capabilities worked into every product in your line, causing extra work for both you and the customer.

Architecture

If you are a member of a large organization, more options might be open to you when it comes to vendor support and available architectures. Because you will most likely be building larger systems, it is probably in your best interest to take advantage of these corporate partnerships. If the same system was being built by a smaller outfit without the same resources available, that company would have to take different approaches when scaling different portions of the system.

In a larger organization, operations tend to move more slowly, but you have partnerships that the smaller outfits might not be privy to. Smaller businesses can get vendor support too, although it is generally a very different class of support, given the difference in available funds. Whether it is simply a more powerful architecture or a deal that allows massive discounts on large volumes, taking advantage of the options available can result in a system that is much more scalable and more likely to fulfill your capacity needs over a longer period of time.

Overall, when you are involved in a larger organization, factors are, for the most part, good with respect to capacity planning. Vendor relationships might be useful, in-house expertise likely will be available, and your system target usage ranges are probably more well known. As long as sufficient research is done within the company to ensure that work duplication isn't occurring, constructing a good capacity plan should be feasible. The smaller the number of unknowns is, the more likely accurate predictions can be made. In general, larger organizations are more stable, making your job that much easier.

Medium Business

In a medium-size business, capacity planning might involve a little more work than in a large enterprise to be effective. More unknowns might exist, you might have a smaller user base to start from, and you might have a staff with less expertise. However, you might have more flexibility in possible approaches to the problem. In the previous section, it sounded as if working within a large corporate structure is always perfect—in reality, though, it might not be. As far as capacity planning goes, a large organization does have a lot of advantages, but don't feel that all is lost if you are in a medium-size business. What follows are factors involved in medium-sized businesses.

Determining Actual and Potential Growth of a Smaller Base

As mentioned, you might start out with a smaller user base than in a large corporation, which can directly effect system architecture and planned growth rate. In a large business in which a system might start out with thousands of users, yours might begin with a couple hundred or less. In this case, extensive research must look at possible impacts of the system outside the normal customer base. Careful consideration needs to be done to balance the possibilities between actual capacity growth and the potential from a possible influx of new users.

If you build the system according to the normal growth rate with an average customer base for your business and the product takes off immensely, your system capacity will be met in short order. Constructing the system with extra costs and hardware potential to handle a possible large audience might be appropriate for your model, depending on the amount of risk that is appropriate for the situation. In a medium-sized business, there is a better chance of there being a larger fund base to build a more capable system moving forward. Although these factors are not necessarily as clear-cut as in a larger outfit, they should be relatively predictable, given enough market research.

Cost

Cost is an obvious factor. Larger businesses have more money to devote to planning and deployment for a system. In a medium-sized business, some of these relationships might not be open to you. However, many vendors have specific groups and models for dealing with businesses of your size, which should help your cause.

Cost also can be a factor in terms of just being able to accept the risk of developing a new product and system. With your business's size, you might not have a lot of spare resources to put together a large, infinitely scalable system with all the latest hardware. Assuming a lot of growth can indicate up-front needs for large-capacity servers, networks, and other components. Building a system today that can scale to any potential need three years down the road might not be feasible within your company's financial model. This fact needs to be taken into account to find the right balance between appropriate use of existing funds and acceptable levels of growth potential in the future.

Current Business Models and Focus

Besides cost, when working in a smaller environment, you need to make sure that the system fits your current business model. If you have a specific set of business needs, like most smaller businesses focus on, the system's similarities with other products in place probably need to be fairly close. If the system lies outside the core set of capabilities, there might be a larger risk factor involved that can directly impact the amount of money injected into capacity planning for the future.

Even if the system is within the core competencies of the business, large-scale capacity planning might incur too much overhead for the business to handle up front, and a smaller scale might need to be adopted. In general, a great deal of thought must go into the system, to determine whether the risks involved in doing a large-scale capacity projection are worth the risks to the current cash flow. You also should determine whether scaling down the projection model likely will incur significant growth problems down the road.

For many medium-size businesses that have a core focus, new development and capacity planning could involve areas in which the normal groups don't have expertise. In most of these cases, this need must be recognized and external expertise must be brought in to help with the planning process. Without a clear understanding of what might be involved, a capacity plan is worthless. But by making sure that the right talent reviews the process and that possible bottlenecks are avoided, a capacity plan can be constructed to safely move the system onward under future growth patterns. Failing to take everything into account can be disastrous, and this fact cannot be repeated enough.

Overall, capacity planning can be safely done within a medium-size business without much more risk than in a large enterprise. Although cost risks can be more destructive in this size business than in a large environment (because the customer base might be more predicted than existing), the business should still have a core competency used to apply domain-specific knowledge to the problem at hand. Then they should construct reliable models about how the system's capacity should be tested in the future. Any further unknowns, such as a lack of in-house expertise in a new software technology, can be mitigated so that the impact on the capacity plan is absolutely minimal.

Small Technical Outfits

Capacity planning within a small outfit can take many forms, and it's hardly ever as nicely projectable as it is within a large stable environment. This is not to say that all small businesses are unstable and are completely incapable of capacity planning—it's much more difficult to do, though. Listed here are some factors to take into careful consideration when planning your capacity.

Domain Expertise

In a small business, there might be significant gaps in the amount of domain knowledge needed to correctly plan, build, and deploy the system. Even when the business is made up purely of people with solid technical backgrounds, some areas probably just aren't covered well enough.

You might have some people who are coding wizards and some great system administrators, along with a good networking core. These people might have been put together to work on a difficult problem, but when it comes to this specific problem, there might not be anyone with a specific background in the area. Although you can build a great system, no one really knows the exact intricacies that the problem could present down the line as it scales. This can just as easily happen in other larger businesses, but there is usually a better chance that an in-house expertise there can help solve all aspects of the problem.

Monetary Factors

Money is especially important in the scale of a small business. Chances are, very little money can be allocated to planning and building the system, let alone making extensive plans and building in large amounts of scalability so that it can grow to any possible need. That said, there are financial ways around this. For the most part, however, the smaller business must think in smaller-capacity growth scales. Even if there is a great desire for the system to take off (there should be), it still makes sense to project in smaller scales, at least initially, as deploying a large SAN on a small company budget is probably out of the picture. Should the system take off, the capacity management timeline could shorten, and there could be room to deploy a SAN years ahead of schedule, but this is rarely the case in the real world.

All is not lost, though: With today's hardware prices and capacity, most small businesses can effectively build systems at a low price point that will scale effectively up to the point at which the business should have enough money to deploy a more significant architecture. This implies growing pains in the system, and sometimes this cannot be avoided with the monetary restrictions in place. With the right amount of foresight, some of these can be accounted for in the initial system without incurring initial costs. An example would be some code or application that is known to scale well on higher-end hardware. Beginning the system with this application might result in a more stable configuration over time: As things do grow, hardware can be swapped in and out without causing massive rewrites or reconfigurations of all components involved.

Projected Usage

With a small business, you might not have a clear idea of how large your system will grow to be. Maybe you've come together to work on a new product with an as-yet-undefined market, or perhaps the company is the underdog in an already large market and it's difficult to project how much of the established market it can coerce to its product.

A larger factor might be the fact that you don't already have a large customer base from which to start. Allowances for lots of growth need to be built into the architecture, as compared to what is expected initially. Let's take a closer look at that last sentence. If you assume that you have an initial set of two customer groups that are definitely interested in your product, you cannot reliably build performance expectations and growth patterns based on these numbers. Assume that you did and that you built your system's capacity plan around this simple baseline, given that customer information plays a large part in the mechanics of your system. Assuming normal industry growth rates in your market, you might have accounted for a 20% annual storage growth rate. Compound this rate—imagine that you will double your storage needs in four years. At this point, your capacity plan allows for double the number of user groups. So, in four years, you've gone from two groups to four groups. This is obviously not a valid method of planning.

You might be thinking that the previous example was kind of absurd. Well, it was in a way, but it shows the value that needs to be placed on accurate planning. As mentioned, some of this accuracy might not be achievable with a small group, but every step that can be done to minimize this should be taken. Although a small organization might never have the accuracy that can be achieved in a large environment, reasonable assurances should be made so that all usage unknowns are nailed down as much as possible.

Management

In a smaller business environment, system management factors must be carefully considered. Because of limitations in raw manpower—and possibly expertise—systems need to be developed and deployed that have minimal impact on the business. This also should take into account growth as a prime factor. It might take a little bit more work to plan and build the system with a certain software package, but, in the end, this might be more suitable for scaling. Otherwise, as you need to add more servers, more day-to-day management might be needed to keep the system operational. This impacts overall profitability and also steals manpower from an already limited pool.

Requirements Communication

In all likelihood, this can have the largest negative impact on the capacity planning process, and it is most likely to occur within a small group. This might sound somewhat counterintuitive, but it is quite common in practice. In a large environment, groups tend to be segmented into different areas, either logically or physically. Within that larger organization, though, there tends to be a stricter requirement placed on a definition of system requirements and planning. Formal review processes are common, ensuring that all affected parties are involved in the process. This makes sure that as groups scale larger, communication still takes place among them.

Now let's look at the group dynamic in a smaller system. Assume that there are a handful of developers, and some management is driving the operation. It would be simple to assume that on this order of scale, communication is very easy and everyone involved has a clear idea of what should be happening going forward.

In a perfect world, that view might work. But in reality, because the smaller group is generally less oriented toward rigid structures and formal processes, communication can easily break down. The future vision as conceived by the management side might be completely different than what the technical people see, and large disparities will grow in the development of the architecture. Without some kind of requirements specification, it is assumed that everyone involved picks up a common vision from the interaction within the group. In reality, though, everyone tends to come away with a different idea of what should be done next.

This disparity must be avoided at all costs: There is no way to perform any kind of capacity planning or even the basic construction of a system when everyone involved has a different idea of how things should fit together. A formal review process as implemented by a large enterprise might be overkill and could overwhelm the people involved, but some kind of requirements definition and description of future goals should be put forward and debated until a final plan can be put together. When everyone knows exactly what is being built, it becomes much easier to determine usage rates and growth patterns so that capacity planning can go on.

Although this makes it sound as if working in a small group is full of risks, it shouldn't scare you away from attempting to build a capacity plan in that environment. The only thing that is different is that more care needs to be focused in the areas described.

In addition, a small outfit brings one solid advantage to the table that simply isn't present in most larger organizations: flexibility. Within a large organization, capacity planning involves planning for systems that, because of their size and management nature, might as well be written in stone. Large degrees of flexibility simply don't enter the picture on a large scale. In a smaller organization, however, if something does not work as planned or a certain component is found that could greatly simplify both management and operational speed, dropping it into the environment is usually more of an option than on the larger scale. So, in exchange for more unknowns in the capacity-planning process itself, more flexibility plays a part in the implementation down the road—if mistakes are made in planning or certain factors weren't taken into consideration at first, they can easily be rectified in the final solution with minimal impact.

Summary

When you are looking at how to plan system growth, make sure that you utilize all information open to you to the fullest. In any prediction of the future, some unknowns will exist. But if you use all the domain knowledge present, all requirements data that you can get your hands on, all relevant performance data, and any other bit of research available, a fairly clear picture of the system over time should begin to form. By taking into account your individual business needs, these factors should come together and allow you to devise a good plan that will make good use of today's technology and also provide a clean growth path for the future of the system. The end result is a system that can keep up with the load, both present and future, resulting in both satisfied management and a loyal customer base over time.

Methods for Capacity Planning

A Blueprint for Capacity Planning

In the previous chapter, you worked through many of the factors that go into capacity planning. Depending on what kind of enterprise you are in, what kind of business model you follow, and other factors, you might face a lot of competing pressures when trying to actually put together a solid capacity plan. To really be effective, you must take into consideration everything that you can find to be relevant. As mentioned in the last chapter, you might have lots of data that needs to go into your analysis, all coming from different sources.

General Principles

So how do you make sense of this? Looking at it from a higher level, this can appear to be just a large mess of data and interweaving factors, with some very complicated interrelationships. This isn't likely to be an illusion—rarely will some planning data be completely independent of everything else in the set. That's just the nature of the beast. To construct a plan from all this, though, you should approach the process in a structured manner. As you move forward, individual components of the data will become clear, and the plan can come together out of these pieces. The following sections give some general principles to follow when performing effective capacity planning. These should provide a blueprint to follow in most situations.

Gathering Requirements

When people first think about requirements gathering, it is usually associated with software development. But when doing capacity planning, you need to make sure that you completely understand every requirement involved in the system.

It is important to make it fairly all-encompassing. You need to take all aspects of the system's needs into account. This includes existing user agreements for time turnarounds on data, expected network behavior, expected transaction rates through the database, and so on. Consider every aspect of the existing system, or, in the case of a new system, everything that it will need to do. Track down every minute detail about every minor task that the system must perform.

Gathering Statistics

Raw statistics can be as helpful in predicting system usage as any business plan document describing the anticipated usage over time. Although the document is describing a potentiality, the statistics are working with an actuality. Your job is to make sure that this system can scale to future needs, so the plan is definitely needed. However, raw numbers on how the whole system has worked up until now are just as valuable in piecing together an accurate view of the future.

As mentioned in Chapter 13, "Thinking About Capacity Planning," when dealing with your system statistics, you need to find every bit of relevant data that you can. Of course, *relevant* is the key word here. As with gathering requirements, you need any bit of data that might have the slightest bit of relevance to the system's operation. Then you must determine what kinds of loads the system has handled in the past. This includes disk statistics, network usage, and anything that might give information on past usage and indication of future trends.

Make it a point to determine what is commonly collected, and attempt to collect that data on all present systems for your capacity plan. For the most part, data that you collect on multiple systems generally will have some fundamental similarities when it comes to what individual types of data are kept. In terms of your business's planning structure, it is probably beneficial to find these patterns and make sure that everyone collects at least the same baseline statistics. Not only will this give you more data for analysis, but it also might uncover unknown bottlenecks in some systems as you compare the sets.

Achieving a Global View

As mentioned before, it is important to take a global view of the system over time. The more you know about where a system came from and where it is intended to go, the more accurate your capacity plan will be. This search for a high-level view most likely will unearth some aspect that a certain business director could want to extend in the future. Without this knowledge, the capacity plan will end up getting blindsided somewhere down the road when these plans come out of the closet and the system is expected to be capable of handling them.

If you are working on planning the future of an already existing system, another angle could helpful: information about where the system came from. This includes information on what group originally put it together and, more importantly, what kind of growth patterns the system has already sustained. If you know that the system historically has had bottlenecks in drive utilization and network slowdown during high rates of growth, you should most definitely take this into account. This indicates that a large portion of the work involved is I/O-bound and that extra capacities must be incorporated into the capacity plan to ensure smooth growth patterns in the future.

Using Upcoming Technologies

When you are projecting the path of the system in the foreseeable future, it is important to know what is coming up in the relevant technology markets that might have an impact on your system. This can be difficult—it requires in-depth knowledge of what is going on in the relevant markets and an understanding of how well the new technologies might impact the system. You must consider this from an increased performance perspective, and you also must know how disruptive it will be to implement them.

Let's look at a couple examples. Assuming that one of your primary components is an application server, consider a scenario in which a vendor is intending to release a version in six months that will increase the throughput of your system through some architectural changes within the server. The bar might be raised slightly with hardware requirements, but the associated savings will improve your business tremendously and allow you to seamlessly introduce some of the capabilities for which users are screaming.

In this case, assuming that the software is a quick upgrade, the disruption to the system should be minimal. It will require maybe only the amount of time needed to perform the installation upgrade. By testing your later code extensively, you can add extra capability without severely disrupting the users of the system. Assuming a lot of online tests, this likely will work into the system nicely. As such, it should be figured into the capability plan. The slight hardware change also should be reflected there so that everything is ready for it when the time comes.

Now take a look at another possibility. When you're planning the storage needs of the system, you find out that a new SAN system is being offered by a certain vendor. Although it is new—and, therefore, expensive—it would fit your needs perfectly and allow your system to maintain its growth rate very well. But it might be difficult to get that hardware in place now. Instead, you have the option to save a lot of money by getting a small storage array and working with that. This assumes that in a year or so, its capacity will be maximized, and the SAN hardware will be within a price range that is agreeable to those in charge of purchasing. You must strike a balance here between cost savings and disruption of the system. Choosing which is appropriate depends on the situation, of course. In a perfect world, the higher-end hardware is the obvious choice. In reality, however, a cap must be placed on the system's construction.

The point of all this is that there is a trade-off between disruption and capabilities when planning a system. Because the software world is always changing, an attempt must be made to allow for these paradigm shifts. Some of them will be required to allow the system to grow, some might just allow for different capabilities down the road, and some might prevent the need for in-depth tuning. All will likely cause disruptions to the system, either now or later. Determining the best route is up to you.

These are the general principles that should be applied when approaching the problem. Although they cannot be necessarily executed in a clean order, they make chronological sense. Some of them might require you to back up a step and reevaluate the data you gathered. It makes sense to understand the basic set of requirements up-front. This should give a clear view of what the system is originally specified to do, and any questionable requirements can be fleshed out easily before getting mixed up with the rest of the process.

Now that you understand your requirements, you must gather statistics on how the system has behaved in the past. This should be a fairly straightforward process because you have your requirements and know what to look for.

The next step is where things get interesting. When you step back and look at how the larger picture fits together, all kinds of hidden requirements could start to come out of the woodwork. Suddenly the waters that had cleared might become fuzzy again. With these new ideas, you might need to step back a bit and reorganize. This should involve defining requirements for the new ideas, which means getting back to the first step. Some of these new requirements might impose different loads on the system's future as they come online. Because this could stress different aspects of the system, you might need to get more statistics from the current system as implemented. With purely new requirements, there might not be relevant statistics; in general, though, it should be possible to glean more information from your existing system.

Next, figure in the upcoming technologies. This point has already been hammered home, so we won't explain the importance again. But the implications of these new technologies could impact your requirements as specified, causing a rollback to the first step again. When the new set of requirements makes it back to the global view with the new technology included, you might find another angle on what the system can do. And so the process continues.

As you can see, this can be a highly iterative process, but it can be very effective and not necessarily utilized in this strict sequence. Rather than run through the whole set several times, if you find an obvious technology that would be a good fit when gathering the original requirements, by all means roll it in then. That way, when you start looking at achieving the global view, the technology is already worked in and won't cause an extra full pass through the process.

Keep in mind that, in the end, there is room for play; you should never follow a strict procedure only as it is presented to you in a book. Every situation is different, and allowances must be made in all cases. If everything were so cut and dried, capability planning and tuning would be as simple as just picking out what you need and plugging it in.

Identifying the Way Forward

When all the system's requirements have been specified, an actual plan needs to be constructed to lay out the capacity plan as needs dictate. All the requirements that have been found need to be translated into real-world implementation details. A plan also needs to be drawn up to make sure that the system is deployed as needed for growth, or to determine how and when to insert the upgrades into the system as usage levels rise.

Software and Hardware Requirements

Based on the individual requirements details, you have a clear picture of what the system capabilities need to be. The first step is to take these notes, which might be expressed in abstract form, and make them specific software and hardware requirements. In general, they should be translated into software requirements first because, in most situations, the present software dri-ves the need for the underlying hardware.

Sometimes the distinction might not be perfectly clear, and the software needed might operate on multiple architectures. This enables you to choose the best hardware and software combina-tion for your needs. Finally, the dependency might swing the other way, forcing you to specify your software based on the set available for the hardware you need to use. Depending on your needs, the process can be done either way. In the end, though, there are two very simple ques-tions to answer, to make sure that the right choices have been made:

- Based on the requirements presented, does the resulting hardware and software configu-ration offer the capability to handle the raw numbers of requests that the system needs to be able to handling?

- Do those numbers or the architecture allow for sustained growth, according to your model?

If your requirements are spelled out in depth, most situations should enable you to do the math and compare the raw throughput of the system to the raw throughput defined by the require-ments. In the end, with enough data, the decision of whether the system will scale should be a question of raw numerics, not a hunch.

Determining Planned Component Update Points

When you have selected your physical and logical configuration by building your hardware and software selection, you need to determine how and when upgrading of components should take place. This is applicable both when you are building the system from scratch and when you are performing planning and analysis for an existing system.

When you're building the system from scratch, trade-offs in the design process likely will need to be dropped into place farther down the road, as needs arise. This case was described earlier, when we debated the merits of spending extra resources on a full SAN versus just getting a minimal drive array and upgrading later. Or, maybe some components couldn't be put together in time for the initial system launch. The possibility exists that the component is present but that the drivers were not production-ready at the start. As those components come online down the road, they will need to be integrated into the rest of the system, with minimal impact on system operation. The core capabilities of the system can be active in the meantime, but adding the new pieces needs to be handled carefully so that it does not impact existing services.

When performing capacity planning and upgrade paths for an existing system, extra care must be taken. Tuning modifications might have been made to the system to make it perform reason-ably until the upgrade could be performed. Also, the potential exists that, from the current point on, the system's growth could be more susceptible to overload than anticipated. That is, the system might have been designed years ago, and the current implementation might be using old technology that, when faced with a large increase in usage, might not be capable of handling the shift smoothly. In this case, a tighter upgrade schedule might need to be planned.

In either case, upgrades should be prepared well ahead of time, when possible. Given a strong understanding of the system's requirements and growth patterns, determining the point at which a system will need upgrades should be an objective decision based on statistics exhibited by the system. If these upgrades are planned and prepared for, handling the growth of the system should be a relatively straightforward, manageable process.

Handling Configuration Management Migration

Over time, especially in an already existing system, various components, both hardware and software, will have their configurations modified in some fashion. Usually this is to handle a tuning issue that required attention or that was a response to a need that the original planning cycle did not predict. This change might not have modified the plan going forward where capacity management is concerned, but it still must be taken into account.

In reality, this should be a separate problem of simple configuration management, but it does require coordination with the capacity plan. If a year goes by and an application needs to be upgraded, that is definitely a capacity planning issue. But if during the course of that year various alterations were made to the software that caused it to deviate from the configuration norm, that should have been tracked through a configuration-management system and policy.

During the update, these two plans should coordinate, or the system could fall apart. As the application is upgraded, not all of the configuration changes might be kept—they might not even be applicable anymore. Without considering all the repercussions inherent in the upgrade, interruptions in service could occur. This is why all plan implementations should have built-in assurances that configuration management details are applied to the process going forward. It also should go without saying that, to be safe, all these changes should be surrounded by a comprehensive set of backups.

In the end, taking into account all factors affecting the system, you should be able to build a plan that specifies fairly precise instructions over the course of the planned lifetime. Turning requirements into raw numbers for hardware and software requirements should be feasible with enough data, and applying growth rates over time will project the system into the future. When you have a plan for what the system can handle over time, you can predict component drop-ins with reasonable accuracy. Although coordinating all these changes can be time-consuming, it can be handled effectively as far as the system's operation is concerned if you consider all factors during the growth cycle.

14

How to Develop a Structure

Now you have your requirements, the system, a growth rate, and a capacity plan to manage the growth. There is still a large hole in the process, if left at this point: You need an underlying structure to implement this plan over time as the system grows, hopefully according to plan. A plan won't do anyone any good if it's written and then dropped into a filing cabinet somewhere and forgotten about. A team of some sort must be put together and bound in some manner to make sure that the plan is carried out effectively.

Determining Who Is Involved

Now you're back to the idea of having a global view of requirements. If you have a clear view of all the highest levels of the requirements, it should be a fairly straightforward matter to drill down through these and determine what groups will be involved in the architecture of the system. This list should include the people who developed it, the maintenance group, sections that might be implementing business plans that use it, and people who plan to integrate with it in the future.

Applying this data likely will depend on your infrastructure and environment. If everything is handled within a single company, the best route could be to figure out who is involved, in what manner, and build your structure from that—this could be from a manpower perspective or from an incurring cost perspective. Cost distribution can be set up at this point through internal billing infrastructures so that the cost of managing the system is balanced among all involved parties.

If the system is built to be used by both internal and external groups, this might involve a more complex approach. In general, service agreements need to be written to ensure that all parties involved are guaranteed levels of use of the system. It goes without saying that these kind of assurances need to be in place when bridging organizations, especially when individual corporations are involved. This is where your capacity plan can start to shine. Because it takes into account all these groups involved and their respective growth strategies, along with the allotted system availability guarantees, you can truly plan for the growth track and bring together the management infrastructure.

Creating the Group

Many times part of the structure definition for the capacity plan will involve laying out a new management infrastructure to implement the plan over time. Given the capacity plan, you need to determine management overhead and calculate the number of people it will take to effectively manage the system going onward, especially as the system grows. Can the system handle a quadrupling of load without adding more employees to staff it? If the system was designed carefully, this should generally be fine with self-sufficient systems, but a defined list still must identify administrators and services performed over the growth cycle, even if it is only for minimal component upgrades and operational maintenance such as backups. In general, the plan should account for at least a minimal increase in management over time because as the end of the plan is reached, the hardware's capacity will need to be tested and will require tuning as implemented by administrators.

As with any group created for this kind of work, it is important to select people with the correct domain expertise. If the system is bridging several internal business structures, it might be helpful to enlist help directly from the groups involved because there likely will be specific domain expertise in each group involved. By making sure that this expertise is used correctly, you can build a more efficient team, resulting in a smoother implementation of the plan. In addition, this can prevent overlap of expertise, prevent extra resources from being brought in, and generally make better use of the resources available within the organizations involved.

Outsourcing

The previous section extolled the virtues of making sure that all the in-house talent was used to implement the capacity plan effectively. Why would outsourcing be an issue at this point? Simple: The system still might have needs that your organization is not equipped to handle. It doesn't make sense to lay out an internal infrastructure to do it yourself. It might make sense to have someone else perform some part of the operation. After all, the party in question might already have learned the lessons involved; to relearn those lessons in-house would present risks that shouldn't be taken.

A classic example of this is with bandwidth management. Most businesses are interested in developing and managing an application because they have the domain expertise relevant to the problem. But when it comes to making sure that users get adequate bandwidth to the application and guaranteeing uptime, doing all the work inside the existing groups would result in bringing in a whole new set of experts. If you're working on a product that does customer relationship management, you don't necessarily have a full staff on hand that understands the bandwidth-management issues that might come up when deploying it.

In this case, some kind of co-location company should be brought in to handle all of this for you and perform all the work on bandwidth management, guaranteed reliable power, and so on. This saves the trouble of bringing the bandwidth to the company to manage it, providing a 24-hour maintenance infrastructure, and so on.

For example, consider the concept of laying the lines to the company to provide bandwidth. When this bandwidth is exhausted, upgrading the land line can be a costly undertaking. But if this is managed by the service provider, it can result in significant cost savings. Realizing what should be done in-house, along with what should be outsourced, and then applying it to the capacity plan can result in a much more effective use of available expertise.

Ensuring Flexibility in the Future

This can be difficult to determine in objective terms, but you should keep it in mind when reviewing the structure being built. What will happen to the structure if some of the business systems are reorganized? Can the existing infrastructure handle the subsequent reorganizations? These are very important questions because they can directly affect the future viability of the system. Having a global view can help mitigate risks because the predicted patterns are somewhat clearer. However, it is ludicrous to assume that all factors can be accounted for. Large, unforeseen business reorganizations can still have a large impact, but it is important to account for all known pending or possible organizational changes in the structure.

Building a Contract

Obviously, the details of forming a contract based on the ideas presented here will depend greatly on your needs. Contractual negotiation varies from company to company, and your needs likely will be very unique. In the end, though, especially with systems that bridge external organizations, there needs to be some kind of contractual obligation concerning the system in question. By solidifying the growth patterns as much as possible and specifying the requirements, the capacity plan accounts for every known contingency and for all the factors presented here.

A contract should be put in place to ensure that every resource needed will be present. This can cover anything regarding the system, from usage rates to management hours, to the capability to call on domain expertise in other departments as needed. By building this into a binding contract, you solidify many of the remaining unknowns that pertain to the system's growth patterns, further ensuring the viability of your capacity plan.

Handling Project Management

Capacity planning should be treated as a normal project-development problem. Although it can be viewed as a service contract, it generally makes sense to look at it as a normal project, the same as other projects within the organization. Stepping back to look at the factors involved, this makes sense—it has all the classic factors involved in normal project management: employee burn rates, research into individual technologies as time goes on, hardware deployment costs, code updates in most situations, and so on.

The details of implementing the plan as a normal project within your organization will vary, but you definitely should treat this no differently than any other project. The plan should be subjected to periodic review, should have internal resources allocated to it as if it were a normal project, and so on. By viewing it as a standard procedure, you better ensure that it will receive the same amount of internal attention over time and that the plans won't fall by the wayside as time moves on and resources are reallocated. Devoting specific resources to manage it ensures that the built-in deadlines are handled effectively in a prepared manner as they occur. When combined with a binding contract laid out in the structure segment, the capacity plan should have enough resources dedicated to it that it consistently meets its requirements.

Navigating Political Aspects

Now we get to the ugly side of capacity planning and deployment. If handled correctly, political problems shouldn't affect your plans for moving the system forward. However, if you mishandle them, you can face serious repercussions. Either way, it helps to know the environment to make sure that it works *for* the system, not against it.

Let's look at the possible negative repercussions. In implementing your system, there could be significant overlaps with other groups. This is a good thing, but not necessarily from everyone's perspective. Although it might make sense for the overall health of the product line, some groups involved might not want to release the work that they are doing, to maintain their status quo within the infrastructure. This likely will happen if you are deploying a system that involves a SAN or something else that implies a centralization of different sources. Another group might already have that information, so it would make sense to move that group's databases into your management infrastructure and consolidate efforts. From the group's perspective, however, this could mean a loss of management costs in the budget, a loss of employees, or other factors. Steps should be taken to reduce the impact of this centralization, possibly by getting the employees over to the new system to maintain the expertise in the company, or possibly just matrixing operations among the groups involved.

Another pitfall that can occur, mostly as a result of the previous example, is groups withholding data. If a group determines that the system is a threat to its line of business, it might not be as forthcoming with relevant data as it should be. If you are attempting to build an effective capacity plan, the lack of this data can open large holes in your prediction models, resulting in a much less effective plan. For this reason, you should take every possible step to work with the groups involved, to alleviate their fears so that you can be sure that you are getting the data you need.

Management also might have some fears when looking at your proposed system. If you do not allay these fears, management might prevent the project from happening, rendering all the work you have done useless. Many factors can contribute to this: Maybe the business model isn't quite believable and there isn't as much of a market as believed. Perhaps the management team believes that there is no need for the system, let alone a capacity plan to go along with it. Or, maybe the new product is just so far outside the company's core competency group that fears have arisen about its viability within the current structure. Whatever the reason, these fears need to be considered and built into the current plan. Without the support of upper management, your plan's chances of survival, let alone growth, are slim.

This is not to say that all political aspects are bad. If care is taken, you can avoid these harmful factors and find some bonuses. Working within a larger infrastructure doesn't have to be painful—it obviously has some merit, or so many people wouldn't choose this environment.

Many of the bonuses of political influences are based on the idea of obtaining a global view of the project, an idea espoused throughout this text. Although you might need to rely on the help of an upper-level proponent to get operations pushed through, opening your requirements to the enterprise could ultimately offer some large rewards. First, there will be more eyes looking at your project. This means insight from more people of different core competencies, which is always good for obtaining visibility within the enterprise and externally as a product. In addition, you'll get better insight into what could be planned more efficiently. As more people analyze your system, they might find ways to consolidate into preexisting infrastructures, which could already have capability layouts to handle your load. This reduces your cost factor and the cost factor within the company, and it removes variables from your capacity plan. Thus, the model that you are trying to project into the future is simplified. Fewer variables are always better from the standpoint of planning simplicity and also from the perspective of those looking at the business's bottom line.

Working through the political minefield with care, you might come out with a more capable system that faces fewer unknowns. At the same time, you might get free exposure within the enterprise. These factors can help bring together different groups that historically might have had different core competencies, further helping the business's bottom line. As you can see, the political aspects aren't always bad; they just need to be carefully addressed.

Knowing Your Application Needs

The most important part of defining a structure for your capacity planning is knowing your application needs. This can be viewed as just another angle on requirement specification, but its importance cannot be overstated. Whether it is the system as a whole or the applications that comprise it internally, nearly all of your capacity requirements will be driven by what they require. Any bit of knowledge that can be applied here should be considered, and any spare bit of research that can be done to eliminate ambiguities should be performed.

Software drives hardware, and hardware drives the capability set of the system. If the software's needs aren't fully known, you end up with a system that either doesn't work as needed or something that won't scale over time. If there is one rule to be followed in defining the planning structure, it should be that application needs should be considered first and foremost in moving forward.

When you're attempting to find the best path for your capacity plan, you could have too many factors to consider or too many unknowns in the potential growth patterns to be sure that you're looking down the right path. Sometimes this is a result of poor requirement specifications. Many times, though, especially if the system is in a new market area that hasn't been proven yet, you might just have a number of unknowns that cannot be predicted.

What do you do in this situation? Being faced with complete unknowns and still being expected to formulate a reliable capability plan could be frightening. You might not be able to get rid of all unknowns. With some software utilities, however, you might be able to get enough data back to get rid of some of them—or at least minimize their impact. Specific software packages could help in this regard. Depending on the path you choose, they can be fairly expensive, but it is important to make the right choice to minimize your risk going forward.

Commercial Products

In the realm of commercial offerings, some fairly large players are involved in the market. BMC and SAP, two of the larger ones, offer products that work as enterprise resource planners. These products test your network to see if it can handle the strain of the resources that are planned. Many large corporations are vying for the market, but they are all focused on the same areas, including consolidation of existing functional areas into a single system and predictive resource analysis for your network.

These are very effective tools, but they also tend to be very expensive. In most situations, they're overkill for what you need. Deploying these kinds of systems might require large amounts of time, effort, and cash to get any kind of real value from them. The resulting overhead could be more than you can afford to implement in your scale. If you are planning a very large system, though, it might be worthwhile to look closely at these options because they can provide both software implementations and contracted manpower of domain expertise in planning your system.

Network Analysis Tools

All is not lost if you can't afford the time or resources to get a large enterprise-planning system in place. Some valid options can get you the data you need to complete your model and finish implementing your plan so that the system can be built and deployed.

Many analysis tools rely on simply using SNMP to gather their data, and they then add value by calculating statistics based on these values for you. (Many poke at data not available via SNMP, but most of this data can be retrieved without external software.) Sometimes this model might be overkill because much of this data can be gotten by hand; for the most part, rough statistics also can be generated to indicate usage statistics. Some simple math can go a long way and can save the large costs involved in deploying a large-scale product. (This is not to say that the large products don't have their place; for most small, medium, and even large businesses, however, the cost is too high or the problem at hand is so domain-dependent that local analysis needs to be done anyway.)

14

So, given a little knowledge about how to use SNMP, you might be able to do predictive analysis on your network yourself. This precludes the need for expensive applications, enables you to get the exact data you need, and even lets you tune your statistics generation to what might be domain-specific needs. The downside of this is that it requires a little bit of in-house knowledge about using the protocol. This is fairly straightforward, though, and it's very easy to get up to speed. The other downside is that some of the custom statistics packages that come with the large applications might not be directly available to you, but that situation could be changing in the near future.

We've talked a lot about SNMP throughout the book, but what exactly is it? The acronym stands for Simple Network Management Protocol, and it really does what its name suggests. Most management applications and services imply that this is a complex system to use, but it's really not difficult to work with at all.

Although SNMP can have different capabilities beyond this, here is the overall explanation of the protocol: It enables you to look at a system from over the network and watch various system usage parameters presented in a tree-like format. Every node in this tree has a numeric path, such as 1.3.6.1, which is called an *object identifier (OID)*. This numeric sequence is mapped to a meaningful name known as an object identifier through a Message Information Base (MIB). A MIB defines the names in ASN.1 notation.

Different places in the tree of data are reserved for different types. This provides a standard for establishing normal places to find specific data about things such as uptime values. It also provides trees of application-specific data for vendors to implement. Keep in mind that this is an extremely simplistic view of what SNMP does; more research is encouraged to make sure that you know how to use it correctly for your needs.

Pollers

Many applications out there speak SNMP and can retrieve data for you to analyze. At their basic level, though, they simply poll specific resources at defined intervals. For the sake of simplicity, we will call these pollers. Applications that fall into this group include Hewlett-Packard's Network Node Manager (NNM), known as OpenView, and BMC's PATROL software, among others. In the open source world, there are several means of doing some of the same work, using more simplistic tools such as Big Brother. Although Big Brother doesn't come close to the commercial application's support for various reports and bells and whistles, an upstart named OpenNMS will provide much of that functionality in the near future.

Because it is so expensive to deploy an infrastructure based on tools such as HP's NNM, the coders at www.opennms.org have been putting together a framework application that provides much of the same functionality, but with a fresher look. This will provide a flexible system in the face of changing network standards. Some people view network-management systems as ways to automate detection of problems on the network or as a means of configuration management, but this is also a very valid way of doing predictive analysis on your systems. Assuming that all your machines have SNMP daemons installed and running, (which should be the case—many daemons ship by default with many distributions), you should be able to use SNMP over time to get valuable data about your usage patterns.

In the network-management market, many trend-analysis tools sit on top of NNM or talk to NNM to collect data and piece it together into meaningful statistics. This solution can be easier to implement than a full capacity planning suite, and it will still give you the custom statistics you need. But the OpenNMS project has an explicit goal of doing trending and reporting on historical data. In time, either the collection facilities present in OpenNMS will surpass those of commercial tools, or the commercial tools will allow OpenNMS to provide the data for analysis. At the time of this writing, OpenNMS is in a beta form, usable in some respects, and is working with an early adoption group to test deployments. However, OpenNMS is moving forward at a breakneck pace and likely will have a full release by the time you read this book.

Example

Enough of the abstract talk of how this should be done. Let's walk through a couple instances of getting SNMP data for you to work with. With an analysis or correlation tool, you probably won't ever have to get data this way, but it's a good way to see how things are done. For simplicity, assume that the SNMP daemon is running on the local machine (of course, it could be anywhere) and that you're interested in getting the value for the value in the tree named .iso.org.dod.internet.mgmt.mib-2.ip.ipInDelivers. (This corresponds to the raw numeric tree value of .1.3.6.1.2.1.4.9, with an instance number tagged on the end of 0.) By reading the MIB file, this value will give you the total number of input datagrams successfully delivered to IP user-protocols (including ICMP). This number can be used to determine the relative load on the network stack (although probably some other data points in the SNMP tree would be more indicative of IP usage, either on their own or together in aggregate). Look at how this would be done from the command line:

```
# snmpget 127.0.0.1 public ip.ipInDelivers.0
ip.ipInDelivers.0 = 39746134
```

Now wasn't that simple? (The public name is a community string—refer to normal SNMP guides for more data on how it might relate within your environment.) Of course, other switches can be used, such as the -O f or -O n switches (this assumes that the UCD-snmp set of utilities is installed, but your installation/distribution might vary slightly). Getting the data with these switches retrieves the data with the full naming path through the tree and the full numeric path, respectively, as shown here:

14

METHODS FOR
CAPACITY
PLANNING

```
# snmpget -O n 127.0.0.1 public ip.ipInDelivers.0
.1.3.6.1.2.1.4.9.0 = 39746142
# snmpget -O f 127.0.0.1 public ip.ipInDelivers.0
.iso.org.dod.internet.mgmt.mib-2.ip.ipInDelivers.0 = 39746144
```

Besides the normal command-line command `snmpget`, there is a whole family of commands, such as `snmpbulkget`, which, as you might guess, does bulk requests of SNMP data. The `snmpwalk` command is another useful one because it walks through the entire tree for you. A simple pipe to `less` enables you to easily look at your whole SNMP tree.

Command-line tools probably won't cut it for most of your data collection, though. There could be a few exceptions (pieces of data that couldn't be retrieved through normal SNMP means but might otherwise be retrievable from the command line). For the most part, you will rely on a tool that can do at least some of the analysis for you with a minimal amount of work, such as NNM or OpenNMS. Here's a sample of what OpenNMS might show you, taken from its Web site's list of screenshots (`http://www.opennms.org/sections/download/screens/realtime`). (Keep in mind that this is an ongoing project and that the screenshot you are seeing here probably will be classified as ancient by the time you read this.)

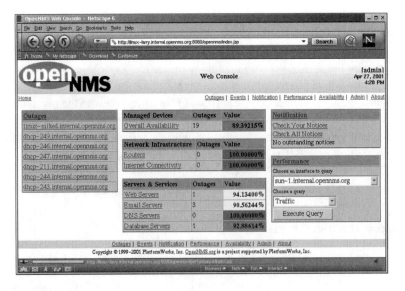

FIGURE 14.1

An example of OpenNMS in action.

Although this is a very high-level view of some router data, the statistical properties should be pretty visible. If the application can present this data to you, it should also be capable of preparing the data for you in other ways. By piecing together different components of what you can see from SNMP, you should get a good picture of what the existing system is doing and determine how to plan the future based on this data. By recording this data over time, the data should point a clear path for your capacity plans.

Summary

Regardless of all the recommendations made here, your individual blueprint for capacity planning likely will vary from this model. The fundamentals might be similar, but you probably will need to weight the various components of the basic rule set differently. If you are in a very dynamic market, you might determine that all your capacity plans must revolve around the capability to drop in new components at any time, or maybe that your global view needs to be revisited on a monthly basis. You might need to include domain-specific factors that were not even mentioned here.

In general, however, you need a solid blueprint when doing capacity planning to help prevent different system deployments from having to relearn the same lessons. With a good blueprint that fits your needs, you should be able to generate a viable capacity plan that will reliably determine your system's future.

Case Studies

IN THIS PART

15 Case Studies: Web Server Performance   281

16 Where to Go From Here   291

Case Studies: Web Server Performance

No performance-tuning manual is good without examples. Sometimes inline examples are not enough to fully explain the processes of troubleshooting a real performance problem. In this chapter, you'll look at some case studies. Symptoms will be gathered, a quick look for the most common causes will ensue, a more in-depth analysis will be performed, and, finally, a list of possible solutions will be drawn up. These cases will not follow the actions verbatim because all the tools needed are explained elsewhere. However, the sections will thoroughly explain all the tools used and what they told the troubleshooter.

It should be noted that these cases are based on fact, although all names have been omitted.

Web Server Performance

The most visual server systems in use today are Web servers (with file servers of all types running close behind). Almost every Unix administrator maintains a Web server in some capacity—most often the sysadmin is the Web master as well. In this case, the main function of this particular Linux system is to serve up some static Web pages, a few CGI-generated Web pages, and some pages generated through PHP scripts that connect to a database server behind a firewall.

The Symptoms

The symptoms are vague, at best: somewhat consistent spotty performance from any client. Obviously, any clients that access the Web server within the network will be faster, but there is still a noticeable performance drop of nearly 50% in download times. The database server can be eliminated quickly because the problem occurs on both static and dynamic pages (albeit the problem is much longer on dynamic ones).

The Quick Checks

The industrious administrator quickly runs top and sees several httpd processes eating up the system. This is still not enough information, though, because httpd requires the use of many subsystems (especially on this system).

The next step is to use tools that are a bit more granular. After employing sar and vmstat, it is discovered that the processor and memory seem I/O-bound, but disk I/O seems okay.

This tells the administrator that the problem could be a CPU problem. Even though memory is being used more than it normally is, there is no excessive paging.

Some Quick Guesses

Because the problem is directly related to the Web server and not the database, this points to the only part of the Web server that could be the culprit: the pages in general. This does not make much sense, though—static Web pages hardly cause any overhead by themselves.

The administrator takes a look at the HTML documents and discovers that they have all been modified recently along with the Web server's configuration files.

After viewing the configuration files, the culprit is finally revealed.

The Web Server Culprit

Someone (a virtual person?) has activated server-side includes and added a whole host of SSI scripts that get called repeatedly by each document (even dynamically generated ones). The scripts range from date/time, last modification times, file sizes, and owner names to hit counters for each page.

Possible Solutions

The first solution might be to remove anything that is not necessary. For example, hit counters on each page are a bit excessive, and the Web server logs provide a much more accurate picture anyway. In addition to the counter, file sizes of current documents and owner names could go as well.

If the user simply cannot live without the scripts, alternatives might be offered. For example, PHP can do almost all of the functions that these new scripts do within PHP itself (without relying upon calling external scripts).

Ultimately, the best solution is a combination of the first two:

- Eliminate scripts that are not necessary.
- Find a better way to run the ones that remain.

A Classic Memory Problem

No performance-tuning example would be complete without a memory problem. Although this time the troubled subsystem is revealed, the solution is not exactly what most people might consider.

The System Configuration

This system has three SCSI hard drives, all the same size and model. Additionally, the system has a tape backup device and a CD-ROM drive. It is used as test server for compiling programs and running them. The drives are all on the same chain.

The Beginnings of a Problem

In any development environment, eventually critical mass will be reached. In today's ever-changing environment, new tools are created, downloaded, and installed daily. It finally becomes apparent that this system is getting beaten up. The compile time for the ever-growing projects is getting larger, and test runs are going slower. This is because of the obvious feature creep of the software being developed.

Detailed Analysis Says...

It is discovered that although the programs are larger, they still are not large enough to hog memory. The stalwart administrator employs sar again and discovers that the swap disk is getting I/O-bound. The swap disk is the first disk in the system, and also it is used to contain a lot of tools used for compiling.

Quick Solutions

The obvious quick solution is to upgrade the system—first memory, then perhaps the motherboard, and finally the disks. In the Linux world (and most of the open source OS community in general), this hardly seems appropriate. Furthermore, it is not always that easy; rarely (if ever) does an administrator have funds available to stop such sneaking types of problems. Instead, more fundamental solutions are necessary.

Changing the Disk Configuration(s)

You've probably already figured out the possible plausible solutions (especially if you thoroughly read Chapter 11, "Linux and Memory Management").

One method is to juggle the swap partitions onto lower-used disks, thus splitting off the load. The great thing about this solution is that no downtime is required (hopefully). This is not the best solution, though.

Perhaps the best (but most time-consuming) method is to back up all the data files and reinstall the system. This time, however, use striping across all three disks, including the swap partition. Then load the data back after the system is configured. This will evenly allocate all disk resources.

Increasing Network Latency

Network problems plague even non-network administrators. With chatty protocols, a seemingly endless list of new file-sharing protocols, and everyday changes to network security systems, it is a wonder that more administrators are not locked away in asylums. This case study reveals an extraordinarily succinct problem that actually has little to do with Linux but certainly seems that way.

A Day in the Life of an FTP Server

In this case, an internal FTP server is the troubled child. The problem is file transfer times. In a nutshell, these times are steadily getting worse, although in almost unnoticeable increments. Large differences are noticed only over weeks, and the situation is getting worse.

The First Look

Initially, the administrator looks at netstat and ntop and notices that the system itself seems to be dropping a lot of packets in and out. The administrator tries to adjust the media settings, changing a few other parameters and the like. None of this seems to have any effect, however, other than mutating the problem—for example, expanding the MTU of the NIC results in more packets being dropped.

Even after more in-depth analysis, nothing seems to stand out. After several (worsening) weeks, the administrator surrenders and installs a new NIC. After monitoring the interface for nearly a week, the problem begins to creep up again.

And the Answer Is...

It is quite obvious that one of two things is wrong:

1. The networking subsystem is grossly messed up.
2. Some sort of hardware issue is at stake.

The administrator installs a clone of the system on a spare PC and does not see similar results. The administrator then moves the NIC in the FTP server to another slot, and it works fine for several weeks. The problem was the slot itself; it had intermittent problems most likely brought on by cold solder joints.

Another Memory Problem

The Symptoms

Under extremely heavy load, the system behaves erratically, and becomes very slow. This is happening on your database server, during peak hours. The machine keeps going, but it is obvious that something is wrong.

Tracing the Problem

Let's look more closely at the problem. By watching the drive I/O with the standard tool set, it is obvious that it is being hit fairly hard, although the throughput numbers seem to be within reason for the number of users involved.

Next, check the CPUs and memory to see if something is bound by those factors. Watching it, the system again is being worked fairly hard, but it looks like it's weathering the storm pretty well. The CPUs aren't fully hammered, and memory, while high, isn't absolutely gone.

All right. Let's check the database logs, just to make sure the problem is not a software configuration issue. Nothing really looks too bad, but there are some memory errors in a couple of the logs that seem to be lining up closely with the peak usage.

Now things are getting confusing. The system looks all right from most of the normal tools, but the application logs seem to be saying that there is a memory issue. Now it's time to check around the kernel itself, as this one is becoming difficult to check in the normal fashion.

Bingo. Looking at the kernel ring buffer with dmesg, and looking at the /var/log/messages, there are messages in the following form:

```
# tail /var/log/messages
Apr 22 12:15:07 db kernel: VM: do_try_to_free_pages failed for db_proc...
Apr 22 12:15:07 db kernel: VM: do_try_to_free_pages failed for db_proc...
Apr 22 12:23:52 db kernel: VM: do_try_to_free_pages failed for db_proc...
Apr 22 12:53:58 db kernel: VM: do_try_to_free_pages failed for db_proc...
```

Finding a Solution

All right, there's obviously a problem here, but what exactly is going on? By checking the kernel mailing list archives, the current kernel has a problem in which the VM system is under heavy load. The kernel source has been installed by hand since it was necessary to make sure exactly what was built into the system, so the state of the kernel source is known. Based on the current state of the 2.4 series, driver support for the RAID card isn't ready yet. It will be ready in a month or so, which will enable the jump to 2.4 to get rid of the problem. But what about dealing with the problem immediately?

Further research shows that there is an existing patch against the 2.2.18 pre series that has been used by other people in this situation and has been found to be effective. Sources point to the people directory on kernel.org, where there is a patch for the VM patch from Andrea Arcangeli's set of patches. The current one is against 2.2.18pre25, which, as described in the kernel chapter, is Alan Cox's latest patch against the base 2.2.17, which will eventually become 2.2.18. A lot is going on in the series, and there have been 25 patches against the base 2.2.17, with no end in sight. Rather than waiting until the final 2.2.18 comes out, which might not have the patch that is needed, the 2.2.18pre25 patch is retrieved from Alan's directory.

Now, you have your 2.2.17 source base, Alan's 2.2.18pre25 patch, and Andrea's VM patch that was made against 2.2.18pre25. So, patch the base kernel up to pre25, then apply the VM patch and build the kernel as usual. (The configuration parameters were set before, so it's just a build.) Once you reboot with the new kernel, the system's problems will go away, and it will handle the high load (and higher) with ease.

Conclusion

While this was a fairly complex example, the hardest part was diagnosing the problem. The longest path was taken to find the solution, but in reality, it all could have been done in a matter of minutes, and in general, it is just as easy to run dmesg first. In situations where the culprit is not known directly, dmesg is a good first pass just to head off any kernel level issues.

While this was a known issue, it was resolved in the 2.2 series and is not a factor in the 2.4 series. This should not be taken as a common problem with any of the current kernel series.

Linux Virtual Server (LVS) Walkthrough

Concept

As described earlier, the LVS project allows for the clustering of machines so that they appear to be one single service. The most common case for this is in web farms, where there is a need to make a large set of machines to respond to a single routing point. Some people implement round-robin DNS to handle this, but this process in no way is resilient to failures. (If you have three machines in round-robin DNS, and one fails, DNS will still send about one third of all requests to the dead machine.) LVS, with failover applied with services like the Linux High Availability project, provides a nice way to distribute the load safely. Though it was discussed earlier, this does deserve some coverage with an example. It is a core component in most capacity planning operations, due to the fact that it can provide cheap, nearly linearly-scalable solutions for a minimal cost in hardware.

Assumptions

If LVS is selected as an option, there must have been a determination at some point that there is a strict need for this capability over a traditional single web server configuration. While in many cases LVS is used to aggregate bandwidth that could not be achieved with a single machine, in this case, let's assume that the service being clustered is HTTP, and it can't be served from one machine due to processor speed and memory usage.

In our capacity plan, it was determined that with our client base, we need to be able to sufficiently handle 300 simultaneous users. In testing, it is found that with the default server configuration, about 100 users can load a machine to the point that swap begins to become a factor, and the processors begin to hit peak usage. While it is feasible to simply triple the processor capacity and add more memory, this won't fit with the growth model, which assumes a doubling in growth over the next few years as more users migrate in from the previous system. In these tests, since the uplink is relatively slow, the full network throughput is not a factor. But as the system grows, as it is likely to do so quickly, it would be nice to be able to just drop new machines in as needed and add them to the cluster set, which is why LVS is being used.

Configuration

As explained earlier, LVS works by having a central director (with failover) that arbitrates connections for the cluster. To install this, a single central machine (the director) needs to be built and the LVS code installed on it. The details aren't shown here, as they are in the directions for the software, but essentially, some local software is installed, and there is a kernel patch that needs to be put in place on the director. (Your vendor might ship a kernel with the ipvs support already built in.) There are patches for the 2.2 series, which is considered to be in production at this point, and also ones for 2.4, which is stable but still under testing. Once the patch is installed, a series of kernel options needs to be enabled and the kernel rebuilt.

Once the director is built and running, the real servers need to be installed. VS-DR is determined to be the best configuration. As described earlier, LVS can run in a NAT configuration or with Direct Routing. With NAT, services are simpler because everything channels back through the director machine. But this introduces a bottlneck at the NAT director. Direct Routing, or DR, is generally chosen over this solution. In this case, every machine in the cluster is required to have a routable address so that it can directly talk back to the client for the response rather than through the controller. While in this case it is not likely that there will be a huge load on the director, it is generally advantageous to use direct routing if possible in the face of growth. Since it only requires a few IP addresses, the gain of being able to grow the cluster nearly indefinitely is definitely worth the overhead.

Now that the director is configured, and the real servers are in place, there is one more configuration piece to put in place—the failover for the load balancer. With the heartbeat component of the Linux High Availability project, this failover can be handled fairly easily. Again, the actual installation process is covered in the software (from www.linux-ha.org). The heartbeat at least should be configured on the director server. By communicating over two interfaces, it can watch the master server, and in the event of a failure can perform full IP address takeover. This machine needs to be configured in the same way as the master server so that it can reliably take over in an emergency.

In the end, the resulting structure is fairly simplistic—there is a central server (with failover) that handles the incoming traffic, and a set of real servers that are going to do the real work, all connected to the required networks. Services need to be configured on the director, with a file containing all of the relevant network data. From this configuration, a file is generated that needs to be run on the director and all of the real servers with ipvsadm.

Once everything is running, the cluster is ready. Tests can be performed to see which one is responding to each request, which should be a different server each time assuming the normal scheduling rotation. By default, simple round-robin is used, as most clusters consist of identical hardware. However, weighted round-robin can be selected to give more work to larger boxes. LVS also supports least-connection scheduling, which directs new requests against the machine in the cluster with the fewest connections, and weighted least-connection. This again is the same algorithm but with weights toward individual machines.

As you can see, it's really not that hard to deploy a cluster with this technology. All that is needed is an IP address, a director server (and hopefully a failover machine for it), and some real servers to do the work. In some cases, this might be used to distribute access to file data, over several protocols, or as a way to distribute incoming processor-intensive requests. In some situations, it could be used as a way to distribute a view on an even bigger system behind the cluster, if that is what is required. The system is extremely flexible and fairly simple to set up. As it runs on any commodity hardware, deploying a cluster will only cost as much as the hardware involved and the time used to bring up the nodes, assuming normal management of the machines over time.

Summary

Although the case studies in this chapter have attempted to cover the big subsystems, many different types of performance issues can crop up on both server and client Linux systems. Hopefully the case studies in this chapter showed how gradual insights can serve an administrator. A great deal of other resources also are available on the Web and in other publications discussed in the next chapter.

Where to Go From Here

This book is not the ultimate solution to performance tuning on Linux systems. Instead, it is a guide filled with many great suggestions, methodologies, and ideas. This is a good starting point, and it serves as a quick reference for many operations that the Linux administrator might have to perform to tune a Linux system.

World Wide Web Resources

Linux has spawned an incredible number of Web sites. Most are personal, but many are run by groups of people who share a common interest or by a distributor of Linux. These sites range from just "Hey, I like Linux" to massive online archives of detailed information.

In the realm of performance tuning, very few sites are solely geared to it. Many sites are generic Linux sites, so there are far too many to list here. These are a few dedicated sites that cover performance monitoring and tuning only:

- The Linux Performance Tuning Site: `http://linuxperf.nl.linux.org/`
- Dan Kegel's Web Hostel, a personal site with several papers on Linux Tuning: `http://www.kegel.com/`
- Linux.com's performance-tuning section: `http://www.linux.com/enhance/tuneup`
- The Linux Server Performance Checklist: `http://home.att.net/~jageorge/performance.html`
- Linux tuning in general: `http://www.tunelinux.com/`
- Benchmarking rules: `http://oss.sgi.com/LDP/HOWTO/Benchmarking-HOWTO.html`

As you can see, not that many sites are specifically geared just to Linux performance tuning, but rather the knowledge is scattered throughout the net. Always remember to refer to your application distribution for accurate information as well. Samba, for example, ships a large amount of technical documentation with the source.

The ultimate location for documentation on Linux, however, is the Linux Documentation Project (`http://www.linuxdoc.org/`), which has a vast repository of HOWTO-style documents. You should note that many documents in the LDP tend to undergo a long update process before the newest revisions make it to the official Web site, especially since the code is usually being developed at the same time. This ensures that the projects they are describing are solidified and that the documentation is accurate. If you are working on something that could be a little more bleeding-edge than what is described by the document, you might find it worthwhile to email the author or search for the more recent revisions of the document.

Magazines, Journals, and Newsletters

Unlike sites that are only for Linux performance, a plethora of media is available online and in print, at little or no cost to the administrator. The following list covers only a few of the more obvious ones:

- *The Linux Journal*, `http://www2.linuxjournal.com/`; some online and print
- *The Linux Gazette*, `http://www.linuxgazette.com/`; online only
- *Linux Today*, `http://www.linuxtoday.com/`; online only
- *Linux Magazine*, `http://www.linux-mag.com/`; some online and print
- *Linux Weekly News*, `http://www.lwn.net/`; online only

In addition to Linux-related sites, there are sites such as 32BitsOnline, which covers Linux (in addition to many other systems). Most projects have an individual site where project specific news is kept, and this can contain valuable information about upcoming capabilities and different ways to use the software. Many of these have gravitated toward centralized hosting sites such as SourceForge.net, although many application index sites such as `http://www.freshmeat.net` can point you in the right direction for different project categories and keep you up-to-date on releases.

Newsgroups and Mailing Lists

Last but definitely not least, if there is an unanswered question in the administrator's realm, just ask. Eventually an answer of some sort (whether good, bad, or ugly is a whole different topic) will emerge. Although there aren't any hard-and-fast rules, there are some guidelines to follow when posting messages to the world. A rough outline follows:

1. Check for mailing lists devoted to your problem or application, and look for expertise there first. This is likely to be the most centralized collection of knowledge on the subject. RedHat hosts many of the development lists, although the location you pulled the application from will likely have the location for your specific group lists. Archives of these lists might include your answer, and you should check them, if possible. Failure to check for an already solved problem will reduce your chances of getting further help.

2. Subscribe to your local Linux Users Group (LUG) list. You might find local help that can assist you right away.

3. Post to newsgroups as appropriate, minimizing cross-posting within the groups.

4. In some cases, a metagroup might be able to answer your question. For example, if your question pertains to a kernel problem, the best course (besides reading the documentation) is likely to be checking with a local list or the maintainer of the chunk of code in question, possibly followed by a newsgroup posting and, ultimately, the Linux kernel list

itself. It cannot be stressed enough that the kernel list is high-volume and accepts only questions that have been presented in a well thought-out manner—and possibly in a particular format. (Note that you should read the Linux Kernel Mailing List FAQ before sending a question to ensure that you aren't breaking any of the rules.)

With any of these resources, it is very important that you thoroughly describe the problem at hand, along with all factors that are relevant. In the special case of the kernel list, such as when posting an oops message, a specific format of what problems were found should be included, accompanied by a translated version of the oops data itself. Failure to follow these rules usually will get you nowhere. In general, it is a good idea to read the list rules and, if possible, to "lurk" on the list to get a feeling for what should be asked and *how* it should be asked.

Summary

With a little tenacity—and, hopefully, spare time—an administrator can easily fortify his arsenal of information by taking a look on the Web, digging through the LDP, querying mailing lists, or subscribing to newsgroups. As always, remember that the open source and free software movements are extremely fast-moving entities, and pieces of code are coming into the bleeding edge and rapidly being stabilized into the normal distribution channels. If you don't see a specific fix for your problem either in vendor documentation or other normal sources, be sure to check the lists for how to use the latest information.

INDEX

SYMBOLS

#! command, 20

A

-a option
>   hdparm command, 203
>
>   swapoff command, 217

accuracy of metrics, 33

Act field (ntop command), 66

activating swap files, 217

actual needs versus potential growth (capacity planning), 242-244

addresses
>   NAT (Network Address Translation), 146
>
>   PAE (Processor Address Extension), 93-94
>
>   virtual address space, 93

administrators, 244

age_buffer parameter (kernel), 176

age_super parameter (kernel), 176

agreements (performance), 86-87

ALL field (hosts.allow file), 228

-all option (x11perf command), 101

allocating resources, 10

Alpha processor, 88

analysis and interpretation. *See also* case studies
>   application architecture, 33-34
>
>   bottlenecks, 36
>
>   capacity planning, 248-249
>>   *data collection techniques, 250-251*
>>
>>   *data storage, 251*
>>
>>   *need for data, 249*
>>
>>   *performance tuning, 252-253*
>>
>>   *quality versus quantity, 249-250*

compute versus I/O intensive
applications, 33
CPU speed, 34
disk space management, 35-36
disk types, 34-35
network analysis tools,
273-274
resource saturation, 36-37
resource starvation, 37
unsatisfactory response time,
37
Apache JMeter, 151
**application network tuning,
122-123**
**application-specific require-
ments (capacity planning),
241-242, 272-273**
applications
application network tuning,
122-123
architecture, 33-34
capacity planning requirements, 241-242, 272-273
compute versus I/O-intensive,
33
configuration, 29
effects on memory, 221
loading, 20-22
applying patches, 190-191
**approaches to capacity plan-
ning, 245-246**
Appwatch Web site, 82
architecture
Alpha processor, 88
applications, 33-34
capacity planning, 254-255
kernel
CPU scheduling, 18-20
filesystem caching, 25
*process management,
22-23*
program loading, 20-22
thread management, 22-23
virtual memory, 23-24
NUMA (Non-Uniform
Memory Access), 88

operating system
buffer cache, 16
file interface, 16
filesystems, 17-18
/proc directory, 16-17
**Arguments field (inetd.conf
file), 227**
assessing tuning needs, 28
**assigning swap space,
215-216**
at tool, 157-158
ATA support, 181
**-aux option (ps command),
56**

B

b field (vmstat), 50
background mode, 156-157
**background, sending jobs to,
156-157**
backlogs, 133
balancing load, 145-147
bandwidth, 141-143
batch processing, 19, 158
batch tool, 158
bdflush file, 175-176
benchmarking
Benchmarking HOWTO Web
site, 292
bonnie utility, 53-55
**Benchmarking HOWTO Web
site, 292**
Beowulf clusters, 89
Beowulf project, 137
**-bg option (x11perf com-
mand), 101**
bi field (vmstat), 51
Blk_read field (iostat), 72
Blk_reads/s field (iostat), 72
Blk_wrtn field (iostat), 72
Blk_wrtn/s field (iostat), 72

block device support, 181
**blueprint for capacity
planning**
application-specific requirements, 272-273
capacity planning teams,
268-269
commercial products, 273
contracts, 270
example, 275-277
flexibility, 270
general principles
capacity plans, 265
global view, 263
*requirements gathering,
262*
statistics, 262-263
*upcoming technologies,
263-265*
hardware and software
requirements, 265-267
network analysis tools,
273-274
political issues, 271-272
pollers, 274-275
project management, 270-271
bonding, 137-141
bonnie tool, 53-55, 203
bottlenecks, 86
clustering solutions
Beowulf, 89
*MOSIX (Multicomputer
Operating System for
Unix), 90*
CPU-related parameters,
90-92
general application tuning, 89
hardware solutions, 87-88
identifying, 36-38
memory bottlenecks, 92-95
paging and swapping, 96
performance agreements,
86-87
software solutions, 88
system integrity, 97

system usage statistics, 95-96
user expectations, 86
bottom-up approach to capacity planning, 239-240
buff field (vmstat), 50
buffer cache, 16
buffermem file, 176
buffers
  buffer cache, 16
  filesystem buffers, 125
buffers field (free command), 60
building kernel, 183
bus, 207-208
businesses, capacity planning
  actual and potential growth, 255
  architecture, 254-255
  communication, 259-260
  core focus, 256
  costs, 255-258
  current business models, 256
  domain expertise, 257
  group crossover, 254
  management, 258
  medium businesses, 255
  projected usage, 258
  scalability, 253-254

C

-c option
  hdparm command, 203
  iostat command, 73
  mkswap command, 216
  ping command, 63
-C option (ps command), 56
cache
  buffer cache, 16, 94
  filesytem caching, 25
  getwd() calls, 126
  Samba, 129
cache field (vmstat), 50
cached field (free command), 60

calculating swap space, 215
capacity planning
  bottom-up approach, 239-240
  commerical products, 273
  contracts, 270
  creative thinking, 246-247
  defined, 236-238
  example, 275-277
  flexibility, 270
  general principles
    capacity plans, 265
    global view, 263
    requirements gathering, 262
    statistics, 262-263
    upcoming technologies, 263-265
  large businesses
    architecture, 254-255
    group crossover, 254
    scalability, 253-254
  medium businesses
    actual and potential growth, 255
    core focus, 256
    costs, 255-256
    current business models, 256
  network analysis tools, 273-274
  physical RAM requirements
    application effects and memory operations, 221
    determining, 214
    industry guidelines, 220
    multiuser systems, 213
    obtaining additional RAM, 214
    single-user systems, 212-213
    test systems, 221
  planning teams, 268-269
  political issues, 271-272
  pollers, 274-275

predictive analysis, 248-249
    data collection techniques, 250-251
    data storage, 251
    need for data, 249
    performance tuning, 252-253
    quality versus quantity, 249-250
  preventing need for performance tuning, 247-248
  project management, 270-271
  relationship with performance tuning, 247
  reliability, 240-241
  requirements
    application-specific requirements, 241-242, 272-273
    classic system requirements, 241
    communication, 244
    gathering, 262
    global view of, 238-239, 263
    hardware and software, 265-267
    potential growth, 242-244
  small businesses
    communication, 259-260
    costs, 257-258
    domain expertise, 257
    management, 258
    projected usage, 258
  statistics, 262-263
  structured approaches, 245-246
  swap files
    activating, 217
    advantages and disadvantages, 219
    creating, 24
    initializing, 217
  swap space, 214-215
    assigning, 215-216
    calculating, 215

configuring, 216-217
managing, 216
swap priorities, 218
swap strategies, 204
top-down approach, 239-240
case studies
classic memory problem
analysis, 284
development of problem, 283
disk configuration, 284
solutions, 284
system configuration, 283
complex memory problem
diagnosis, 285-286
solution, 286-287
LVS (Linux Virtual Server) walkthrough
assumptions, 287
configuration, 288-289
network latency, 284-285
Web server performance, 282-283
changing job priorities, 161
character devices, 182
checking
available memory, 60-61
status of processes
output format control, 56
output modifiers, 56
process forest, 58
process selection by list, 56
sample output, 56-58
simple process selection, 55
singling out users, 58-59
chipset-specific configuration options, 110
choosing drivers, 187-188
classic system requirements (capacity planning), 241
clients (X Window), 116-118

clustering solutions
Beowulf, 89
MOSIX (Multicomputer Operating System for Unix), 90
code maturity level, 180
collecting data (capacity planning)
performance tuning, 252-253
techniques, 250-251
color depth, 107-108
COMMAND field (top command), 49
Command Line field (ktop tool), 75
commands, 46-47, 70
#! prefix, 20
at, 157-158
batch, 158
bonnie, 53-55, 203
cron, 158-160
dd, 217
depmod, 166
diff, 189-190
dmesg, 286
dt, 202
executing
at specific time, 157-158
batch processing, 158
nice priority, 160-161
periodic execution, 158-160
free, 25, 60-61
gtop, 74-77, 79
hdparm, 203-204
interpreting results of, 47
iostat, 71-73
JMeter, 151
jobs, 156
ktop, 74-79
lmdd, 202
lsmod, 166
make bzImage, 183
make bzlilo, 184
make config, 180

make dep, 183
make menuconfig, 180
make modules, 183
make xconfig, 180
mkraid, 207
mkswap, 24, 216-217
mpstat, 73-74
Netwatch, 149-150
nice, 105, 160
ntop, 65-66
patch, 190-191
ping, 62-63
pollers, 274-275
ps
output format control, 56
output modifiers, 56
process forest, 58
process selection by list, 56
sample output, 56-58
simple process selection, 55
singling out users, 58-59
pvcreate, 200
raidstart, 207
raidstop, 207
renice, 106, 161
rmmod, 166
sard, 202
sg_dd, 202
smnpbulkget, 276
smnpget, 276
smnpwalk, 276
swapoff, 216-217
swapon, 24, 216-218
tcpdump, 64-65, 149
time, 61
top, 47-49
traceroute, 63-64
uptime, 53
vgcreate, 200
vgextend, 200
vgreduce, 200
vmstat, 50-51
x11perf, 100-103

x11perfcomp, 104
xload, 52
xosview, 52-53
xset, 111-112, 116-117
commerical capacity-planning products, 273
common causes, looking for, 39
communication, 244, 259-260
Compaq Alpha processor, 88
compute applications, 33
configuration files
inetd.conf, 225-226
X Window servers, 107
configuration management migration, 267
configuring
applications, 29
drivers, 188
kernel
ATA/IDE/MFM/RLL support, 181
block device support, 181
character devices, 182
code maturity level, 180
filesystems, 182
general setup, 181
loadable module support, 180
multimedia devices, 182
network device support, 181
networking options, 181
processor type, 180
SCSI support, 181
sound, 182
USB devices, 182
ramdisks, 208-209
software RAID (redundant array of independent disks), 206-207
swap space, 216-217
system configuration, 28
connections, testing, 62-63
contiguous memory spaces, 94

contracts, 270
controlling jobs
at tool, 157-158
background mode, 156-157
batch tool, 158
cron tool, 158-160
nice tool, 160
renice tool, 161
converting kilobytes to megabytes, 108
core focus (businesses), 256
costs of capacity planning, 255-258
Cox, Alan, 192
CPU field
ktop tool, 75
mpstat command, 74
top command, 49
vmstat tool, 51
CPU States field (top command), 48
CPU-related parameters, 90-92
cpuinfo file, 170
CPUs (central processing units)
CPU-related parameters, 90-92
PAE (Processor Address Extension), 93-94
scheduling
batch processes, 19
epochs, 18
interactive processes, 19
priorities, 20
quantums, 18
real-time processes, 19
speed of, 34
critical resources
identifying, 9
minimizing requirements of, 9-10
cron tool, 158-160
crontab files, 158
cs field (vmstat), 51
current business models, 256

D

-d option
hdparm command, 203
iostat command, 73
Daemon field (inetd.conf file), 227
daemons
inetd, 224-228
tcpd, 227-228
data collection
performance tuning, 252-253
techniques, 250-251
data storage, 251
data-presentation areas (kernel), 172-173
databases, 122-123
dbe module, 109
dd command, 217
deactivating ICMP, 133
decreasing
color depth, 107-108
display resolution, 107-108
dentry-state parameter (kernel), 172
dependency checking, 166, 183
depmod command, 166
-depth option (x11perf command), 101
desktop environments, 115-116, 123-124
device backlogs, 133
Device Memory Export Protocol (DMEP), 196
devices file, 170
DFSA (Direct File System Access), 90
diff tool, 189-190
Direct File System Access (DFSA), 90
directives, 111-113
directories
/etc
hosts.allow file, 227
hosts.deny file, 227

inetd.conf file, 224-227
raidtab file, 206-207
rc.d scripts, 228-230
starting and stopping services, 231
/proc, 16-17
cpuinfo file, 170
devices file, 170
filesystems file, 170
interrupts file, 170
iomem file, 170
ioports file, 170
kcore file, 170
kmsg file, 170
ksyms file, 170
loadavg file, 170
meminfo file, 170
modules file, 170
monitoring system activities with, 79-82
mounts file, 170
mtrr file, 171
partitions file, 171
pci file, 171
per-process data, 171-172
slabinfo file, 171
support for, 169
swaps file, 171
uptime file, 171
disabling
ICMP, 133
modules, 108-110
server extensions, 108-110
disk space management, 35-36
alternative solutions, 208-209
bus limitations, 207-208
GFS (Global File System), 196-197
hdparm tool, 203-204
LVM (Logical Volume Manager), 198-202
RAID (redundant array of independent disks), 204-205
level 0, 205
level 1, 205

level 10, 205
level 5, 205
software RAID, 205-207
SANs (Storage Area Networks), 196-197
swap strategies, 204
testing throughput, 202-203
disks, hard. See hard disk drives
-display option (x11perf command), 101
display resolution, 107-108
displaying statistics
CPU utilization, 71-72
device utilization, 71-73
processor-related statistics, 73-74
system load average, 52
system uptime, 53
top CPU-intensive processes, 47-49
virtual memory statistics, 50-51
DMEP (Device Memory Export Protocol), 196
dmesg command, 286
documentation
Linux Documentation Project, 292
local documentation, 11
metric documentation, 32
domain expertise, 257
domains, 123-124
downloading kernel source code, 178-179
dquote-max parameter (kernel), 173
dquote-nr parameter (kernel), 173
dri module, 109
drivers
kernel drivers, 187-188
modular drivers, 165-166

drives, hard. See hard disk drives
-dry-run option (patch command), 191
dt tool, 202
duration of problem, 30
dynamic buffer cache, 94

E

-e option (ps command), 56
e-mail mailing lists, 194, 293-294
ECN system, 134-135
enforced bandwidth limitations, 141-143
environment variables, LD_PRELOAD, 21
epochs, 18
error trapping, 193-194
/etc directory
hosts.allow file, 227
hosts.deny file, 227
inetd.conf file, 224-227
raidtab file, 206-207
rc.d scripts
example, 228-230
rc file, 230
rc.local file, 230
rc.sysinit file, 230
starting and stopping services, 231
Ethereal, 148
evaluating need for capacity planning
large businesses
architecture, 254-255
group crossover, 254
scalability, 253-254
medium businesses
actual and potential growth, 255
core focus, 256
costs, 255-256
current business models, 256

small businesses
  communication, 259-260
  costs, 257-258
  domain expertise, 257
  management, 258
  projected usage, 258
executing jobs
  at specific time, 157-158
  batch processing, 158
  nice priority, 160-161
  periodic execution, 158-160
**expectations for perfor-
  mance, 29**
expectations of users, 86
**extensions, disabling,
  108-110**
extmod module, 109

F

**-f option (ping command),
  62-63**
**fake oplocks (opportunistic
  locks), 126**
fake oplocks parameter, 126
fbdevhw module, 109
**-fg option (x11perf com-
  mand), 101**
Fiber Channel drives, 34
fields
  free command, 60
  hosts.allow file, 228
  inetd.conf file, 227
  iostat tool, 72-73
  ktop tool, 75
  mpstat tool, 74
  system usage statistics
    RSS, 95-96
    SHARE, 96
    SIZE, 95
  top tool, 48-49
  vmstat tool, 50-51
FIFO (first in, first out), 142
file I/O (input/output), 26

file interface, 16
**file-max parameter (kernel),
  173**
**file-nr parameter (kernel),
  173**
**files. *See also* directories;
  filesystems**
  bdflush, 175-176
  buffermem, 176
  cpuinfo, 170
  crontab, 158
  devices, 170
  file interface, 16
  freepages, 176
  hiding, 127
  hosts.allow, 227
  hosts.deny, 227
  I/O (input/output) layers, 26
  inetd.conf, 225-227
  interrupts, 170
  iomem, 170
  ioports, 170
  kcore, 170
  kmsg, 170
  kswapd, 176-178
  ksyms, 170
  loadavg, 170
  meminfo, 170
  modules, 170
  mounts, 170
  mtrr, 171
  partitions, 171
  pci, 171
  raidtab, 206-207
  rc, 230
  rc.local, 230
  rc.sysinit, 230
  server configuration files, 107
  slabinfo, 171
  swap files
    activating, 217
    *advantages and disadvan-
      tages, 219*
    creating, 24
    initializing, 217

  swaps, 171
  uptime, 171
  vetoing, 127
  XF86Config-4, 107
filesystems, 17-18, 170
  buffers, 125
  caching, 25
  GFS (Global File System),
    196-197
  limitations, 172-173
  NFS (Network File System),
    27-28, 130-131
  support for, 182
filters, 49
first in, first out (FIFO), 142
**flexibility in capacity plan-
  ning, 270**
focus (businesses), 256
**-fomit-frame-pointer parame-
  ter, 91**
FontPath directive, 111, 113
fonts
  font servers, 113
  loading, 111-113
**foreground, bringing jobs to,
  157**
**fragmentation thresholds,
  134**
free command, 25, 60-61
free field
  free command, 60
  vmstat command, 50
free memory, 60-61
freepages file, 176
Freshmeat Web site, 82
functions
  getwd(), 126
  refill_freelist(), 175
-funroll-loops parameter, 91

G

**gathering relevant data
  (capacity planning), 250-251**
Gavrilov, Constantine, 138

general setup (kernel config-uration), 181
generating patches, 189-190
get mem script, 80-82
getwd cache parameter, 126
getwd() function, 126
GFS (Global File System), 196-197
GLCore module, 109
Global File System (GFS), 196-197
global view of capacity plan-ning requirements, 238-239, 263
glx module, 109
GNOME desktop system, 115-116, 123-124
goals, prioritizing, 40
Godard, Sebastien, 70
Grand Unified Bootloader (GRUB), 184-186
group crossover, 254
GRUB (Grand Unified Bootloader), 184-186
gtop tool, 74-79

H

hard disk drives, 34
　disk space management, 35-36
　　alternative solutions, 208-209
　　bus limitations, 207-208
　　GFS (Global File System), 196-197
　　hdparm tool, 203-204
　　LVM (Logical Volume Manager), 198-202
　　SANs (Storage Area Networks), 196-197
　Fiber Channel, 34
　RAID (redundant array of independent disks), 204-205
　　level 0, 205
　　level 1, 205

level 5, 205
level 10, 205
software RAID, 205-207
ramdisks, 208-209
SCSI (Small Computer Systems Interface), 34
solid-state disks, 35, 208
swap space, 214-215
　advantages and disadvan-tages, 219
　assigning, 215-216
　calculating, 215
　configuring, 216-217
　managing, 216
　swap priorities, 218
　swap strategies, 204
throughput, testing, 202-203
hardware solutions
　bottlenecks
　　Alpha processor, 88
　　faster CPUs, 87
　　NUMA (Non-Uniform Memory Access), 88
　　SMP machines, 87-88
　capacity planning require-ments, 265-267
　network performance, 120-121
　upgrades, 114-115
hdparm tool, 203-204
hiding files, 127
high-availability networks, 145-147
host connections, testing, 62-63
Host field (ntop command), 66
hosts.allow file, 227
hosts.deny file, 227
HTTP (Hypertext Transfer Protocol)
　HTTP speed-ups, 123
　TUX server, 143-144

I

I/O (input/output), 25
　disk I/O utilization, 202-204
　I/O-intensive applications, 33
　layers, 26
　monitoring
　　gtop tool, 74-79
　　iostat tool, 71-73
　　ktop tool, 74-79
　performance management, 26
ibiblio FTP site, 82
ICMP (Internet Control Message Protocol), 133
icmp_echo_ignore_all paramter, 133
icmp_echo_ignore_broadcasts paramter, 133
id field (vmstat), 51
IDE support (kernel), 181
identifying
　bottlenecks, 36-38
　critical resources, 9
%idle field (iostat), 72
in field (vmstat), 51
industry guidelines, 220
inetd daemon, 224-228
inetd.conf file, 225-226
initializing swap files, 217
inode-nr parameter (kernel), 173
inode-state parameter (ker-nel), 173
input/output. *See* I/O, 25
installing kernel, 183-187
integrity of system, 97
interactive processes, 19
interfaces (file), 16
Internet Control Message Protocol (ICMP), 133
Internet Server
　inetd.conf file, 225-227
　TCP (Transmission Control Protocol) wrappers, 227-228

interpretation and analysis
(performance tuning)
application architecture, 33-34
bottlenecks, 36
compute versus I/O intensive
applications, 33
CPU speed, 34
disk space management, 35-36
disk types, 34-35
resource saturation, 36-37
resource starvation, 37
unsatisfactory response time,
37
interrupts file, 170
intr/s field (mpstat), 74
IO section (vmstat tool), 51
iomem file, 170
ioports file, 170
iostat tool, 71-73
IP (Internet Protocol) tunneling, 146
ipfrag_high_thresh value,
134
ipfrag_low_thresh value, 134
IPTOS_LOWDELAY option,
129
IPTOS_THROUGHPUT option,
129

J

-j option (ps command), 56
JMeter, 151
job control
at tool, 157-158
background mode, 156-157
batch tool, 158
cron tool, 158-160
nice tool, 160
renice tool, 161
jobs
bringing to foreground, 157
controlling, 156

executing
batch processing, 158
nice priority, 160-161
periodic execution,
158-160
at specific time, 157-158
sending to background,
156-157
jobs command, 156
journals, 293

K

K Desktop Environment
(KDE), 115-116
-K option (hdparm com-
mand), 203
kcore file, 170
KDE (K Desktop
Environment), 115-116
keepalive times, 135
Kegel, Dan, 292
kernel, 7-8, 164
/proc filesystem
cpuinfo file, 170
devices file, 170
filesystems file, 170
interrupts file, 170
iomem file, 170
ioports file, 170
kcore file, 170
kmsg file, 170
ksyms file, 170
loadavg file, 170
meminfo file, 170
modules file, 170
mounts file, 170
mtrr file, 171
partitions file, 171
pci file, 171
per-process data, 171-172
slabinfo file, 171
support for, 169
swaps file, 171
uptime file, 171

architecture
CPU scheduling, 18-20
filesystem caching, 25
monolithic architecture,
165
process management,
22-23
program loading, 20-22
thread management, 22-23
virtual memory, 23-24
building, 183
configuring
ATA/IDE/MFM/RLL
support, 181
block device support, 181
character devices, 182
code maturity level, 180
filesystems, 182
general setup, 181
loadable module support,
180
multimedia devices, 182
network device support,
181
networking options, 181
processor type, 180
SCSI support, 181
sound, 182
USB devices, 182
data-presentation areas, 172
dependency checking, 183
downloading source code,
178-179
drivers, 187-188
installing, 184-187
modules
creating from source code,
168
dependency checking, 166
installing, 183
loadable module support,
180
loading, 166-167
modular drivers, 165-166
removing, 166

network manipulation, 174
network performance tuning,
    132-133
    device backlogs, 133
    ECN, 134-135
    fragmentation thresholds,
        134
    ICMP, 133
    keepalive times, 135
    large windows, 136
    local port range, 133
    path discovery, 134
    selective packet acknowl-
        edgement, 135-136
    TCP timestamps, 136-137
    urgent pointers, 136
    window scaling, 136
parameters, 90-92
    age_buffer, 176
    age_super, 176
    bdflush file, 175-176
    buffermem file, 176
    dentry-state, 172
    dquote-max, 173
    dquote-nr, 173
    fake oplocks, 126
    file-max, 173
    file-nr, 173
    fomit-frame-pointer, 91
    freepages file, 176
    getwd cache, 126
    funroll-loops, 91
    icmp_echo_ignore_all,
        133
    icmp_echo_ignore_
        broadcasts, 133
    inode-nr, 173
    inode-state, 173
    kswapd file, 176-178
    level2 oplocks, 127
    max_map_count, 177
    max xmit, 127
    msg*, 174
    ON, 91
    overcommit_memory, 177

overflowgid, 173
overflowuid, 173
page-cluster, 177
pagecache, 177
pagetable_cache, 178
panic, 173
printk, 173
read prediction, 128
read raw, 128
read size, 128
read write, 128
shm*, 174
super-max, 173
super-nr, 173
swap_cluster, 177
threads-max, 174
tries_base, 176
tries_min, 176
wide links, 126
patching
    advantages of, 188-189
    diff tool, 189-190
    example, 193
    obtaining patches,
        192-193
    patch tool, 190-191
    potential problems, 191
    testing patches, 191
reasons to modify, 165
recompiling
    building kernel, 183
    dependency checking, 183
    downloading source code,
        178-179
    driver configuration, 188
    driver selection, 187-188
    kernel configuration,
        180-182
    kernel installation,
        184-187
    module installation, 183
    patches, 188-193
risks of performance tuning,
    40-41
trapping errors, 193-194

virtual memory
    bdflush file, 175-176
    buffermem file, 176
    freepages file, 176
    kswapd file, 176-178
Kernel Traffic Web site, 192
kilobytes, converting to
    megabytes, 108
kmsg file, 170
KNOWN field (hosts.allow
    file), 228
known peak periods, 29
kswapd file, 176-178
ksyms file, 170
ktop tool, 74-79

L

-l option
    ntop command, 66
    x11perfcomp tool, 104
-labels option (x11perf com-
    mand), 101
large businesses, capacity
    planning, 253
    architecture, 254-255
    group crossover, 254
    scalability, 253-254
latency case study, 284-285
layers of file I/O (input/
    output), 26
LD_PRELOAD environment
    variable, 21
level 2 oplocks (opportunistic
    locks), 127
levels of RAID (redundant
    array of independent disks)
    level 0, 205
    level 1, 205
    level 5, 205
    level 10, 205
    software RAID, 205-207
liability, 87

libraries
  bottlenecks, 95
  linking, 21
limitations of performance tuning, 40
linking libraries, 21
Linux Documentation Project, 292
The Linux Gazette, 293
The Linux Journal, 293
Linux kernel. *See* kernel
Linux Magazine, 293
Linux Performance Tuning Site, 292
Linux Server Performance Checklist (Web site), 292
Linux Today, 293
Linux Virtual Server (LVS)
  case study
    assumptions, 287
    configuration, 288-289
      Web sites
    performance-tuning resources, 292
Linux Weekly News, 192, 293
linux-kernel mailing list, 194
Linux.com, 292
listings
  color depths, 108
  modules, disabling, 109
  x11perf tool
    results, 103
    tests, 102
  x11perfcomp tool, 104
  xset command, 112
lmdd tool, 202
load averages, 31-32, 52
load balancing, 145-147
loadable module support, 180
loadavg file, 170
loading
  fonts, 111-113
  modules, 166-167
  programs, 20-22

local documentation, 11
LOCAL field (hosts.allow file), 228
local port ranges, 133
log levels (Samba), 127
logical extents, 200
Logical Volume Manager (LVM), 26, 198-202
logical volumes, 200
lsmod command, 166
LVM (Logical Volume Manager), 26, 198-202
LVS (Linux Virtual Server)
  case study
    assumptions, 287
    configuration, 288-289
    performance-tuning resources, 292

M

-m option (hdparm command), 203
magazines, 293
mailing lists, 194, 293-294
make bzImage command, 183
make bzlilo command, 184
make config command, 180
make dep command, 183
make menuconfig command, 180
make modules command, 183
make xconfig command, 180
management factors (capacity planning), 258
managing
  disk space, 35-36
    alternative solutions, 208-209
    bus limitations, 207-208

    GFS (Global File System), 196-197
    hdparm tool, 203-204
    LVM (Logical Volume Manager), 198-202
    RAID (redundant array of independent disks), 204-207
    SANs (Storage Area Networks), 196-197
    swap strategies, 204
    testing throughput, 202-203
  processes, 22-23
  services, 224
    inetd.conf file, 225-228
    rc.d scripts, 228-231
    TCP (Transmission Control Protocol) wrappers, 227-228
  swap space, 216
  threads, 22-23
max_map_count parameter (kernel), 177
max_xmit parameter (kernel), 127
measurements
  epochs, 18
  load averages, 31-32
  metric accuracy, 33
  metric documentation, 32
  per-process CPU metrics, 32
  qualitative versus quantitative measurements, 33
  quantums, 18
  queues, 31-32
medium businesses, capacity planning
  actual and potential growth, 255
  core focus, 256
  costs, 255-256
  current business models, 256
%MEM field (top command), 49

meminfo file, 170
memory
  bottlenecks, 92-95
  cache
    buffer cache, 16, 94
    Samba, 129
  case studies
    classic memory problem,
      283-284
    complex memory problem,
      285-287
    performance-tuning,
      283-285
  filesystem buffers, 125
  free memory, 60-61
  NUMA (Non-Uniform
    Memory Access), 88
  physical RAM requirements
    application effects and
      memory operations, 221
    determining, 214
    industry guidelines, 220
    multiuser systems, 213
    obtaining additional RAM,
      214
    single-user systems,
      212-213
    test systems, 221
  swap files
    activating, 217
    advantages and disadvan-
      tages, 219
    creating, 24
    initializing, 217
  swap space, 214-215
    advantages and disadvan-
      tages, 219
    assigning, 215-216
    calculating, 215
    configuring, 216-217
    managing, 216
    swap priorities, 218
    swap strategies, 204

system usage statistics
    RSS field, 95-96
    SHARE field, 96
    SIZE field, 95
  virtual memory, 23-24
    bdflush file, 175-176
    buffermem file, 176
    freepages file, 176
    kswapd file, 176-178
    returning statistics about,
      50-51
memory bottlenecks, 92-93
  contiguous memory spaces,
    94
  dynamic buffer cache, 94
  PAE (Processor Address
    Extension), 93-94
  shared libraries, 95
  virtual address space, 93
Memory field (ktop tool), 75
**memory section (vmstat
  tool), 50**
**methodology of perfor-
  mance tuning**
  application configuration, 29
  assessment, 28
  duration of problem, 30
  known peak periods, 29
  local documentation, 11
  performance expectations, 29
  proactive/reactive, 6, 11-12
  solution options, 31
  sudden changes, 30
  system configuration, 28
metrics
  accuracy, 33
  documentation, 32
  per-process CPU metrics, 32
MFM support (kernel), 181
**minimizing critical resource
  requirements, 9-10**
mkraid tool, 207
**mkswap command, 24,
  216-217**
modes, background, 156-157

modular drivers, 165-166
modules (kernel)
  creating from source code,
    168
  dbe, 109
  dependency checking, 166
  disabling, 108-110
  dri, 109
  drivers, 165-166
  extmod, 109
  fbdevhw, 109
  GLCore, 109
  glx, 109
  installing, 183
  loadable module support, 180
  loading, 166-167
  removing, 166
modules file, 170
monitor fields (top tool), 48
monitoring performance
  Linux tools, 70
    gtop, 74-79
    iostat, 71-73
    ktop, 74-79
    mpstat, 73-74
    online resources, 82
    /proc directory, 79-82
  Unix tools, 46-47
    bonnie, 53-55
    free, 60-61
    interpreting results of, 47
    ntop, 65-66
    ping, 62-63
    ps, 55-56, 58-59
    tcpdump, 64-65
    time, 61
    top, 47-49
    traceroute, 63-64
    uptime, 53
    vmstat, 50-51
    xload, 52
    xosview, 52-53
**MOSIX (Multicomputer
  Operating System for
  Unix), 90**

mounts file, 170
mpstat tool, 73-74
msg* parameter (kernel), 174
mtrr file, 171
Multicomputer Operating
  System for Unix (MOSIX),
  90
multimedia devices, 182
multiuser systems, 213

N

Name field
      inetd.conf file, 227
      ktop tool, 75
namespaces, 196
NAT (Network Address
  Translation), 146
Netwatch, 149-150
Network Address Translation
  (NAT), 146
network analysis tools,
  273-274
Network File System (NFS),
  27-28, 130-131
network latency case study,
  284-285
networks
      application network tuning,
        122-123
      device support, 181
      domains, 123-124
      hardware, 120-121
      kernel network stack behavior,
        174
      kernel options, 132-133, 181
          device backlogs, 133
          ECN, 134-135
          fragmentation thresholds,
            134
          ICMP, 133
          keepalive times, 135
          large windows, 136

      local port range, 133
      path discovery, 134
      selective packet acknowl-
        edgement, 135-136
      TCP timestamps, 136-137
      urgent pointers, 136
      window scaling, 136
monitoring
      ntop tool, 65-66
      ping tool, 62-63
      tcpdump tool, 64-65
      traceroute tool, 63-64
NAT (Network Address
  Translation), 146
network latency case study,
  284-285
performance tuning
      bonding, 137-141
      enforced bandwidth limi-
        tations, 141-143
      kernel options, 132-137
      load balancing, 145-147
      NFS (Network File
        System), 130-131
      NIS (Network Information
        System), 132
Samba, 124-125
      filesystem buffers, 125
      getwd() calls, 126
      hiding/vetoing files, 127
      oplocks, 126-127
      packet transmit size, 127
      raw reads and writes, 128
      socket options, 129
      write cache size, 129
SANs (storage area networks),
  35, 196-197
tools, 147
      Ethereal, 148
      Netwatch, 149-150
      ntop, 65-66
      ping, 62-63

      SNMP (Simple Network
        Management Protocol),
        150
      tcpdump, 64-65, 149
      testing tools, 150-152
      traceroute, 63-64
      zero-copy networking,
        144-145
new features
      TUX server, 143-144
      zero-copy networking,
        144-145
newsgroups, 293-294
newsletters, 293
NFS (Network File System),
  27-28, 130-131
NI field (top command), 49
%nice field
      iostat command, 72
      mpstat command, 74
nice command, 105
nice priority, 105-106
nice tool, 160
NIS (Network Information
  System), 132
Non-Uniform Memory Access
  (NUMA), 88
ntop tool, 65-66
NUMA (Non-Uniform
  Memory Access), 88

O

object identifiers (OIDs), 274
objectives of performance
  tuning, 8
OIDs (object identifiers), 274
-ON parameter (kernel), 91
online resources
      journals, 293
      magazines, 293
      mailing lists, 293-294
      newsgroups, 293-294
      newsletters, 293
      performance-tuning sites, 292

OpenNMS Web site, 276
operating system structure, 16
   buffer cache, 16
   file interface, 16
   filesystems, 17-18
   /proc directory, 16-17
oplocks (oportunistic locks), 126-127
optimizing performance. *See* performance tuning
outsourcing, 269
overcommit_memory parameter (kernel), 177
overflowgid parameter (kernel), 173
overflowuid parameter (kernel), 173

P

-p option
   ntop command, 66
   swapon command, 218
-p0 option (patch command), 190
packets
   Samba, 127
   selective acknowledgement, 135-136
PAE (Processor Address Extension), 93-94
page-cluster parameter (kernel), 177
pagecache parameter (kernel), 177
pagetable_cache parameter (kernel), 178
paging, 96
panic parameter (kernel), 173
parameters, 90-92
   age_buffer, 176
   age_super, 176
   bdflush file, 175-176

buffermem file, 176
dentry-state, 172
dquote-max, 173
dquote-nr, 173
fake oplocks, 126
file-max, 173
file-nr, 173
fomit-frame-pointer, 91
freepages file, 176
getwd cache, 126
funroll-loops, 91
icmp_echo_ignore_all, 133
icmp_echo_ignore_broad-
   casts, 133
inode-nr, 173
inode-state, 173
kswapd file, 176-178
level2 oplocks, 127
max_map_count, 177
max xmit, 127
msg*, 174
ON, 91
overcommit_memory, 177
overflowgid, 173
overflowuid, 173
page-cluster, 177
pagecache, 177
pagetable_cache, 178
panic, 173
printk, 173
read prediction, 128
read raw, 128
read size, 128
read write, 128
shm*, 174
super-max, 173
super-nr, 173
swap_cluster, 177
threads-max, 174
tries_base, 176
tries_min, 176
wide links, 126
PARANOID field (hosts.allow file), 228
partitions file, 171

partitions, swap. *See* swap space
patch tool, 190-191
patches
   applying, 190-191
   example, 193
   generating, 189-190
   obtaining, 192-193
   potential problems, 191
   testing, 191
patching kernel
   advantages of, 188-189
   diff tool, 189-190
   example, 193
   obtaining patches, 192-193
   patch tool, 190-191
   potential problems, 191
   testing patches, 191
path discovery, 134
pci file, 171
peak periods, 29
per-process CPU metrics, 32
per-process data, 171-172
performance agreements, 86-87
performance analysts, 12
performance expectations, 29
performance monitoring
   Linux tools, 70
      gtop, 74-79
      iostat, 71-73
      ktop, 74-79
      mpstat, 73-74
      online resources, 82
      /proc directory, 79-82
   Unix tools, 46-47
      bonnie, 53-55
      free, 60-61
      interpreting results of, 47
      ntop, 65-66
      ping, 62-63
      ps, 55-59
      tcpdump, 64-65
      time, 61

top, 47-49
traceroute, 63-64
uptime, 53
vmstat, 50-51
xload, 52
xosview, 52-53

performance tuning
advantages of, 7
bottlenecks
    clustering solutions, 89-90
    CPU-related parameters,
        90-92
    general application tuning,
        89
    hardware solutions, 87-88
    memory bottlenecks, 92-95
    paging and swapping, 96
    performance agreements,
        86-87
    software solutions, 88
    system integrity, 97
    system usage statistics,
        95-96
    user expectations, 86
case studies
    classic memory problem,
        283-284
    complex memory problem,
        285-287
    LVS (Linux Virtual Server)
        walkthrough, 287-289
    network latency, 284-285
    Web server performance,
        282-283
common causes, 39
critical resources
    identifying, 9
    minimizing requirements
        of, 9-10
data collection, 252-253
defined, 6-7
disk space management
    disk I/O utilization,
        202-204
    GFS (Global File System),
        196-197

LVM (Logical Volume
    Manager), 198-202
    SANs (Storage Area
        Networks), 196-197
    filesystem caching, 25
    I/O (input/output), 25-26
    interpretation and analysis
        application architecture,
            33-34
        bottlenecks, 36
        compute versus I/O-inten-
            sive applications, 33
        CPU speed, 34
        disk space management,
            35-36
        disk types, 34-35
        resource saturation, 36-37
        resource starvation, 37
        unsatisfactory response
            time, 37
    job control
        at tool, 157-158
        background mode,
            156-157
        batch tool, 158
        cron tool, 158-160
        nice tool, 160
        renice tool, 161
    kernel, 7-8, 18, 164
        /proc filesystem, 169-172
        building, 183
        configuring, 180-182
        CPU scheduling, 18-20
        data-presentation areas,
            172
        dependency checking, 183
        downloading source code,
            178-179
        drivers, 187-188
        installing, 184-187
        modules, 165-168, 183
        monolithic architecture,
            165
        network manipulation,
            174
        parameters, 172-173

patching, 188-193
    process management,
        22-23
    program loading, 20-22
    reasons to modify, 165
    thread management, 22-23
    trapping errors, 193-194
    virtual memory, 175-178
limitations, 40
Linux-specific tools, 70
    gtop, 74-79
    iostat, 71-73
    ktop, 74-79
    mpstat, 73-74
    online resources, 82
    /proc directory, 79-82
measurements
    load averages, 31-32
    metric accuracy, 33
    metric documentation, 32
    per-process CPU metrics,
        32
    qualitative versus quanti-
        tative measurements, 33
    queues, 31-32
methodology
    application configuration,
        29
    assessment, 28
    duration of problem, 30
    known peak periods, 29
    local documentation, 11
    performance expectations,
        29
    proactive/reactive, 6,
        11-12
    solution options, 31
    sudden changes, 30
    system configuration, 28
networks
    application network tun-
        ing, 122-123
    bonding, 137-141
    domains, 123-124

enforced bandwidth limita-
tions, 141-143
hardware, 120-121
kernel options, 132-137
load balancing, 145-147
NFS (Network File
System), 27-28, 130-131
NIS (Network Information
System), 132
objectives, 8
online resources
general Web sites, 292
journals, 293
magazines, 293
mailing lists, 293-294
newsgroups, 293-294
newsletters, 293
operating system structure,
16-18
performance analysts, 12
physical RAM requirements
application effects and
memory operations, 221
determining, 214
industry guidelines, 220
multiuser systems, 213
obtaining additional RAM,
214
single-user systems,
212-213
test systems, 221
preventing need for, 247-248
prioritizing goals, 40
relationship between users and
performance, 13
relationship with capacity
planning, 247
resource allocation, 10
risks, 40-41
Samba, 124-125
cached getwd( ) calls, 126
filesystem buffers, 125
hiding/vetoing files, 127
oplocks, 126-127
packet transmit size, 127

raw reads and writes, 128
socket options, 129
write cache size, 129
services
inetd.conf file, 224-227
rc.d scripts, 228-231
starting, 224
TCP (Transmission
Control Protocol) wrap-
pers, 227-228
swap files
activating, 217
advantages and disadvan-
tages, 219
creating, 24
initializing, 217
swap space, 214-215
advantages and disadvan-
tages, 219
assigning, 215-216
calculating, 215
configuring, 216-217
managing, 216
swap priorities, 218
swap strategies, 204
Unix performance-monitoring
tools, 46-47
bonnie, 53-55
free, 60-61
interpreting results of, 47
ntop, 65-66
ping, 62-63
ps, 55-59
tcpdump, 64-65
time, 61
top, 47-49
traceroute, 63-64
uptime, 53
vmstat, 50-51
xload, 52
xosview, 52-53
virtual memory, 23-24
when to use, 38-40
X Window System
chipset-specific configura-
tion options, 110

client performance,
116-118
color depth, 107-108
desktop environments,
115-116
display resolution,
107-108
fonts, 111-113
hardware upgrades,
114-115
rebuilding server, 110-111
server configuration file,
107
server extensions, 108-110
server priority, 105-106
server upgrades, 113-114
unused modules, 108-110
x11perf tool, 100-103
x11perfcomp tool, 104
performance-monitoring
tools, 46-47, 70
bonnie, 53-55
free, 60-61
gtop, 74-77, 79
interpreting results of, 47
iostat, 71-73
ktop, 74-77, 79
mpstat, 73-74
ntop, 65-66
online resources, 82
ping, 62-63
/proc directory, 79-82
ps
output format control, 56
output modifiers, 56
process forest, 58
sample output, 56-58
simple process selection,
55-56
singling out users, 58-59
tcpdump, 64-65
time, 61
top, 47-49
traceroute, 63-64
uptime, 53

vmstat, 50-51
xload, 52
xosview, 52-53
physical extents, 200
physical RAM requirements
    application effects and memory operations, 221
    determining, 214
    industry guidelines, 220
    multiuser systems, 213
    obtaining additional RAM, 214
    single-user systems, 212-213
    test systems, 221
physical volumes, 200
PID field
    ktop command, 75
    top command, 48
ping tool, 62-63
planning. *See* **capacity planning**
pointers, urgent, 136
political aspects of capacity planning, 271-272
pollers, 274-275
ports, 133
POSIX threads, 22-23
potential growth, 242-244, 255
predictive analysis, 248-249
    data collection techniques, 250-251
    data storage, 251
    need for data, 249
    performance tuning, 252-253
    quality versus quantity, 249-250
preventing need for performance tuning, 247-248
PRI field (top command), 49
principles of capacity planning
    capacity plans, 265
    global view, 263
    requirements gathering, 262

    statistics, 262-263
    upcoming technologies, 263-265
printk parameter (kernel), 173
priorities, 20
    of goals, 40
    nice values, 105-106, 160-161
    resource allocation, 10
    swap priorities, 218
    X Window servers, 105-106
Priority field (ktop tool), 75
proactive performance tuning, 6, 11-12. *See also* **performance tuning**
/proc directory, 16-17
    cpuinfo file, 170
    devices file, 170
    filesystems file, 170
    interrupts file, 170
    iomem file, 170
    ioports file, 170
    kcore file, 170
    kmsg file, 170
    ksyms file, 170
    loadavg file, 170
    meminfo file, 170
    modules file, 170
    monitoring system activities with, 79-82
    mounts file, 170
    mtrr file, 171
    partitions file, 171
    pci file, 171
    per-process data, 171-172
    slabinfo file, 171
    support for, 169
    swaps file, 171
    uptime file, 171
process fields (top tool), 48-49
processes
    batch processes, 19
    checking status of
        output format control, 56
        output modifiers, 56

        process forest, 58
        process selection by list, 56
        sample output, 56-58
        simple process selection, 55
        singling out users, 58-59
    interactive processes, 19
    managing, 22-23
    priorities, 20
        nice values, 105-106, 160-161
        swap priorities, 218
    real-time processes, 19
    scheduling, 18-20
    top CPU-intensive processes, 47-49
processes field (top command), 48
Processor Address Extension (PAE), 93-94
processor type (kernel configuration), 180
processor-related statistics, 73-74
procs section (vmstat tool), 50
profiles (usage), 100
programs. *See* **applications**
project management, 270-271
projected usage, 258
Protocol field (inetd.conf file), 227
<protocol> field (ntop command), 66
protocols
    DMEP (Device Memory Export Protocol), 196
    HTTP (Hypertext Transfer Protocol)
        HTTP speed-ups, 123
        TUX server, 143-144
    ICMP (Internet Control Message Protocol), 133

IP (Internet Protocol) tunneling, 146
NAT (Network Address Translation), 146
NIS (Network Information System), 132
Samba, 124-125
SNMP (Simple Network Management Protocol), 150
TCP (Transmission Control Protocol)
TCP wrappers, 227-228
timestamps, 136-137
ps tool
output format control, 56
output modifiers, 56
process forest, 58
sample output, 56-58
simple process selection, 55-56
singling out users, 58-59
pvcreate command, 200

Q-R

qualitative measurements, 33
quality of data (capacity planning), 249-250
quantitative measurements, 33
quantity of data (capacity planning), 249-250
quantums, 18
queues, 31-32
"quick fixes," 237-238

r field (vmstat), 50
-r option
hdparm command, 203
ntop command, 66
ping command, 63
rmmod command, 166
x11perfcomp command, 104

-R option (patch command), 191
RAID (redundant array of independent disks), 204-205
level 0, 205
level 1, 205
level 5, 205
level 10, 205
software RAID, 205-207
raidstart command, 207
raidstop command, 207
raidtab file, 206-207
RAM (Random Access Memory)
application effects and memory operations, 221
determining, 214
industry guidelines, 220
multiuser systems, 213
obtaining additional RAM, 214
single-user systems, 212-213
test systems, 221
ramdisks, 208 209
Random Access Memory. See RAM
-range option (x11perf command), 101
ranges (ports), 133
raw reads and writes (Samba), 128
rc file, 230
rc.d scripts
example, 228-230
rc file, 230
rc.local file, 230
rc.sysinit file, 230
stopping and starting services, 231
rc.local file, 230
rc.sysinit file, 230
Rcvd field (ntop command), 66

reactive performance tuning, 6, 11-12. See also performance tuning
read prediction, 128
read raw parameter, 128
read size parameter, 128
reads (Samba), 128
real-time processes, 19
rebuilding X Window servers, 110-111
recompiling kernel
building kernel, 183
dependency checking, 183
downloading source code, 178-179
driver configuration, 188
driver selection, 187-188
kernel configuration
ATA/IDE/MFM/RLL support, 181
block device support, 181
character devices, 182
code maturity level, 180
filesystems, 182
general setup, 181
loadable module support, 180
multimedia devices, 182
network device support, 181
networking options, 181
processor type, 180
SCSI support, 181
sound, 182
USB devices, 182
kernel installation, 184-187
module installation, 183
patches
advantages of, 188-189
diff tool, 189-190
example, 193
obtaining, 192-193
patch tool, 190-191
potential problems, 191
testing, 191

redundant array of independent disks. *See* RAID
refill_freelist() function, 175
relationship between capacity planning and performance tuning, 247
relationship between users and performance, 13
reliability, 240-241
removing kernel modules, 166
renice command, 106, 161
-repeat option (x11perf command), 101
requirements of capacity planning
  application-specific requirements, 241-242, 272-273
  classic system requirements, 241
  communication, 244
  gathering, 262
  global view of, 238-239, 263
  hardware and software, 265-266
    configuration management migration, 267
    upgrades, 266-267
  potential growth, 242-244
Resident field (ktop tool), 75
resource allocation, 10
resource saturation, 36-37
resource starvation, 37
resources
  allocating, 10
  critical resources
    identifying, 9
    minimizing requirements of, 9-10
  journals, 293
  magazines, 293
  mailing lists, 293-294
  newsgroups, 293-294
  newsletters, 293
  performance-tuning Web sites, 292

saturation, 36-37
starvation, 37
response time, 37
restarting services, 231
risks of performance tuning, 40-41
RLL support (kernel), 181
rmmod command, 166
routes, tracing, 63-64
RSS field
  memory usage statistics, 95-96
  top command, 49
running jobs
  at specific time, 157-158
  batch processing, 158
  nice priority, 160-161
  periodic execution, 158-160
runtime queues, 31

S

-s option
  free command, 60-61
  ping command, 63
Samba, 124-125
  cached getwd() calls, 126
  filesystem buffers, 125
  hiding/vetoing files, 127
  oplocks, 126-127
  packet transmit size, 127
  raw reads and writes, 128
  socket options, 129
  write cache size, 129
SANs (storage area networks), 35, 196-197
sard tool, 202
saturation of resources, 36-37
scalability, 90, 253-254
scheduler
  batch processes, 19
  epochs, 18
  interactive processes, 19

priorities, 20
quantums, 18
real-time processes, 19
scheduling processes, 18-20
scripts
  get mem, 80-82
  rc.d scripts
    example, 228-230
    rc file, 230
    rc.local file, 230
    rc.sysinit file, 230
    starting and stopping services, 231
SCSI (Small Computer Systems Interface) drives, 34, 181
selective packet acknowledgement, 135-136
sending jobs to background/foreground, 156-157
Sent field (ntop command), 66
server extensions, 108-110
servers
  DMEP (Device Memory Export Protocol), 196
  extensions, 108-110
  font servers, 113
  Internet Server
    inetd.conf file, 224-227
    TCP (Transmission Control Protocol) wrappers, 227-228
  LVS (Linux Virtual Server), 287-289
  Samba
    cached getwd() calls, 126
    filesystem buffers, 125
    hiding/vetoing files, 127
    oplocks, 126-127
    packet transmit size, 127
    raw reads and writes, 128
    socket options, 129
    write cache size, 129

TUX, 143-144

Web servers, 282-283

X Window

   color depth, 107-108

   configuration files, 107

   display resolution,
     107-108

   priority, 105-106

   rebuilding, 110-111

   testing performance of,
     100-104

   upgrading, 113-114

services

   restarting, 231

   risks of performance tuning,
     41

   starting, 224, 231

   stopping, 231

sg_dd tool, 202

SHARE field

   memory usage statistics, 96

   top command, 49

Shared field

   free command, 60

   ktop tool, 75

shared libraries

   bottlenecks, 95

   linking, 21

shm* parameter (kernel), 174

si field (vmstat), 51

Simple Network
  Management Protocol
  (SNMP), 150

single-user systems, 212-213

SIZE field

   memory usage statistics, 95

   top command, 49

slabinfo file, 171

small businesses, capacity
  planning

   communication, 259-260

   costs, 257-258

   domain expertise, 257

   management, 258

   projected usage, 258

Small Computer Systems
  Interface (SCSI) drives, 34

SMP machines, 87-88

sniffers, 64-65

SNMP (Simple Network
  Management Protocol), 150

snmpbulkget command, 276

snmpget command, 276

snmpwalk command, 276

so field (vmstat), 51

sockets, 129

software

   bottleneck solutions, 88

   capacity planning require-
     ments, 265-266

     configuration management
       migration, 267

     upgrades, 266-267

   CPU-related parameters,
     91-92

   software RAID (redundant
     array of independent disks),
     205-207

solid-state drives, 35, 208

sound, 182

source code (kernel), down-
  loading, 178-179

SO_KEEPALIVE option, 129

speed

   CPUs, 34

   HTTP speed-ups, 123

   response time, 37

speed-ups (HTTP), 123

starting services, 224, 231

starvation (resources), 37

State field

   ktop command, 75

   top command, 49

statistics

   capacity planning, 262-263

   displaying

     CPU utilitization, 71-72

     device utilitization, 71-73

     free memory, 60-61

     processor-related statis-
       tics, 73-74

     status of processes, 55-59

     system load average, 52

     system uptime, 53

     top CPU-intensive
       processes, 47-49

     virtual memory statistics,
       50-51

   memory usage, 95-96

status of processes, 55-56,
  58-59

stopping services, 231

storage

   drives. *See* hard disk drives

   SANs (storage area networks),
     35, 196-197

storage area networks
  (SANs), 35, 196-197

structured approaches to
  capacity planning, 245-246

studies. *See* case studies

subsystems (kernel), 7-8,
  25-26

sudden changes, 30

super-max parameter (ker-
  nel), 173

super-nr parameter (kernel),
  173

Swap field (top command),
  48

swap files

   activating, 217

   advantages and disadvantages,
     219

   creating, 24

   initializing, 217

swap priorities, 218

swap section (vmstat tool),
  51

swap space, 214-215

   advantages and disadvantages,
     219

   assigning, 215-216

   calculating, 215

   configuring, 216-217

   managing, 216

swap priorities, 218
swap strategies, 204
swapoff command, 216-217
swapon command, 24, 216-218
swaps file, 171
swap_cluster parameter (kernel), 177
swpd field (vmstat), 50
sy field (vmstat), 51
sync time adjustment, 103
%sys field (iostat), 72
sysstat tools, 70
gtop, 74-79
iostat, 71-73
ktop, 74-77, 79
mpstat, 73-74
%system field (mpstat), 74
system administrators, 244
system configuration, 28
system integrity, 97
system load average, 31-32, 52
system section (vmstat tool), 51
system services. *See* **services**
system usage statistics, 95-96

T

-t option (hdparm command), 203
-T option (ps command), 55
Tarreau, Willy, 138
TCP (Transmission Control Protocol)
TCP wrappers, 227-228
timestamps, 136-137
tcpd daemon, 227-228
tcpdump tool, 64-65, 149
TCP_NODELAY option, 129
tcp_stdurg value, 136
tcp_window_scaling value, 136

teams (capacity planning)
choosing team members, 268
creating, 268-269
outsourcing, 269
testing
host connections, 62-63
networks, 150-152
patches, 191
physical RAM requirements, 221
throughput, 202-203
X Window performance
x11perf tool, 100-103
x11perfcomp tool, 104
thinking "outside the box," 246-247
threads, 22-23
threads-max parameter (kernel), 174
throughput, testing, 202-203
Time field
ktop command, 75
top command, 49
-time option (x11perf command), 101
time tool, 61
timestamps, 136-137
tools, 46-47, 70, 147
#! prefix, 20
at, 157-158
batch, 158
bonnie, 53-55, 203
cron, 158-160
dd, 217
depmod, 166
diff, 189-190
dmesg, 286
dt, 202
Ethereal, 148
executing
at specific time, 157-158
batch processing, 158
nice priority, 160-161
periodic execution, 158-160

free, 25, 60-61
gtop, 74-79
hdparm, 203-204
interpreting results of, 47
iostat, 71-73
JMeter, 151
jobs, 156
ktop, 74-77, 79
lmdd, 202
lsmod, 166
make bzImage, 183
make bzlilo, 184
make config, 180
make dep, 183
make menuconfig, 180
make modules, 183
make xconfig, 180
mkraid, 207
mkswap, 24, 216-217
mpstat, 73-74
Netwatch, 149-150
network analysis tools, 273-274
network testing tools, 150-152
nice, 105, 160
ntop, 65-66
patch, 190-191
ping, 62-63
pollers, 274-275
ps
output format control, 56
output modifiers, 56
process forest, 58
process selection by list, 56
sample output, 56-58
simple process selection, 55
singling out users, 58-59
pvcreate, 200
raidstart, 207
raidstop, 207
renice, 106, 161
rmmod, 166
sard, 202

sg_dd, 202
SNMP (Simple Network
    Management Protocol), 150
smnpbulkget, 276
smnpget, 276
smnpwalk, 276
swapoff, 216-217
swapon, 24, 216-218
tcpdump, 64-65, 149
time, 61
top, 47-49
traceroute, 63-64
uptime, 53
vgcreate, 200
vgextend, 200
vgreduce, 200
vmstat, 50-51
x11perf, 100-103
x11perfcomp, 104
xload, 52
xosview, 52-53
xset, 111-112, 116-117
top CPU-intensive processes,
    47-49
top tool, 47-49
top-down approach to capac-
    ity planning, 239-240
Torvalds, Linus, 192
total field (free command),
    60
tps field (iostat), 72
traceroute tool, 63-64
tracing network routes,
    63-64
Transmission Control
    Protocol. *See* TCP
trapping kernel errors,
    193-194
tries_base parameter (ker-
    nel), 176
tries_min parameter (kernel),
    176
troubleshooting patches, 191
TuneLinux.com Web site, 292
tuning performance. *See* per-
    formance tuning

tunneling (IP), 146
turning off ICMP (Internet
    Control Message Protocol),
    133
TUX server, 143-144
Type field (inetd.conf file),
    227

U

-u option
    hdparm command, 203
    ps command, 58-59
Ultra 160 drives, 34
Unix performance-monitor-
    ing tools, 46-47
    bonnie, 53-55
    free, 60-61
    interpreting results of, 47
    ntop, 65-66
    ping, 62-63
    ps, 55-59
    tcpdump, 64-65
    time, 61
    top, 47-49
    traceroute, 63-64
    uptime, 53
    vmstat, 50-51
    xload, 52
    xosview, 52-53
UNKNOWN field (hosts.allow
    file), 228
unsatisfactory response
    time, 37
unused modules, disabling,
    108-110
up field (top command), 48
upcoming technologies,
    263-265
upgrading
    hardware/software, 266-267
    X Window system
        hardware, 114-115
        servers, 113-114

uptime file, 171
uptime tool, 53
urgent pointers, 136
us field (vmstat), 51
usage profiles, 100
USB devices, 182
used field (free command),
    60
Usenet newsgroups, 293-294
%user field
    iostat, 72
    mpstat, 74
user expectations, 86
User field
    inetd.conf file, 227
    top command, 48
user-space threads, 23
Username field (ktop tool),
    75
users
    expectations, 86
    relationship to performance,
        13
utilities. *See* tools

V

variables, LD_PRELOAD, 21
Venema, Weitse, 227
verifying server configura-
    tion files, 107
vetoing files, 127
vgcreate command, 200
vgextend command, 200
vgreduce command, 200
virtual address space, 93
virtual memory (VM), 23-24
    bdflush file, 175-176
    buffermem file, 176
    freepages file, 176
    kswapd file, 176-178
    returning statistics about,
        50-51
VM. *See* virtual memory

vmstat tool, 50-51
volume groups, 200

W

w field (vmstat), 50
-W option (hdparm command), 203
Wait-status field (inetd.conf file), 227
Web Hostel Web site, 292
Web servers case study, 282-283
Web sites
  Appwatch, 82
  Beowulf, 89
  Ethereal, 148
  Freshmeat, 82
  ibiblio, 82
  journals, 293
  Kernel Traffic, 192
  magazines, 293
  mailing lists, 293-294
  newsgroups, 293-294
  newsletters, 293
  Open NMS, 276
  performance-tuning resources, 292
wide links parameter, 126
window managers, 115
window scaling, 136
wrappers (TCP), 227-228
write cache, 129
write raw parameter, 128

X-Z

X Window system, 100
  performance tuning
    chipset-specific configuration options, 110
    client performance, 116-118
    color depth, 107-108
    desktop environments, 115-116
    display resolution, 107-108
    fonts, 111-113
    hardware upgrades, 114-115
    rebuilding server, 110-111
    server configuration file, 107
    server extensions, 108-110
    server priority, 105-106
    server upgrades, 113-114
    unused modules, 108-110
  testing performance of
    x11perf tool, 100-103
    x11perfcomp tool, 104
x11perf tool, 100-103
x11perfcomp tool, 104
XF86Config-4 file, 107
XII-based tools, 52-53
xload tool, 52
xosview tool, 52-53
xset command, 111-112, 116-117

zero-copy networking, 144-145